Who Speaks for the Climate?

The public rely upon media representations to help interpret and make sense of the many complexities relating to climate science and governance. Media representations of climate issues – from news to entertainment – are powerful and important links between people's everyday realities and experiences, and the ways in which they are discussed by scientists, policymakers and public actors. A dynamic mix of influences shapes what becomes climate 'news' or 'information'. From internal workings of mass media such as journalistic norms, to external political, economic, cultural and social factors, this book helps students, academic researchers and interested members of the public explore how the media portrays influence. Providing a bridge between academic considerations and real-world developments, this book makes sense of media reporting on climate change as it explores 'who speaks for the climate' and what effects this may have on the spectrum of possible responses to modern climate challenges.

Maxwell T. Boykoff is an assistant professor in the Cooperative Institute for Research in Environmental Sciences's Center for Science and Technology Policy Research at the University of Colorado Boulder. He teaches in the Environmental Studies Program and is Adjunct Faculty in the Geography Department. In addition, he is a senior visiting research associate in the Environmental Change Institute at the University of Oxford. Max has ongoing interests in climate adaptation, cultural politics and environmental governance, science–policy interactions, and political economy and the environment. His research has been mentioned in a range of outlets such as *Science*, *Nature*, the *Guardian*, the *New York Times*, *Columbia Journalism Review*, the *Los Angeles Times*, *Christian Science Monitor*, *Grist*, *Utne Reader*, *La Rázon* (Spain) and (US) National Public Radio.

Who Speaks for the Climate?

Making Sense of Media Reporting on Climate Change

MAXWELL T. BOYKOFF

CAMBRIDGE
UNIVERSITY PRESS

CAMBRIDGE UNIVERSITY PRESS
Cambridge, New York, Melbourne, Madrid, Cape Town,
Singapore, São Paulo, Delhi, Tokyo, Mexico City

Cambridge University Press
The Edinburgh Building, Cambridge CB2 8RU, UK

Published in the United States of America by Cambridge University Press, New York

www.cambridge.org
Information on this title: www.cambridge.org/9780521133050

First published 2011

Printed in the United Kingdom at the University Press, Cambridge

A catalogue record for this publication is available from the British Library

Library of Congress Cataloguing in Publication data
Boykoff, Maxwell T.
   Who speaks for the climate? : making sense of media reporting
on climate change / Maxwell T. Boykoff.
      p.   cm.
   Includes bibliographical references and index.
   ISBN 978-0-521-11584-1
   1. Climatic changes–Public opinion.   2. Mass media and the environment.
   3. Global warming–Prevention–Public opinion.   I. Title.
   QC903.B68 2011
   070.4'4936373874–dc23
   2011026308

ISBN 978-0-521-11584-1 Hardback
ISBN 978-0-521-13305-0 Paperback

I dedicate this book to the memory of Stephen H. Schneider (1945–2010).

I also dedicate this to my sons Elijah and Calvin.

Contents

Figures

Preface

It is my hope that this volume inspires ongoing thinking and research that interrogates *why* and *how* media representations of climate change are produced, negotiated and disseminated through unequal power and inequalities of access and resources. In so doing, I hope my work will expand the spectrum of possibility for enhanced decision-making and action on climate change.

This book has been an opportunity to weave a coherent narrative through quantitative and qualitative work that I have produced on the subject of media and climate change over the last decade or so. In particular, Chapter 1 derives from cooperative work that I have undertaken with Michael K. Goodman and Ian Curtis on 'the cultural politics of climate change'. Chapters 5 and 6 draw from collaborations with Jules Boykoff on US newspaper coverage of climate change, and with Maria Mansfield on tabloid coverage in the UK. Parts of Chapters 7 and 8 draw on materials once assembled with J. Timmons Roberts as well as with S. Ravi Rajan, while considerations of new and social media in Chapter 8 stem from ongoing discussions with Saffron O'Neill. In addition, close readers will certainly detect the imprints of many scholars, mentors and friends who have influenced my considerations in the volume you now hold.

The perspective in this book derives from my interdisciplinary path through both formal and informal academic commitments and pursuits. I have been heavily influenced by exposure and formal as well as informal training in intersecting disciplines such as Environmental Studies, Geography, Sociology, Psychology, Politics, Chemistry, Physics and the History of Consciousness.

I am not a trained journalist. The observations and arguments that I put forward come from many interviews with those inside the profession, analyses of the content of media representations, and interrogations of how these communities relate to science, policy and the public. Yet, these explorations remain from the standpoint of a scholar outside the quotidian practices of journalism. Moreover, I am from the United States. This influences how the book has approached the material from a Western perspective, with many examples and illustrations emanating from the United States and Western Europe.

Media representations of climate change and other environmental issues are areas of burgeoning research. In this volume, I have been tempted to extensively catalogue this work. However, doing so would quickly expand this book to twice the size it is now. Therefore, I have had to be very economizing with the research I have mentioned here.

In addition, I have not been able to satisfyingly address all of the many dimensions and intersections between this topic and themes such as media and democracy, as well as media and political ecology. While it has been necessarily beyond the scope of the book to take up such themes comprehensively, it is my intention that this volume can be read usefully with these other literatures.

These days, a great deal of interesting and innovative research seems to be coming from undergraduate, masters and PhD students around the world. Many researchers have contacted me over the years and shared their insights, approaches, findings and conclusions. Some of the innovative thinking may be attributed to the new generation of new media consumers as well as those who have grown up in a time when climate change was already evident on the public agenda. I worry a bit that much of these contributions haven't yet made it into the formal peer-reviewed literature, and instead remain confined to their respective department and campus library archives, or on a family bookshelf. However, there is a lot that can be gained from these contributions: methodologically, empirically, theoretically. So I do hope that my work here will inspire all its readers (you!) to continue to take up these vexing yet vital twenty-first century questions.

Acknowledgements

My grandfather, Alvin 'the silent swimmer' Schoenbeck, roots this scholarship. He worked in the stock room for the *Milwaukee Journal/Sentinel* for over fifty years, and his mantra of 'Work, Study, Play, Relax' has kept me thinking and reflecting over time.

My brother Jules Boykoff deserves recognition for the co-creation and initial research on this project. While accompanying me on a fieldwork expedition many years ago, this project was concocted together in the waters off the North Coast of Honduras. I admire his ongoing work as a true public intellectual, and appreciate his critically important research on social movements and the suppression of dissent.

I have Ami Nacu-Schmidt at the University of Colorado Boulder and Debs Strickland at the University of Oxford to thank for their work on the figures found in this volume. Ami also deserves credit for her help in formatting the book, as well as for the cover design. I also thank Sarah Erskine for her help with data collection in the later stages of the assembly of this book manuscript.

Thanks go out to John Haslam, Josephine Lane, Matt Lloyd, those involved in the two stages of anonymous peer review, and others at Cambridge University Press for their kind patience, guidance and support throughout the process from nascent idea to published book. I also wish to thank Monica Boykoff and Kita Murdock in particular for their close readings of draft manuscripts, and for their comments as interested and 'real-people' readers on the topic.

There are many people that deserve my deep gratitude. Among them, I've been fortunate to interact with and find academic inspiration from Diana Liverman, Stephen H. Schneider, Angela Y. Davis, David Goodman, Tim O'Riordan, Margaret Fitzsimmons, Mike Hulme, S. Ravi Rajan, Steve Rayner, Jerry Ravetz, Ross Gelbspan, Susi Moser, Alan Richards, Terry Root, Roberto Sanchez-Rodriguez,

Mike Urban, Bud Ward, Midori Aoyagi-Usui, Sue Weiler, Ron Mitchell, Dale Willman, Coleen Vogel, Bryce Sullivan and Andrew Schwebel.

In the process of pursuing these questions, I've also deeply appreciated friendship and collegial support from Michael K. Goodman, J. Timmons Roberts, Scott Prudham, Chukwumerije Okereke, Emily Boyd, Peter Newell, Sam Randalls, David Frame, Emma Tompkins, Heike Schroeder, Nate Hultman, Judith Pallot, Mark Sheehan, Brian Gareau, Maria Carmen Lemos, Maria Mansfield, Roger Pielke Jr, Ben Hale, Tom Yulsman, Waleed Abdalati, Konrad Steffan, Mark Serreze, Lisa Dilling, William Travis, Roberta Klein, Mark McCaffrey, Patrick Luganda, Joe Smith, Rose Cohen, Dustin Mulvaney, Melanie Dupuis, Daniel Press, Janet Wharton-Goodman, Marcos Lopez, Anna Zivian, Chris Dixon, Sean Burns, Alexis Shotwell, Rebecca Schein, Doug Bevington, Dana Takagi, Michael Loik and Simon Batterbury.

In addition to individuals, I would like to acknowledge the influence that particular collectives and organizations had on my considerations here. These include the James Martin 21st Century School, the Environmental Change Institute, and Christ Church at the University of Oxford, the Cooperative Institute for Research in Environmental Sciences (CIRES), the Center for Science and Technology Policy Research, the Environmental Studies Program and the Department of Geography at the University of Colorado Boulder, the Political Ecology Working Group and Environmental Studies department at the University of California-Santa Cruz, the community of Duyure Honduras, New Natives, Three Americas and Free Radio Santa Cruz.

I have many to thank in my support system of friends and family: Monica Boykoff, Susan Schoenbeck, Thomas Boykoff, Carl and Leah Moore, Molly Boykoff, Alan Graves, Derek Riebau, Ignacio Fernandez-Amenategui, la familia Bustillo, Toby Murdock, Phil Sustronk, Andy Horning, David 'DeeBee' Banghardt, Bert and Lois Muhly, Kevin Coleman, Tara Pisani-Gareau, Noel Kinder, Andrew 'Scooter' Marcin, Gitta Ryle, Erik Ragatz, Ian Davies, Clay Sinclair, Jon Stewart, Polly Ericksen, Anthony Tukai, Ken Kimes, Sandra Ward, Jim and George Cadman, Daria Kotys-Schwartz and my sons Elijah and Calvin.

1 | *The world stage*
Cultural politics and climate change

All the world's a stage, and all the men and women merely players. They have their exits and their entrances ...
> William Shakespeare, *As You Like It*

As we progress in the twenty-first century, climate change has become a defining symbol of our collective relationship with the environment. Diagnoses (what it is) and prognoses (what we should do) make for high-stakes, high-profile and highly politicized science and policy deliberations. They cut to the heart of how we live, work, play and relax in modern life, and thus critically shape our everyday lives, lifestyles and livelihoods.

Nowadays 'climate change' is no longer thought of merely as an environmental or scientific issue. Rather, the Kautskian 'climate question' is considered one that, now more than ever, permeates our individual, as well as shared, economic, political, cultural and social lives. As the notion of climate change has increasingly dominated the contemporary science and policy landscapes, it has also more visibly inhabited public discourse, through news and entertainment media representations and 'popular' cultures. Considerations of climate change and reductions in greenhouse gas (GHG) emissions have become engrained in cultural and social behaviour, where being Politically Correct ('PC') has often given way to being Climate Correct ('CC').

In this volume, with a focus on mass media, I take up questions of *how* and *why* these interactions have unfolded, by considering the Lorax-like question 'Who speaks for climate?'

Most broadly, references to 'mass media' include television, films, books, flyers, newspapers, magazines, radio and internet. They involve publishers, editors, journalists, content producers and members of the communications industry who produce, interpret and communicate texts, images, information and imaginaries.

1

Over the last decade or so, there has been a significant expansion from consumption of traditional mass media – broadcast television, newspapers, radio – into consumption of 'new' and 'social' media. Essentially, in tandem with technological advances, this expansion in communications is seen to be a fundamental shift from broadcast, or 'one-to-many' (often one-way), communications to 'many-to-many' more interactive webs of communications (van Dijk, 2006; O'Neill and Boykoff, 2010a). This movement has signalled substantive changes in how people access and interact with information, who has access, and who are authorized definers of the various dimensions of climate issues. At present, new and social media have been accompanied by democratizing influences, as these channels of communication often offer a platform for more people to become content producers, and therefore have the potential to more readily shape the public agenda.

Together, these media are constituted by a diverse and dynamic set of institutions, processes and practices that together serve as 'mediating' forces between communities such as science, policy and public citizens. Mass media have (vigorously) debatable limits in terms of potential conduits to attitudinal and behavioural change. Nonetheless, as unparalleled forms of communication to wide audiences, it remains vitally important to examine the ways in which media representations and symbols are produced, interpreted and consumed, thus influencing a spectrum of possibilities for governance and decision-making. From visceral influences such as 'Hey, that's me on television!' to measured interrogations such as how corporate control of media potentially constrains dissent, the multifarious contributions that mass media make to public discourse deem it worthy of careful reflection and scrutiny.

Connections between media information and policy decision-making, attitudes, perspectives, intentions and behavioural change are far from straightforward. Coverage certainly does not determine engagement; rather, it shapes possibilities for engagement (Boykoff, 2008a; Carvalho and Burgess, 2005). Media representations – from news to entertainment – are critical links between people's everyday realities and experiences, and the ways in which these are discussed at a distance between science, policy and public actors. People throughout civil society rely upon media representations to help interpret and make sense of the many complexities relating to climate science and governance. Furthermore, media messages are critical inputs to what becomes public discourse on today's climate challenges. As such, this book examines media coverage of climate change as it seeks to make sense of the implications of media representations on a 'scope of politics', as Clayton Rosati has put it (Rosati, 2007, 1008).

Furthermore, the explorations in this volume spring from an expansive view of science in society, where scientific understanding is part of, rather than separate from, public uptake. Mass media have thereby influenced a range of processes, from formal climate science and policy to informal notions of public understanding. Media representations are convergences of competing knowledge, framing climate change for policy, politics and the public, and drawing attention to how to make sense of, as well as value, the changing world. Emanating from these processes, public perceptions, attitudes, intentions and behaviours, in turn, often link back through mass media into ongoing formulations of climate governance.

Throughout, I work from Maarten Hajer's definition of 'discourse', as 'an ensemble of ideas, concepts, and categories through which meaning is given to phenomena. Discourses frame certain problems; that is to say, they distinguish some aspects of a situation rather than others ... discourses provide the tools with which problems are constructed ... [and they] dominate the way a society conceptualizes the world' (Hajer, 1993, 45–46).

So, this book sets out to make sense of how media reporting has made climate change meaningful for different Shakespearean 'players', and in various contexts, scenes and settings (as the quote to begin the chapter indicated). These pursuits have been referred to as the 'cultural politics of climate change': dynamic and contested spaces where various 'actors' battle to shape public understanding and engagement. This is a place where formal climate science, policy and politics operating at multiple scales permeate the spaces of the 'everyday'.

Cultural politics refer to dynamic and contested processes behind which meaning is constructed and negotiated, and involves not only the portrayals that gain traction in discourses, but also those that are absent from them or silenced (Derrida, 1978; Dalby, 2007). Framing processes have important effects on marginalizing some discourses while contributing to the entrenchment of others (Castree, 2004). Tim Forsyth has stated, 'assessments of frames should not just be limited to those that are labelled as important at present, but also seek to consider alternative framings that may not currently be considered important in political debates' (Forsyth, 2003, 1).

Media representational practices can confront power as they critically engage with pressing contemporary issues. However, portrayals can also service political and economic power. Jaclyn Dipensa and Robert Brulle have warned that, 'The news media [can] serve as an important institution for the reproduction of hegemony' (Dipensa and Brulle, 2003, 79). Through complex, dynamic and messy processes, media have taken on varied roles, from watch dog to lap dog to guard dog for the public sphere.

Both discursive and material elements comprise the cultural politics of climate change. Discourses are tethered to material realities, perspectives and social practices (Hall, 1997).

Examples from politics, economics, culture, the environment and society surround us. We can briefly consider three instances from the malignant to the benign. First, in 2001 the United States (US) Army renamed 'School of the Americas' as the 'Center for Inter-American Security Cooperation'. This was seen partly as an effort to quell protests and shed their reputation as a training facility for human rights abuses. Second, in 2007, the US plum growers won permission from government regulators to move from 'prunes' to 'dried plums'. The alleged motive behind such a linguistic twist was to increase the appeal and sales of dried plums among a younger consumer base.

Third, in the aftermath of the 2010 Gulf of Mexico oil spill, many responsible parties that were involved actively sought to 'name the disaster' in order to minimize damage to their interests and to shift blame. Among them, BP, Transocean and Halliburton attempted to scrub their name from the disaster title by using names like 'the Macondo well incident' or 'the Deepwater Horizon spill' or 'the MC252 oil spill incident' (Soraghan, 2010). These acts of discursive positioning demonstrated the importance that carbon-based industry placed on how naming and shaming linked to perception and potential behavioural change.

Examining interactions between discourses and material lives in this way facilitates our consideration of questions regarding how power flows through the capillaries of our shared social, cultural and political body. It also helps us to ponder how this, in turn, constructs and maintains knowledge, norms, conventions and (un)truths (Foucault, 1980). Power here is not a thing to be bought and sold, but is relational, shaping everyday interactions between individuals and communities. In this way, power is situated in professional and disciplinary practices, making actors both the object of discipline and the instruments of its exercise (Foucault, 1984). Furthermore, this power saturates social, political, economic and institutional conditions (Wynne, 2008).

Yet, these conditions and practices are inextricably shaped by the power of ongoing climate processes themselves. This has been referred to by Dennis Cosgrove and others as the inseparable dialectic of nature and culture (Cosgrove, 1983). In other words, nature is not a backdrop upon which various actors contest and battle for epistemological and material successes. Rather, (scientific) interpretation and knowledge is constructed, maintained and contested through intertwined socio-political and biophysical processes (Blaikie, 1985; Whatmore, 2002). Importantly then, meaning is constructed and manifested through *both* ontological conditions of nature and contingent social, political, cultural and scientific processes involved in interpretations of nature (Robbins, 2004).

Approaching these spaces of the cultural politics of climate change in this way helps to interrogate 'how social and political framings are woven into both the formulation of scientific explanations of environmental problems, and the solutions proposed to reduce them' (Forsyth, 2003, 1). These 'framings', then, are inherent to cognition, and effectively contextualize as well as 'fix' interpretive categories in order to help explain and describe the complex environmental processes of climate change.

It is instructive to consider more specifically how and why these forces have interacted with media representations of climate change. Historically entrenched cultural preoccupations with free markets and economic growth in capitalist societies – along with the concomitant politics of interest groups – have resulted in a naturalized consideration of market-led approaches to policy action (see Chapter 8 for more). Commitments to economic growth, and deeply entrenched technological optimism, have been significant forces influencing the wider cultural politics of climate change. In this context, it is often the case that those deemed as permissible discourses have remained encased in the logic of neoliberal late capitalism (Bailey, 2007).

Many associated critiques have emerged regarding the dangers of emergent 'carbon capitalism' associated with commodifying the atmosphere, and the fixation with market mechanisms as primary tools to 'answer' climate questions, among others (Liverman, 2004; Bumpus and Liverman, 2008). Moreover, these movements are deemed problematic to the extent that these activities, at their core, 'render the messy materiality of life legible as discrete entities, individuated and abstracted from the complex social and ecological integuments' (Prudham, 2007, 414), and in so doing, reduce the need for decarbonization to a matter of simple (neoliberal) political economics. As the following chapters in this book discuss, these critiques have remained largely absent in mainstream mass-media representations to date, while representations of market-led solutions have been dominant. Nonetheless, largely within these discursive tropes, business groups, ideologically driven think tanks and environmental non-governmental organizations (ENGOs) have continued to heartily debate and discuss associated features and consequences in the landscapes of mass media.

Climate change by any other name?

Mike Hulme has traced the term 'climate' back to third century BC Greece (Hulme 2009a). Aristotle's student Theophrastus made early connections between deforestation, water management and the cooling and warming of the climate (Glacken, 1967).

The climate on planet Earth is regulated by way of input from energy of the sun and the loss of this back into space. Incoming solar radiation enters the atmosphere here on planet Earth and is partly absorbed or trapped, and partly reflected back to space. The composition of the atmosphere dictates the balance between these forces, and this is called the 'planetary energy budget'. Certain atmospheric GHGs are critical to this balance, and these include carbon dioxide (CO_2), methane (CH_4), nitrous oxide (N_2O), tropospheric ozone (O_3), halocarbons (CFCs, HFCs, HCFCs) and water vapour (H_2O_v). Emissions of GHGs into the atmosphere cause changes in the climate.

Today, there are differences in strict scientific definitions of each of the terms 'climate change' and 'global warming'. While 'climate change' is a broader term that accounts for changes in many climate characteristics, such as rainfall, ice extent and sea levels, 'global warming' refers to a more specific facet of climate change: the increase in temperature over time. Clearly, temperature increases do not occur in isolation from other climate characteristics; rather, many other sources and feedback processes contribute to changes across time and space. Temperature (particularly atmospheric temperature increases) is seen as the most clear and distinguishable climate characteristic that indicates more general climate change, and has been called the 'fingerprint' for climate change (Wigley, 1999).

These scientific distinctions might seem relatively straightforward. Yet, as the term 'global warming' migrates to the policy realm, things can get muddled. For instance, the United Nations Intergovernmental Panel on Climate Change (IPCC) and the United Nations Framework Convention on Climate Change (UNFCCC) define the term 'climate change' differently. The IPCC definition is more closely aligned with the strict scientific definition. It calls climate change, 'any change in climate over time whether due to natural variability or as a result of human activity' (Houghton *et al.*, 1995). However, the UNFCCC departs from this phrasing as it focuses on the human component. The UNFCCC defines it as, 'a change of climate which is attributed directly or indirectly to human activity that alters the consumption of the global atmosphere and which is in addition to natural climate variability over comparable time periods' (quoted in Pielke Jr, 2005, 549). Roger Pielke Jr has argued that differences between IPCC and UNFCCC definitions of 'climate change' have confused considerations of 'what to do about it', and have 'set the stage for the politicization of climate science' (2005, 548).

Over time, mass media have taken these potentially insular etymological science and policy definitions and thrust them into popular vernacular. However, throughout various media and across different countries, representations have often deployed these terms interchangeably or inconsistently. Needless to say, this has fuelled colloquial confusion amongst the general public.

For example, some press coverage has invoked these in contrast with one another, where global warming has referred to human activity and 'climate change' has signified natural variation. Illustrations abound: in a 2002 *News of the World* commentary in the United Kingdom (UK), the editors wrote, 'Ireland and Britain are set for 100 years of wetter winters because of global warming ... they *blame man for the global warming which is causing the climate change*' (2002, 2, emphasis added). In 2004 in the *Mirror*, deputy political editor Bob Roberts wrote, 'Tony Blair yesterday issued a doomsday warning

about the threat *from climate change because of global warming*'
(2004, 2, emphasis added).

Over time, many have debated which of the terms 'climate change'
and 'global warming' should be invoked when. Others have argued
that neither term adequately captures the meaning behind it. For
example, Frank Luntz – a well-known US political strategist and
advisor to the George W. Bush administration – issued a memo in
2003 called 'Winning the global warming debate – an overview'. He
argued that, 'It's time for us to start talking about 'climate change'
instead of global warming ... 'Climate change' is less frightening than
'global warming' (2003, 142).

Similarly recognizing the power of language, in 2005 *ActionMedia*
produced a report called 'Naming Global Warming'. In efforts to
deliberately shape perceptions, they recommended, 'DO NOT call
the problem "climate change". "Climate change" is understood as
the natural process the earth's climate has undergone in the past. DO
call the problem "global warming". "Global warming" is the result of
human activity' (2005, 6, emphasis in original).

This report came on the heels of a study released by the non-profit
group EcoAmerica, who argued that the terms 'global warming' and
'climate change' needed re-branding. In their place, the group recommended that the phrase 'our deteriorating atmosphere' be invoked,
and to re-frame discussions about atmospheric reductions of carbon
dioxide instead as 'moving away from dirty fuels of the past'.

Focusing on carbon can be seen as somewhat reductionist: there
are greenhouse gases that do not contain carbon (e.g. nitrous oxide),
and not all carbon-containing emissions (e.g. carbon monoxide) trap
heat. However, this element provides helpful 'exchange value' and, as
Gavin Bridge has noted, 'a common denominator for thinking about
the organization of social life in relation to the environment ... from
fossil-fuel addiction and peak oil to blood barrels and climate change,
carbon's emergence as a dominant optic for thinking and writing
about the world and human relations within it is tied to the various
emergencies with which it is associated' (2010, 2).

As these examples indicate, awareness, concern and possible actions
are critically shaped by what the phenomenon may be called, or how
it is described. Through a survey in southern England, Lorraine
Whitmarsh found that 'global warming' was frequently associated
with heat-related impacts, human causes, ozone depletion and the

greenhouse effect. Meanwhile, the survey data showed that 'climate change' was most often associated with observed weather and climate impacts, and natural variation in the climate (2008). She concluded that citizens considered 'global warming' as 'a more emotive term, in part because it suggests a clear direction of change towards *increasing* temperatures', and they found that 'implications of "climate change" are more ambiguous' (2008, 16, emphasis in original).

Moreover, in February 2010, the *New York Times* columnist Tom Friedman commented, 'Avoid the term "global warming". I prefer the term "global weirding", because that is what actually happens as global temperatures rise and the climate changes. The weather gets weird. The hots are expected to get hotter, the wets wetter, the dries drier and the most violent storms more numerous' (Friedman, 2010, A23). Through linguistics, George Lakoff has offered numerous insights on how to successfully activate framing devices, and potential pitfalls therein, within a contentious political landscape (Lakoff, 2010).

Robert Entman has commented that, 'framing essentially involves selection and salience. To frame is to select some aspects of a perceived reality and make them more salient in a communicating text, in such a way as to promote a particular problem definition' (Entman 1993, 52). However, Robert Brulle has cautioned that these approaches 'based exclusively on cognitive science, rhetoric and psychology ... lack any contextual basis within a larger theoretical structure of the role of communication in facilitating large-scale social change processes ... [and] fail to address meaningfully the ecological imperatives defined by global warming. Additionally, the professionalization of political discourse upon which these approaches are based actually reinforces existing relationships of power and institutional dynamics. These factors lead to a weakening of efforts to increase political mobilization over the issue of global warming, and thus undermine the capacity for significant social change' (Brulle, 2010, 83).

Certainly, media representations serve to assemble and privilege certain interpretations and understandings over others (Goffman, 1974; Entman, 1993). This has been the case with the highly charged discourses surrounding climate change. Yet there are dangers that the power behind these terms can be harnessed and manipulated via mass media in order to elicit more (or less) alarmed responses in civil society. These terms have the potential to become empty signifiers or dangerous diversions, filled with desired meanings by those actors with the power to produce and influence content. Meanwhile, Steve Curwood – host of US National Public Radio's 'Living on Earth' – has cautioned, 'Right now we have an alarmed citizenry, but still not a very well-informed one' (Russell, 2008).

As Teun van Dijk and many others have pointed out, discourses themselves must be carefully considered in context (van Dijk, 1988). It is important to acknowledge that particular ways of discussing 'climate change' or 'global warming' are steeped in historically derived and iterative relationships with various ways of knowing and interacting (Fairclough, 1995). Analyzing frames as they relate to ongoing climate discourses are helpful, but they often provide only partial explanations for these wider interactions that comprise 'climate communication'. In fact, there is a clear danger of displacing and decontextualizing important considerations through over-emphasis on analyses of how key actors choose to discuss and 'frame' climate change.

For example, Matt Nisbet has developed a 'typology', where eight categories capture climate-change discourses from 'social progress' to 'public accountability and governance' (Nisbet, 2009). While this approach provides a helpful starting point, such explorations would do well to further consider deeper historical and ontological dimensions of communicating about science and the environment.

Through a wider and context-sensitive lens of cultural politics, we can effectively consider claims and claims-makers, as well as capture the processes and effects of media practices shaping representations of 'climate change' and 'global warming'. Dynamic interactions form nexuses of power–knowledge that shape how we come to understand things as 'truth' and 'reality', and in turn, contribute to managing the conditions and tactics of our social lives (de Certeau, 1984). Rather than brash imposition of law or direct disciplinary techniques, throughout this book I consider how more subtle power–knowledge regimes permeate and create what becomes 'permissible' and 'normal' as well as 'desired' in everyday discourses, practices and institutional processes (Foucault, 1975).

To illustrate, in 2009 it was reported that the Obama administration purposefully began to refer to greenhouse gas emissions as 'carbon pollution' and 'heat-trapping emissions'. This discursive 'switch-eroo' was noted in a series of statements from top officials such as White House science advisor John Holdren, Energy Secretary Steven

Chu, National Oceanic and Atmospheric Administration head Jane Lubchenco, and US Environmental Protection Agency Administrator Lisa Jackson. Lubchenco acknowledged to *Energy & Environment* reporter Lauren Morello that this linguistic shift was deliberate. She commented, 'The choice of that term is intended to make what's happening more understandable and more accessible to non-technical audiences. You know, scientists so often use a lot of jargon without necessarily appreciating that it's jargon. And "heat-trapping pollution" calls a spade a spade, essentially. It says what it is, but in a way that is less jargony' (Morello, 2009).

Many have welcomed these actions as well as working towards more transparent ways to 'smarten up' communication of oft-complex issues. For instance, in the US Susan Joy Hassol has worked with climate scientists, policy actors, communicators, educators and entertainers for many years and on numerous projects to 'translate science into English'. From a scientist's perspective, Drew Westen and Celinda Lake have written, 'we tend to speak to [citizens] in our language – the language of parts per million, carbon emissions, carbon sequestration, and the like – and expect [the public] to make the translation. We would do well to make that translation ourselves ...' (Bowman *et al.*, 2009) Thomas Bowman and colleagues commented in *Science*, 'It is imperative that we improve the exchange of information between scientists and public stakeholders' (Bowman *et al.*, 2009, 37). However, others treat such linguistic manipulation with more suspicion. Robert Brulle commented that approaches such as these are 'cynical and, worse, ineffective. The right uses it, the left uses it, but it doesn't engage people in a face-to-face manner, and that's the only way to achieve real, lasting social change' (Broder, 2009a, A11).

Overall, these negotiations over language and phrasing illustrate the acknowledged interactions between discourse and practices. David Harvey has commented, 'Struggles over representation are as fundamental to the activities of place construction as bricks and mortar' (Harvey, 1990, 422). From subtle to obvious shifts in wording within climate-change stories, media portrayals possess great potential to influence reader perceptions and concern. In turn, these can feed into public awareness and engagement, as well as politics and policy. In other words, the ways in which 'climate change' and 'global warming' are discussed in media representations – as a 'threat', 'problem' or 'opportunity' – impact considerations of possible responses, as well as policy priorities (Hulme, 2009a).

It's here, it's there, it's everywhere

The cultural politics of climate change lurk in a multitude of spaces (recreational centres, neighbourhoods, pubs, workplaces, schools and town centres). 'Actors' on this stage range from climate scientists to business industry interests and ENGO activists. Robert Cox has documented how a range of citizen and organizational voices have shaped considerations of environmental challenges in the public arena through his seminal book *Environmental Communication in the Public Sphere* (Cox, 2006). Also, Peter Newell has examined the role of various pressure groups in shaping the terrain of climate politics in his forerunning book *Climate for Change*. Among his discussions, he focused on the Climate Action Network, a consortium of over sixty ENGOs such as Greenpeace, World Wildlife Fund and Environmental Defence. He found that ENGOs 'constitute an important force for political change by helping to overcome social inertia and bureaucratic resistance to policy (action)' (Newell, 2000, 152).

The critical issue of 'climate change' first unfolded in the public sphere in the late 1980s (see Chapter 2 for more), and media accounts largely turned to climate scientists and policymakers as authorized and expert 'claims-makers'. As journalists, editors, producers and publishers sought to make sense of this newfound issue in the public arena, they faced many competing claims and representations that they worked to sift through. Earlier work in media studies of the environment has looked at the increasing attention paid to environmental issues through varying roles of 'interest group entrepreneurs', or claims-makers who constructed environmental issues as social problems (Schoenfeld *et al.*, 1979).

In addition to climate science and policy 'speaking' on behalf of climate, carbon-based business and industry interests and ENGOs quickly scrambled for discursive and material perches from which to address climate challenges via mass media (Gottlieb, 2002). In their seminal 2007 book *Creating a Climate for Change*, editors Susi Moser and Lisa Dilling demonstrated that in the process of articulating their perspectives on climate change in the public arena, many entities, organizations, interests and individuals battled to shape not only the science but fundamentally the awareness, engagement and possible actions around the climate agenda. In short, these swiftly became dynamic and highly contested battlefields of knowledge(s) and understanding(s).

In the late 1980s and into the 1990s, many predominantly US-based think tanks – often influenced by conservative ideologies and/or funded by carbon-based energy industry actors – amplified uncertainties regarding various aspects of climate science, de-emphasized the human contribution to climate change and called attention to the costs of action, such as mode-switching to renewable energy sources. Prominent groups such as ExxonMobil Corporation and Shell Oil mobilized their considerable financial power and influence to shape public perception and policy prioritization on climate mitigation and adaptation, in line with their interests as a carbon-based industry. Meanwhile, many ENGOs pilloried these industry actions as they sought to raise public awareness and policy-actor concern regarding 'negative externalities' of climate risk as well as impacts. Raymond Bryant aptly commented, 'NGOs do for politics what TV nature documentaries do for culture: motivate, enchant, disturb' (Bryant, 2009, 1540).

In the intervening decades, the approaches that these organizations took became more nuanced and varied, across a range of scales. For example, cooperative efforts such as the World Business Council for Sustainable Development endeavoured to take up low-carbon initiatives to decouple economic growth with environmental impacts. This alliance signed up more than 200 multi-national firms, and has been a powerful demonstration of a break from those staunchly defending carbon-based environmentally damaging practices. At the local level, efforts like the Eco-Renovation initiative in Oxfordshire, England engaged in cross-sectoral community-based enterprises to promote significant low-carbon refurbishment of local homes, reducing GHG emissions at the household level. These alliances and activities illustrated the rapidly expanding engagement in the public sphere with climate-change mitigation challenges.

Moreover, while scientists, business and environmental groups populated the discursive spaces of the climate-change issue through mass media in the 1980s and 1990s, there emerged a broader spectrum of non-nation-state actor (NNSA) voices in the years that followed. The boundaries between who constitutes an 'authorized' speaker (and who does not) shifted (Gieryn, 1999), as voices from science, policy, industry and ENGOs grew to include a wider cast of actors, such as musicians, artists, community groups, science museum curators, sports figures, film and television producers, and others in popular culture. Similarly, moving into the new millennium, these arenas intensified as the number of actors speaking for climate and negotiating how climate change became meaningful in our everyday lives increased.

For example, Katherine Wilkinson has examined how segments of the US evangelical religious movement have worked with other faith groups to address human contributions to climate change. While traditionally associated with political conservatism, or the Republican Party, many initiatives such as an 'Evangelical Call to Action' and a 'What Would Jesus Drive?' campaign have been born from a motivation for environmental stewardship. These endeavours have demonstrated increased NNSA engagement in climate-change issues. Illustrating larger trends, Wilkinson commented, 'Evangelical climate advocacy challenges existing binaries in thought and action related to environmental concerns. Pervasive dichotomous thinking restricts us to such categories as liberal/conservative, secular/religious, human/environment, and material/spiritual, which limit the way we conceive of issues and respond to them. But, clearly, religion and environment are not inimical, nor are scientists and evangelicals or political liberals and theological conservatives on definitively opposing sides. Synergies between them are apparent and increasingly intersect on the issue of climate change' (2010, 55).

In recent years, there has also been a clear surge in engagements with climate change in various segments of popular culture, and these NNSA engagements have brought with them new spaces and dimensions of discursive and material struggles. For instance, many businesses have begun to tout 'carbon neutrality' in their practices. Some ENGOs have praised such activities as a first awareness-raising step towards ongoing decarbonization of industrial practices while others have fiercely critiqued these claims as 'greenwashing' business-as-usual actions. Similar debates have also involved questions regarding 'voluntary carbon offsets' for carbon-unfriendly travel, carbon labelling of food and household products, movements towards 'low carbon diets' by purchasing local goods and the inherent paradoxes of calling on 'clean coal' technologies to reduce GHG emissions.

Over time, individuals, collectives, organizations, coalitions and interest groups have sought to access the power of mass media to influence architectures and processes of climate science, governance and public understanding through various media 'frames' and 'claims'. In an effort to understand and catalogue the growing role of one group of NNSAs – celebrities – King's College London professor Mike Goodman and I defined celebrity interventions through six main types of political or social determinants that shape their actions: actors, politicians, sports figures/athletes, business people, musicians, and public intellectuals (Boykoff and Goodman, 2009).

Some celebrities have focused their energies in media that have traditionally been characterized as 'high culture'. For example, in 2008 British sculptor Antony Gormley worked with human images in ice to demonstrate the ephemeral nature of human existence as part of a *Cape Farewell* project and expedition. This was also associated with a wider project, begun in 2005, entitled *Tipping points: a climate scientists and artists encounter*. The *Tipping Points* initiative arose amongst practising artists, automotive designers and engineering academics. While these endeavours have met a great deal of critical acclaim, others have argued that they enjoy a relatively limited reach into wider spaces of cultural politics through their chosen artistic engagements. Other undertakings in the cultural and political landscapes of climate change include those through more 'popular' forms of mass media such as storylines involving climate change in the popular shows *The Simpsons* and *South Park*, or through the lyrics of Madonna and Spearhead music.

Climate icons and images

When considering media representations of climate change, it is useful to explore how both texts and images are deployed across many media platforms. Doing so provides a more comprehensive understanding of the many ways in which meaning and knowledge are derived from semiotic processes of encoding and decoding. While texts are often privileged as primary means of climate communication, images have been considered as a powerful way to 'bear witness' to climate change (Doyle, 2007, 131).

For many decades, mass-media images have been harnessed and woven into texts in a variety of ways to develop narratives on complex and abstract issues about climate and the environment. Perhaps the first powerful example of this is the well-known Apollo 8 photo 'Earth Rise', taken in December 1968. This was the first view that the general public had of planet Earth in its entirety (Cosgrove, 1994). Images accompanying stories and advertising have served to identify threats and dangers associated with climate change as well as personify the climate-change 'problem' (Smith and Joffe, 2009).

However, Julie Doyle has cautioned that, 'Not all environmental problems can be seen' (Doyle, 2007, 147). She has argued that by the time climate change can be captured visually – a calving iceberg, a drowning polar bear – it might be too late to address these problems. Considered in this way, these images are consistently chasing time, and forcing many invisible features of climate change to be expressed visibly. By relying on 'picturing the clima(c)tic', we collectively allow ourselves to be more reactive than proactive to climate threats, as 'photography cannot visualize the future as a present threat' (Doyle, 2008, 294).

In a groundbreaking 2009 paper entitled 'Fear won't do it', Saffron O'Neill and Sophie Nicholson-Cole sought to empirically test what images raise awareness as well as inspire engagement in the public citizenry. Through work in the UK, they found that dramatic and fearful representations can successfully raise awareness and concern about climate change. However, these kinds of images were 'also likely to distance or disengage individuals from climate change, tending to render them feeling helpless and overwhelmed when they try to comprehend their own relationship with the issue' (2009, 375).

Every day, fear, misery and doom headlines and articles populate the mass media landscape, such as 'It's the end of the world ... mainly for children' in the *Express* in 2000, and 'Pollution is turning the seas into acid' in the *Daily Mail* in 2006. Yet, the dominance of these fear-inducing tropes can be partly attributed to the fact that many aspects of the climate change that get picked up in the media – such as ecological forecasts and societal impacts – are inherently quite gloomy subjects. Therefore, it is difficult to put a hopeful tone on headlines like those covering displaced communities from sea-level rises. Moreover, these fearful themes have fed readily into journalistic norms of dramatization and personalization, making such topics more conducive to story formation (see Chapter 5 for more).

However, Mike Hulme has warned that media coverage of these related issues has developed a discourse of 'catastrophic' climate change. He said, 'It seems that mere "climate change" was not going to be bad enough, and so now it must be "catastrophic" to be worthy of attention' (Hulme, 2006; Hulme, 2007). Moreover, these findings by Saffron O'Neill and Sophie Nicholson-Cole revealed contradictions in efforts that have sought to mobilize consumer-citizens (as Rachel Slocum has called them) in climate mitigation and adaptation actions. They concluded that sensational, shocking and fear-inducing images 'have a place, given their power to hook audiences and their attention. However, they must at least be used selectively, with caution, and in combination with other kinds of representations in order to avoid causing denial, apathy, avoidance, and negative associations that may come as a result of coping with any unpleasant feelings evoked' (2009, 376).

Mike Goodman and I also examined how celebrities have become a new form of 'charismatic megafauna' (2009), displacing images of polar bears and melting glaciers that have been found to occupy the imaginaries of the public minds in the issue of climate change over the years (Leiserowitz, 2006). In so doing, the movements of these new 'actors' may overcome perceptions that climate change is a distant threat (Slocum, 2004; Leiserowitz, 2006).

In research examining icons and climate change, Saffron O'Neill and Mike Hulme found that UK participants in the study found non-expert icons most appealing and relevant to their local communities (2009). Celebrities have certainly 'partnered' with artefacts and images to generate various media messages on climate change. For example, the 2007 cover of the *Vanity Fair* Green Issue portrayed Leonardo DiCaprio and Knut the polar bear appearing together on a slab of Arctic ice. However, in the preface to this issue, the cover was explained in this way:

Polar bears are imperiled by the melting of the Arctic ice. The Bush administration, which has yet to decide whether to list the polar bear as a threatened species, understands the power of symbols, and has warned government scientists not to speak publicly about polar bears or climate change at international meetings. Knut, the cub on our cover, was born in the Berlin Zoo. We brought him together with Leonardo DiCaprio the only way we could, in a photomontage. Knut was photographed by Annie Leibovitz in Berlin. DiCaprio, no stranger to icebergs, was photographed by [Annie] Leibovitz at the Jökulsárlón glacier lagoon, in Iceland. Yes, we know, there are no polar bears in Iceland. If current trends continue, there won't be any in Canada either. (quoted in Boykoff and Goodman, 2009, 395)

The choice to concoct the symbolically-powerful 'photomontage' drove the cover selection, and undoubtedly *Vanity Fair* magazine sales. Along these lines, Anders Hansen and David Machin authored a study called 'Visually branding the environment: climate change as a marketing opportunity' (2008). Getty Images have grown to be an approximately US$1 billion-a-year industry, with a searchable database where companies can buy images for their advertising, web pages and news reporting. Hansen and Machin examined Getty 'Green Issues' Image Collection, and they found distinct trends towards depoliticization, decontextualization and 'genericity'. In other words, these images were found to be abstracted in order to 'promote discourses suitable for branding and marketing' and thus, through the 'commercial appropriation of this discourse [it has] the effect of promoting greater consumption' (2008, 792). Tim Luke has warned that such trends have constricted substantive alternatives for green consumption. He has argued that such green marketing has thus become a bland and impotent environmentalism, 'already defined within the bounds of neoliberal encounters ... we just have to apply them to our lives' (Luke, 1997).

Guy Debord's *Society of the Spectacle* grappled with these questions of imagery-as-signifier, and interrogated how media have mobilized icons and images to represent vexing contemporary issues. Debord warned that in the process of reconciling imagery and capitalism in the way that Hansen and Machin illustrate, 'the real consumer becomes a consumer of illusions. The commodity is the factually real illusion, and the spectacle is its general manifestation' (Debord, 1983, 47). In an analysis of climate action campaigns by Oxfam and Christian Aid in the UK, Kate Manzo illustrated how 'the iconography of climate change is itself inherently political' (Manzo, 2010, 10).

While there can be gains associated with awareness-raising due to powerful media imagery and texts, there are temporal dimensions to consider. Among them, are there long-term costs to providing such a DiCaprio–Knut 'photomontage' and sacrificing accurate representations for attention-grabbing imagery? Do associations of green consumption help to achieve climate mitigation and adaptation goals, or hinder them? How are alarming portrayals of climate impacts potentially numbing rather than sensitizing the general public? Some have dismissed NNSA initiatives harnessing popular culture to address climate challenges as mere distraction (e.g. Weiskel, 2005). However, it is important to acknowledge where NNSAs can in fact reach places where many consumer-citizens reside, discursively, materially and cognitively.

Irish rocker Bono, from U2, once commented about the power of such interventions, saying to *Vogue*, "celebrity is a bit silly, but it's currency of a kind" (Singer, 2002). This influence can sometimes be startling. For example, in 2001 in the State of California, many ENGOs were working to build support for Assembly Bill 1493 (also called 'the Pavley Bill') to limit CO_2 emissions from the tailpipes of personal automobiles. It was a controversial bill as it potentially violated the Federal Clean Air Act rules on fuel efficiency. Moreover, in the US political milieu of the time, many Assembly members were reluctant to commit their support. In order to gather enough votes for the bill to pass the Assembly, Director Russell Long of the ENGO Bluewater Network – now with Friends of the Earth – met with various Assembly members who were to cast swing votes. Among them, he met with the then Assembly Speaker of the house and asked for his support. The Speaker said that if Long could arrange a private meeting between him and actress/singer Jennifer Lopez (a.k.a. J-Lo), then he would support AB1493. While no such meeting was arranged, the Speaker did end up voting for AB1493. While he may have been joking when he made the comment that his support for it hinged on meeting J-Lo, the reported utterance nonetheless demonstrated this power of celebrities on climate governance.

More generally, science organizations have recognized that celebrity voices can raise awareness about climate issues, and have therefore engaged in programmes and projects to employ the help of celebrities to 'get the word out' (Lamb, 2010a). For example, the National Academy of Sciences has set up a 'Science and Entertainment Exchange' programme at the University of Southern California in order to link with professionals from the entertainment industry who are interested in taking up science and environment themes. These examples demonstrate both the power and varied influences of these interactions that this volume will continue to explore in the next chapters.

Rising coverage lifts all awareness?

2009 ended with soaring media coverage of climate change around the world. Climate news seemingly flooded the public arena. The much-hyped and highly anticipated United Nations climate talks in Copenhagen, Denmark (COP15), along with news about the hacked emails of scientists from the University of East Anglia (UEA) Climate Research Unit (CRU) played key parts in this dramatic rise. These events also linked to ongoing stories of energy security, sustainability, carbon markets, green economies and the like. Articles and segments ranged from stories about what role humans play in climate change to questions about how to effectively govern the mitigation of GHG emissions through various Cap-and-Trade market mechanisms as well as other schemes for Reducing Emissions from Deforestation and Forest Degradation (REDD).

The volume of coverage at the end of 2009 was about five times greater than that at the turn of the millennium. Figure 1.1 appraises the trends in media coverage of climate change from 2004 through to the end of 2010 in fifty newspapers around the globe. This figure provides an opportunity to assess and analyze further questions of *how* and *why* there were the apparent ebbs and flows in coverage.

The increases in each of the regions were not symmetrical. For example, the uptick in North American coverage (of which US newspapers are a part) during this time was not as pronounced as the increases in the other regions. North American newspapers had a rise of just 59% from the start of the year, as contrasted with 85%, 79%, 68% and 67% increases in South America/Africa, Oceania, Asia/Middle East, and Europe, respectively. But, the dominance of the ongoing US Congressional debates around healthcare 'reform' served as a contextual factor limiting the 'news hole' for climate stories during this time (see Chapter 5 for more on US coverage). Nonetheless, these increases are dramatic. However, if tragedies in Haiti evidenced by the trigger event of the earthquake on 12 January 2010 were instead on 12 December 2009 (during the COP15 talks), that surely would have reduced this steeply rising slope.

An evident increase in media attention throughout all the regions took place in 2005 and 2006. Again, through examinations of the content of these news articles, it is evident that specific as well as concatenate events contributed to this. For instance, in 2005 the Group of Eight (G8) Summit in Gleneagles, Scotland attracted media attention as climate change was one of the key items on the policy agenda. Moreover, Hurricane Katrina, which made landfall in August 2005 in the Gulf Coast of the US, garnered considerable media coverage as the event tapped into many related issues of risk, hazards and vulnerability, as well as questions regarding what the causes were, who was responsible, and what needed to be done (Liu *et al.*, 2008). In 2006, media coverage of the UK 'Stern Review' on the economic costs of climate-change mitigation, impacts and adaptation further spurred media coverage across the world. Furthermore, the film *An Inconvenient Truth* featuring Al Gore was widely considered an illustrative watershed moment in the media attention to climate change as climate politics met popular culture (Luke, 2008).

Another peak over this period occurred in early 2007. This increase can be attributed to the highly influential IPCC Fourth Assessment Reports, released in stages over the first half of the year amidst a backdrop of highly fluctuating oil and gasoline prices. In addition, continued discussions of the influence of Al Gore's film provided news hooks into climate-change-related stories in Europe, North America and Oceania. However, this intensified media attention in 2007 was greatly surpassed by the news attention focused on climate change that closed out 2009.

The stagnation from mid 2007 until December 2009 can be primarily attributed to a number of intersecting influences. Among them, media attention on the global economic recession displaced/ shrank the news hole for climate stories, where immediate worries regarding job security and economic well-being dominated the news throughout 2008. A public 'caring capacity' for climate change was tested at this time, in the face of these pressing concerns. Stalled-out climate-related news coverage was also compounded by the lack of large-scale Katrina-like disasters that could potentially be hitched to the wagon of climate impacts.

Moreover, climate-related considerations expanded into stories of energy security, sustainability, carbon markets and green economies. An analysis by Curtis Brainard and Cristine Russell in *Columbia Journalism Review* found that stories from October 2008 through to March 2009 in the *New York Times* and the *Washington Post* mentioned 'energy' in their headlines and lead paragraphs over three times more often than 'climate change' or 'global warming'.

Figure 1.1 is most effectively considered as a Rorschach print rather than one to interpret literally. That is because the trends

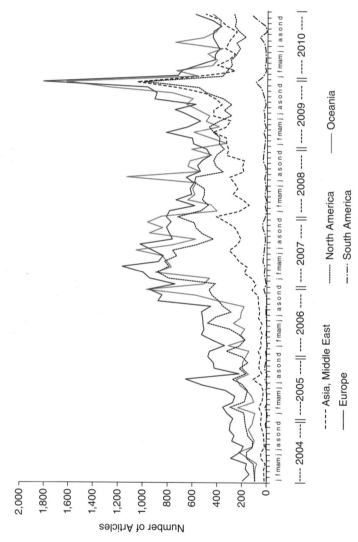

Figure 1.1: World newspaper coverage of climate change/global warming, 2004–2010

This figure tracks newspaper coverage of climate change or global warming in 50 newspapers across 20 countries and 6 continents over a 7-year period (January 2004 – November 2010). These newspapers (appearing alphabetically by newspaper) are: *The Age* (Australia), *The Australian* (Australia), *Business Day* (South Africa), *Clarín* (Argentina), the *Courier-Mail* (Australia), the *Daily Express* (and *Sunday Express*) (United Kingdom), *Daily Mail* (*Mail on Sunday*) (United Kingdom), the *Daily News* (United States), the *Daily Telegraph* (Australia), *Dominion Post* (New Zealand), *Fiji Times* (Fiji), the *Financial Mail* (South Africa), *Globe and Mail* (Canada), the *Guardian* (and *Observer*) (United Kingdom), *The Herald* (United Kingdom), the *Hindu* (India), *Hindustan Times* (India), *The Independent* (and the *Independent on Sunday*) (United Kingdom), *Indian Express* (India), the *Irish Times* (Ireland), *Japan Times* (Japan), the *Jerusalem Post* (Israel), the *Jerusalem Report* (Israel), the *Korea Herald* (South Korea), the *Korea Times* (South Korea), the *Los Angeles Times* (United States), the *Mirror* (*Sunday Mirror*) (United Kingdom), the *Moscow News* (Russia), the *Nation* (Pakistan), *the Nation* (Thailand), *National Post* (Canada), the *New Straits Times* (Malaysia), the *New York Times* (United States), *New Zealand Herald* (New Zealand), the *Prague Post* (Czech Republic), *The Press* (New Zealand), *The Scotsman* (and *Scotland on Sunday*) (United Kingdom), the *South China Morning Post* (China), the *South Wales Evening Post* (United Kingdom), the *Straits Times* (Singapore), the *Sun* (and *News of the World*) (United Kingdom), *Sydney Morning Herald* (Australia), the *Telegraph* (and *Sunday Telegraph*) (United Kingdom), *The Times* (and *Sunday Times*) (United Kingdom), the *Times of India* (India), the *Toronto Star* (Canada), *USA Today* (United States), the *Wall Street Journal* (United States), the *Washington Post* (United States), *Yomiuri Shimbun* (Japan). For monthly updates go to http://sciencepolicy.colorado.edu/media_coverage/

here over time carry more explanatory power than the absolute numbers of stories in each region. University of Oxford researcher Maria Mansfield and I based our decision regarding which newspapers to include on the key factors of their circulation and influence amongst policymakers and the public. Reliable access to the newspapers' archives was important too, additionally influencing the January 2004 starting point.

Furthermore, this figure notes the trends in coverage of climate change or global warming, relative to the amount of coverage of climate change or global warming at other times. More generally, stories tracking issues, events and information on 'environmental issues' (of which climate change is a subset) have continued to occupy a small nook in news overall. In other words, relative to other issues like health, medicine, business, crime and government, media attention to climate change remains a mere blip. Precise data on these trends remain difficult to collect across countries and regions. However, taking a look just at US coverage in 2009, Tricia Sartor and Dana Page found that only 1.5% of news coverage was devoted to all environmental issues (2009). This varied slightly, where newspaper coverage of the environment occupied 2.7% of the overall news hole, while it was 1.6% on radio, 1.3% on network television news, 1% on the internet, and 0.8% on cable television news.

With these sampling issues in mind, this figure also indicates that there remained a relatively low number of stories on climate change or global warming in the regions of South America and Africa throughout this period. This points to a critical regional 'information gap' in reporting on these issues, and relates to capacity issues and support for reporters in these regions and countries (developing and poorer regions/countries). As has been documented by Mike Shanahan, Rod Harbison, James Fahn and others, it is often those who are most at risk from climate impacts who typically have access to the least information about it through mass media (see Chapter 8 for more).

Moving to the national level, Figures 1.2, 1.3 and 1.4 show country-level trends in the US, UK and India. Notably, coverage in the UK increased much more dramatically during 2009. Possible reasons for this include the fact that the UEA CRU email hacking scandal took place in the UK, thereby providing a story of national as well as climatic interest (see Chapter 2 for more). Also, while COP15 provided

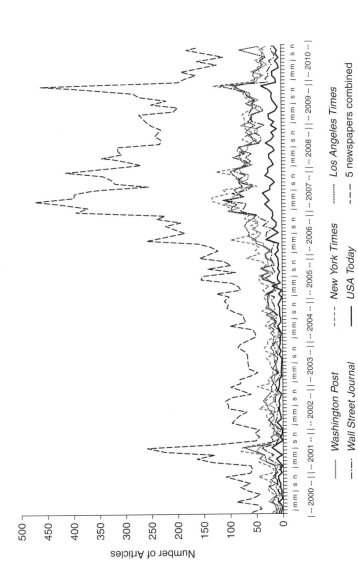

Figure 1.2: US newspaper coverage of climate change/global warming, 2000–2010

This figure tracks newspaper coverage of climate change or global warming in five newspapers in the United States from January 2000 – November 2010). These newspapers are the *Los Angeles Times*, *The New York Times*, *USA Today*, the *Wall Street Journal* and *The Washington Post*. For monthly updates go to http://sciencepolicy.colorado.edu/media_coverage/

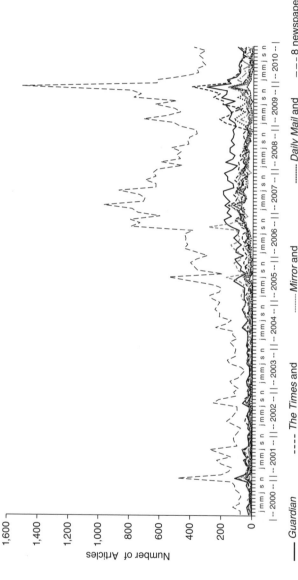

Figure 1.3: UK newspaper coverage of climate change/global warming, 2000–2010

This figure tracks newspaper coverage of climate change or global warming in eight newspapers in the United Kingdom from January 2000 – November 2010). These newspapers are the *Daily Express* (and *Sunday Express*), *Daily Mail* (*Mail on Sunday*), the *Guardian* (and *Observer*), the *Independent* (and the *Independent on Sunday*), the *Mirror* (*Sunday Mirror*), the *Sun* (and *News of the World*), the *Telegraph* (and *Sunday Telegraph*), *The Times* (and *Sunday Times*). For monthly updates go to http://sciencepolicy.colorado.edu/media_coverage/

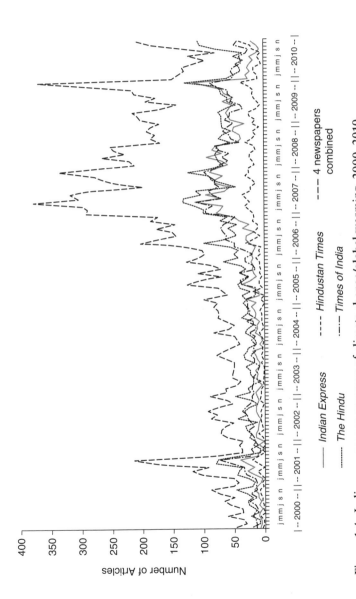

Figure 1.4: Indian newspaper coverage of climate change/global warming, 2000–2010 – This figure tracks newspaper coverage of climate change or global warming in four newspapers in India from January 2000 – November 2010). These newspapers are *The Hindu*, *Hindustan Times*, *Indian Express* and the *Times of India*. For monthly updates go to http://sciencepolicy.colorado.edu/media_coverage/

news hooks aplenty for journalists from all around the globe to cover the talks, the fact that they took place in Europe lowered the transaction costs for UK environment and science content producers to cover the issue, relative to those in the US and India.

Questions remain, such as: how does the quantity of news relate to quality? Now that the quantity of climate-change coverage has increased, to what extent are NNSAs' voices gaining greater traction? What does this mean for information sharing and climate literacy? Also, how much news does it take to generate doubt vis-à-vis confidence in a range of issues, in climate science and governance? To what extent might front-page stories drive policy priorities and public perceptions more than stories buried deep in the newspaper? Placement of climate representations in mass media also matter. For instance, research by Yuki Sampei and Midori Aoyagi-Usui in three Japanese newspapers – *Yomiuri Shimbun*, *Asahi Shimbun* and *Mainichi Shimbun* – found that 'the number of articles on global warming on the front pages of newspapers significantly influenced public concern for global environmental issues' (2009, 210). The importance of content for front-page articles has been described by Tom Yulsman as the kind of climate-change stories that 'make a front-page thought'.

Yet, to the extent that elected officials, (climate) policy negotiators and rank-and-file policy actors view amplified media attention to climate change as a proxy for public attention to climate change (and pressure for action), these trends have the potential to catalyse climate mitigation and adaptation actions. Conversely, a diminished amount of coverage can be seen as detrimental to putting forward strong climate policies.

Introductory conclusions

So, the contemporary cultural politics of climate change operate in a multitude of rapidly expanding spaces. Within these, the media community serves a vital role in communication processes between science, policy and the public. Mass-media representations – from entertainment to news – play a critical role in shaping our perceptions, considerations and action. Media representations of climate science and policy clearly do not drive public opinion, individual action, culture or societal change. Yet they have proven to be a key contributor – among a number of factors – that has stitched together climate science, governance and daily life.

Through all sorts of media forms – from newspapers and books to television and films, radio and the internet – a diverse groundswell of actors and institutions make climate change meaningful, and 'bring climate change home' (Slocum, 2004, 413). While this volume largely focuses on news media, there can often be significant overlaps with entertainment media. Two brief examples can illustrate this point: first, the climate comic *Funny Weather* by Kate Evans has provided both entertainment and instructional value about issues from the greenhouse effect to carbon sequestration; second, the film *Sizzle: A Global Warming Comedy* by Randy Olson has made people laugh while it has attempted to address pertinent and vital themes of climate scepticism as well as alarmism.

Media communications thus unfold within larger political contexts that then recycle into ongoing media coverage and considerations. The chapters that follow will explore *how* and *why* influencing factors at multiple scales – from regulatory frameworks (bounding political opportunities and constraints) and institutional pressures (influencing political and journalistic norms) to individual decision-making about what becomes 'news' – are dynamic and contested spaces of meaning-making and maintenance.

In particular, the next chapter will explore historical pathways and influences on contemporary media representations of climate change. Overall, this way through the material has endeavoured to effectively explore the ways in which mass-media outlets – and the many people and processes comprising them – 'speak for climate' as they give voice to climate issue formulations in various ways, and also then 'frame' the ways in which they are discussed and governed.

2 | Roots *and culture*
Exploring media coverage of climate change through history

People make their own history, but they do not make it just as they please; they do not make it under circumstances chosen by themselves, but under circumstances directly encountered, given and transmitted from the past. The tradition of all the dead generations weighs like a nightmare on the brain of the living

Marx, 1891, *The Eighteenth Brumaire of Louis Bonaparte*, 15

Today's media representations are manifestations of past themes, resonant tropes and collective institutional as well as individual memories. By examining current media narratives, we can delve into histories of scientific and policy endeavours that have sought to understand as well as govern climate processes and effects. Through such undertakings taken up in this chapter, we can identify and ponder moments of critical discourse that have shaped ongoing climate storylines.

Scientific pursuits to make sense of climate change have a long and rich history; however, a historical look at how climate has been communicated through mass media is comparably shorter and much less developed. In *Annals of the Former World*, writer John McPhee provided the analogy that the 4.6 billion-year history of time on Earth can be considered as distance from fingertip to fingertip with one's arms spread wide. He wrote, 'the Cambrian begins at the wrist ... all of the Cenozoic is in a fingerprint, and in a single stroke with a medium-grained nail file you could eradicate human history' (McPhee, 1998). Considered in this way, it would merely take a fine-grained nail file to remove the history of science communications and mass media. In fact, before the late 1980s, media portrayals of 'climate change' or 'global warming' were sporadic, compared to the amount of coverage in most regions around the world today (see Figure 2.1).

Contemporary events provide opportunities to consider histories of climate science and governance via media treatments of various aspects of climate change. For example, in October 2009, claims of possible

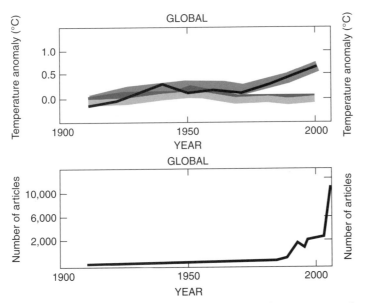

Figure 2.1: Atmospheric temperature and media coverage of climate change

The plot of global temperature anomaly over time (**A**) is from the Fourth Assessment Report Working Group I Summary for Policymakers from the IPCC (2007). The black line depicts decadal averages of observations relative to the corresponding temperature average for 1901–1950. The lower band shows the general range from simulation runs in climate models using only natural forcings due to volcanic and solar activity. The upper band shows the range using both natural and anthropogenic forcings. The plot of number of media articles over time (**B**) shows the general trends in the amount of coverage in fifty influential newspapers, across twenty countries and on five continents.

'global cooling' permeated mass media accounts. The news hook was that the UK Met Office's Hadley Centre reported that the last decade had seen a sputtering rather than a steady increase in global temperatures. Despite the fact that the Met Office commented that "warming is set to resume quickly and strongly" (Hudson, 2009), the report spun out a flurry of associated news reports and web activity (PEJ, 2009).

An iterative back-and-forth took place in the news pages and blogs in the following days and weeks. First, Paul Hudson covered the Met

Office findings in a piece on *BBC News* entitled 'What happened to global warming?' where he commented, 'For the last 11 years we have not observed any increase in global temperatures' (2009). Then, an *Associated Press* piece took a different view, noting that since a high point in 1998, global atmospheric temperatures 'have dipped, soared, fallen again and are now rising once more'. Journalist Seth Borenstein quoted climate scientist Ken Caldeira, who asserted, 'To talk about global cooling at the end of the hottest decade the planet has experienced in many thousands of years is ridiculous' (2009). Nonetheless, a few days later, in a piece called 'The Earth Cools and Fight over Warming Heats Up' in the *Wall Street Journal*, Jeffrey Ball (2009) then claimed that the Met Office report 'has reignited debate over what has become scientific consensus: that climate change is due not to nature, but to humans burning fossil fuels'.

Careful news consumers might have pointed out the misguided and binary logic of the Ball piece. But, such details were swamped by the attention it drew to questions such as whether humans play a role in climate change and whether the climate is changing at all. Moreover, comments and quips that alluded to possible global cooling drew on resonant tropes from many decades earlier. Amidst a downward trend of atmospheric temperatures from the 1940s to the 1970s, numerous people made claims that these trends were indications of entry into a new glacial period. While this cooling was later found to be largely attributable to the short-term effects of aerosols (small particulates) in the atmosphere, in the meantime a great deal of conjecture was perpetuated and amplified through mass-media accounts. For instance, a 1974 article in *Time* magazine ran with the headline 'Another ice age?' while a 1975 *Newsweek* story was entitled 'The cooling world'. Despite the fact that the notion of global cooling had been refuted by experts in climate science, scientific accuracy was displaced by effective argumentation in the mass media. Fuelled by media representational practices, the 2009 example also illustrated how outlier perspectives quickly and capably populated, constructed and influenced public discourse in the highly contentious and highly politicized milieu of climate science and governance. Through traditional media coverage and blog posts representing this October 2009 Met Office report, what began as a mundane communication became a lightning rod for larger battles to make sense of the science and politics of climate change.

Cultural characteristics and psychological factors also influence underlying attitudes to climate-change science and governance (see Chapter 7 for more). Looking at this historically, deeply entrenched scepticism regarding scientific claims of environmental decline was evident during British colonialism. In the first half of the nineteenth century, numerous members of the scientific community – mainly botanists and doctors – warned governments in the UK and the colonial periphery about the dangers of damaging ecosystem services during this process of 'taming' the wild and migrating to new parts of the planet (Boykoff and Rajan, 2007). Although British government officials were responsive to immediate and major crises – such as famine or drought – these creeping environmental challenges were given very low priority. Often, with the passage of the immediate crisis, civil administrators would raise sceptical objections about the claims of the scientists regarding environmental decline. For example, Robert Baden-Powell – a lieutenant general in the British Army and colonial forestry advocate – observed that:

In the official mind up to the highest, we find various degrees of disinclination towards vigorous conviction: and just as we find in the people the progress of conviction barred by self-interest, so it is with their rulers. Considerations of interest, such as the desire to have no complaints and have everything snug and quiet in the district, to show a good revenue sheet by yielding forest produce ... affect their capacity for the reception of a sure belief in forest economy. (Rajan, 2006)

Such to and fro over time in the cultural politics of climate change has also elucidated issues of trust: in science, in media, in experts, in authority. These questions of scepticism and confidence in claims as well as claims-makers are evident in historical examples such as the one above, and also pervade the contemporary arena of climate science and governance. Much of our current understanding of trust is systematically interpreted through polling data. In the issue of climate change in the US, levels of trust have been shown to be fickle in civil society. For example, Anthony Leiserowitz, Ed Maibach, Connie Roser-Renouf, Nicholas Smith and Erica Dawson found a significant loss of trust in scientists in the wake of 'Climategate' (2010). In another example, Kyun Soo Kim found that low trust in media correlated with a perception of a 'hostile media bias', or the view that media representations were skewed away from their own views on climate science and policy (2010).

Moreover, in issues associated with climate change, trust can conflict with expertise. In one study, two-thirds of respondents deemed television weathercasters trustworthy on information about climate change. This figure was higher than trust in religious leaders, corporations or Al Gore (Homans, 2010). However, research by Kris Wilson has shown that these trusted authorities are not necessarily well-trained and well-informed experts on the intricacies of climate science. Journalist Charles Homans has commented, 'There is one little problem with this: most weathercasters are not really scientists' (2010, 26). Nonetheless, Wilson has pointed out that weathercasters are often considered public intellectuals in their communities, where they have high levels of audience credibility. He surmised, 'There isn't a politician, entertainer, or athlete in the world who wouldn't kill for a fraction of the power that television weathercasters command from the public's attention' (Wilson, 2007, 84).

But through avenues of trust as well as discursive traction through mass media, outlier views have gained access to decision-making and have influenced the cultural politics of climate change. These outlier perspectives have come in many shapes and sizes and across multiple axes of understanding. Considerations of power and influence are important here as well as dimensions of expertise and authority (see Chapter 3 for more). Moreover, the discourses themselves have ranged in content and tone from perspectives referred to as 'alarmists', 'climate panics' or 'warmistas' to those commonly referred to as 'sceptics' (spelled 'skeptics' in the US), 'contrarians' or 'denialists'. By drawing on historicized cultural themes, characteristics and traditions, and in combination with these issues of power, knowledge and perspectives, media representations have at times worked against efforts to enlarge rather than constrict the spectrum of possibility for mobilizing the public to address ongoing climate challenges. The 2009 case of 'Climategate' serves as a useful and concrete illustration of these complex interacting factors by way of media representational practices.

The UEA CRU email hacking scandal (a.k.a. 'Climategate')

In November 2009, thousands of emails and documents were leaked from a server used by the Climate Research Unit (CRU) at the University of East Anglia (UEA) and posted to various publicly accessible internet locations. The scandal – swiftly dubbed 'Climategate' – was not dominated by the hacking of the server, but instead mainly focused on how some of these emails raised questions about the integrity of scientific practices. Messages between expert climate scientists such as Michael Mann and Phil Jones revealed allusions to efforts to stave off dissenting views from dominant perspectives on climate science. These developments also followed on the media attention paid to the aforementioned 2009 UK Met Office Hadley Centre report. Journalist Komila Nabiyeva found that the term 'Climategate' was first invoked by James Delingpole in the *Telegraph* blog (Delingpole, 2009; Nabiyeva, 2010). The response in new and social media was swift and fierce. Journalist Christopher Booker of *The Times* named it the 'worst scientific scandal of our generation' (2009), while *Guardian* journalist George Monbiot wrote in an opinion piece, 'the emails are very damaging', calling for CRU Director Phil Jones to resign (2009).

After six months of independent investigations into possible wrongdoing by data manipulation and the violation of UK Freedom of Information laws, Phil Jones and the other climate scientists were cleared of the legal charges (Adam, 2010). Nonetheless, media coverage at the time of this unfolding story flourished, as the many dimensions of the story fed into journalistic norms of personalization, dramatization, novelty and authority–order bias (see Chapter 5 for more). The timing of the email and document hack was also just before the commencement of the much anticipated COP15 climate talks in Copenhagen, where the successor treaty to the Kyoto Protocol was set to be negotiated. Despite the many months and years of preparations for those particular COP15 negotiations, both traditional and new/social media attention swiftly shifted to 'Climategate'. Moreover, story narratives were driven by how the recent conflict and contention stemming from the hacking scandal strained these international negotiations. For example, the *New York Times* front-page story went with the headline: 'Facing skeptics, climate experts sure of peril' (Revkin and Broder, 2009, A1). Also, *CNN* featured a segment called 'Global Warming – trick or truth?' where anchor Campbell Brown began, 'Stolen emails, conspiracy theories – what's the bottom line on global warming? ... Billions of dollars and the future of the planet hang in the balance. Who is telling the truth? ... We'll take you inside the university where the scandal started and to Copenhagen where world leaders are about to make major decisions about how we live our lives. Tonight, a global investigation into what's being called "Climate-gate", hacked e-mails that some say call into question the very science behind global warming. We are looking at all of the angles tonight. We've got coverage from Copenhagen to London, skeptics and scientists' (2009).

In the end, this COP15 gathering – while widely hyped in the wake of the US Presidential Election of Barack Obama in the previous year – failed to assemble a substantive and binding agreement to reduce greenhouse gas (GHG) emissions, the successor to the Kyoto Protocol. Although a pledged 'Copenhagen Accord' emerged from the eleventh-hour negotiations by world leaders, a more substantive Protocol was hampered by perennial challenges along risk/responsibility and global north/south dimensions manifested in mechanisms such as REDD+ to address climate mitigation, and an Adaptation Fund through a Clean Development Mechanism levy.

Yet, the combination of 'Climategate' and COP15 failures provided news hooks aplenty for continued stories on climate change, even beyond the exoneration of Phil Jones and others. For example, a July 2010 article by Fiona Harvey in the *Financial Times* covered a new report by the US National Oceanic and Atmospheric Administration (NOAA) and began: 'International scientists have injected fresh evidence into the debate over global warming, saying that climate change is "undeniable" and shows clear signs of "human fingerprints" in the first major piece of research since the "Climategate" controversy' (2010, 1). The article continued with a back-and-forth between duelling personalities. On one side were Jane Lubchenco and Bob Ward who commented that 'Climategate was a distraction'. On the other were 'prominent climate sceptic(s)' such as Pat Michaels and Myron Ebell who continued to claim, 'It's clear that the scientific case for global warming alarmism is weak. The scientific case for [many of the claims] is unsound and we are finding out all the time how unsound it is' (2010, 1). By flatly reporting the many claims that were associated with the 'Climategate' affair – without some assessment of their veracity relative to their wider peer communities – a gestalt 'climate-change debate' was perpetuated in the public arena (see Chapter 3 for more).

However, while 'Climategate' was a hot topic during this time, it still remained a relatively weak 'signal' over this period amidst the 'noise' of overall climate change or global warming coverage.

Figure 2.2 shows coverage of climate change and global warming from 2009 to 2010 in five US and UK newspapers. This figure also then compares this with more specific coverage of 'Climategate' and COP15 in Copenhagen, Denmark. While questions remain about how much coverage is 'needed' to raise and sustain doubts or uncertainty (see Chapter 6 for more), these trends nonetheless set the table for discussions of climate science and governance in the public arena. Figure 2.3 shows the percent contribution that each of eight UK newspapers – quality press and tabloids – made to the total amount of coverage of climate change or global warming each month. These data draw attention to the high number of articles that appeared in November 2009 in *The Times* in the wake of the UEA CRU email hacking scandal, as well as the numerous articles that appeared in the *Guardian* in February 2010 as part of an investigative series by Fred Pearce into the 'Climategate' affair.

Figure 2.2 shows that the amount of coverage of climate change or global warming diminished after COP15 in December 2009. These trends are also tracked in global media coverage of climate change or global warming in Figure 1.1. Despite this decrease in the quantity of coverage, a great deal of the content of media representations focused on ongoing and contentious issues in climate science and governance, particularly scrutinizing the processes and products of the Intergovernmental Panel on Climate Change (IPCC). For example, many stories in early 2010 were generated through the news hook of errors that were revealed in Himalayan glacier melt-rate claims in the IPCC Fourth Assessment Report. Furthermore, a number of 'climate stories' emerged in reporting on the 2010 InterAcademy Council (IAC) review of IPCC processes. In mid 2010, the IAC ultimately released a report with recommendations for reforming the management structure and assessment procedures of the IPCC (Shapiro *et al.*, 2010).

Furthermore, during this time in 2010, it was revealed through new media coverage that Rajendra Pachauri circulated an email to IPCC Fifth Assessment Report authors stating, 'My sincere advice would be that you keep a distance from the media ...', and included a document assembled by the group 'Resource Media' providing 'tips for responding to the media' (Brainard, 2010). This Pachauri email and document served to demonstrate a rather archaic view of science in society, and inflamed rather than assuaged concerns regarding IPCC openness, transparency, effective communications and dialogue in

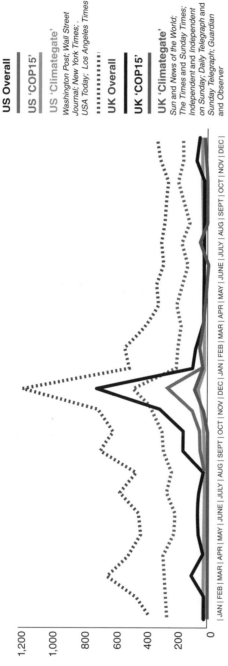

Figure 2.2: US and UK newspaper coverage of climate change, COP15 and 'Climategate', 2009–2010

This figure tracks media coverage of climate change or global warming in US and UK newspapers from 2009 through 2010. The US newspapers are the *Los Angeles Times*, the *New York Times*, *USA Today*, the *Wall Street Journal* and the *Washington Post*. The UK newspapers are the *Guardian* (and *Observer*), the *Independent* (and the *Independent on Sunday*), the *Sun* (and *News of the World*), the *Telegraph* (and *Sunday Telegraph*) and *The Times* (and *Sunday Times*). The 'Climategate' search terms used were 'climate change' (major mentions) OR 'global warming' (major mentions) AND 'climategate' (anywhere) OR 'Climatic Research Unit' (anywhere) OR 'Phil Jones' (anywhere). The 'COP15' search terms used were 'climate change' (major mentions) OR 'global warming' (major mentions) AND 'Conference of Parties' (anywhere) OR 'COP15' (anywhere) OR 'Copenhagen' (anywhere).

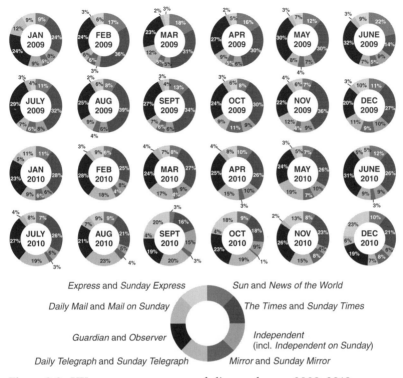

Figure 2.3: UK newspaper coverage of climate change, 2009–2010

This figure tracks media coverage of climate change or global warming in UK newspapers from 2009 through 2010 by percent each newspaper contributed to the total amount of coverage each month. The newspapers included here are the *Daily Express* (and *Sunday Express*), *Daily Mail* (*Mail on Sunday*), the *Guardian* (and *Observer*), the *Independent* (and the *Independent on Sunday*), the *Mirror* (*Sunday Mirror*), the *Sun* (and *News of the World*), the *Telegraph* (and *Sunday Telegraph*), *The Times* (and *Sunday Times*).

the public view (Revkin, 2010b). Moreover, this advice indicated that scrutiny over climate science during the previous year may have had a discernible chilling effect on science–media–public interactions. At a time when the stakes are high and non-nation-state actors (NNSAs) from across the ideological and political spectrum are vying for discursive positions of visibility through mass media, it seemed to be an especially inopportune time to have made efforts to guard IPCC 'experts' from the public arena.

Early media coverage of climate change

An expansive history of media begins with the art of rhetoric in ancient Greece and weaves through the centuries of the Roman Empire, the European Middle Ages and the Renaissance. Over these formative periods, a wide range of activities and modes of communication – performance art, plays, poetry, debate – drew on narratives, arguments, allusions and reports to communicate various themes, information, issues and events (Briggs and Burke, 2005). Organized studies of the art of communications began in these foundational periods for modern expression.

The invention of the Gutenberg printing press in 1450 expanded opportunities for communication on a larger scale. Primarily through the printing and distribution of books and pamphlets, ideas, arguments, stories and commentaries began to circulate throughout various segments of society in the sixteenth and seventeenth centuries. These seeds of 'media' sprouted over a wide extent in the decades that followed. Mass media grew to play vital and varied roles in translation (of information, concepts, developments, debates) between communities, such as the scientific community and the public.

However, such growth was limited by a number of competing factors, such as strong state control over the public sphere, legacies of colonialism, low literacy rates, racial and gender inequalities, as well as ongoing technological capacity challenges (Murdock, 2002). However, conditions during the French Revolution and the First Industrial Revolution in the late 1700s provided opportunities for media communications – newspapers in particular – to emerge with widespread force (Chapman, 2005). The increasing reach of modern media communications through these channels, technologies and innovations has led to the contemporary conception of 'mass media'. However, it still was not until the 1920s that scholars actually began to speak of such activities as 'media', as we do today (Briggs and Burke, 2005).

The late eighteenth century saw continued trends of growing media communications on a mass scale, as well as scientific understanding of the Earth's changing climate. This was a time when the English-led Industrial Revolution was taking hold by way of iron smelting in the coal-rich Shropshire region in the UK, and heavy reliance on carbon-based sources for energy and materials in industry and society began to contribute to substantial changes in the climate. Industrial progress revved up through carbon-based technological advancements driven by the engines of coal, oil and natural gas.

A 'carbon economy' emerged to prop up and connect the workings of everyday life to emergent national and global-level political economic architectures (Boykoff *et al.*, 2009b). Carbon-based activities quickly grew to dominate economies and societies in ways not seen before in human history. Ironically perhaps, it was this carbon economy's 'intertwining evolution with the Earth's inanimate forces, air, sea, rock – and human infrastructure' that was also eventually seen to threaten the very industries and societies it has enabled (Roston, 2008, 1).

At that time, the UK and Europe were considered cultural centres of media development, which then influenced media communications in other cultural contexts throughout the world. Non-democratic societies such as the Ottoman Empire strictly controlled the proliferation of mass media, and printing was not undertaken in Russia until the seventeenth century, nearly 200 years after Gutenberg (McQuail, 2005).

Connections between carbon emissions and climate change were first detected by French physicist Jean-Baptiste Joseph Fourier, British scientist John Tyndall, and Swedish physicist Svante Arrhenius (Bolin, 2007; Fleming, 1998). Such investigations into the 'climate question' were enabled by the establishment of research programmes that investigated factors such as learning about the basic physical processes in the environment, and understanding relationships between deforestation and precipitation (Rajan, 2006; Grove, 2003). Foundational observations and experimental findings gained through these endeavours then enabled further research by scientists such as Guy Stewart Callendar, Milutin Milanković and Gilbert Plass (Weart, 2003).

Meanwhile, early media coverage primarily focused on links between weather, food and climate. This was during a time of particularly cold winters in the Northern Hemisphere. For example, the *Edinburgh Advertiser* ran a story in September 1784 that read, 'The year 1782 proved remarkably cold and wet, the crops over a great part of Europe were more or less injured, and the northern climates experienced a fearcity, amounting to a famine ... Potatoes, which in bad seasons had proved a substitute for grain, were this year frost bitten, and rendered entirely useless. Thus the earth withheld its bounty ...'

The following winters were ones where the cultural mythology of 'ice skating on the Thames' in London was a reality. *The Times* in London captured this in a piece in December 1788, which described how, 'The cold weather has been more than usually severe in the West of England. In Cornwall, the thermometer has been 10 degrees below the freezing point. On the Sussex coast, at Brighton and Hove, the sea at rip tide has been frozen and there has been skating on it. The River Thames above bridge was completely frozen up on Monday evening from St Mary Overer's Dock to the Old Swan Stairs.'

As the nineteenth century commenced, the 'Fourth Estate' continued to flourish as a thirst for mass political communication was coupled with newfound technological and economic capacity. Moreover, in Europe and North America, freedom to participate in democratic processes enabled the proliferation of and development of newspapers into the 1800s. In the mid 1800s, media communications expanded their reach and influence tremendously, where mass-circulation print presses were set up in urban centres and daily newspaper production quadrupled in forty years. Concurrently, the increasing dominance of market-led enterprises served to displace many state-controlled presses, while many capitalist entrepreneurs gained control of influential means of information production (Curran, 2002). Thus, during this time, in Europe and North America mass-media outlets formed increasingly significant and powerful privately-run social, political, economic and cultural institutions (Chapman, 2005).

Sporadic coverage of climate-related themes continued to make connections between weather, food and climate. For instance, an 1841 *Milwaukee Sentinel* article – in the heart of Midwestern US agricultural production – read, 'The moisture of the earth, or the substratum, being continual, facilitates the gradual and constant absorption of carbonic acid gas from the surrounding atmosphere, and hydrogen and carbon, the chief elements of nourishment to vegetables.' As another example, an 1894 article in the *Atlanta Journal Constitution* boasted of a 'warm equable climate' for agricultural production in that southern US region.

These early media representations demonstrate the deep roots of links that have been made between weather and climate over time. When considering how complex processes have been made meaningful in the public arena, discussing the weather as a component of longer-term climate change has been commonplace. Connections made between weather and climate have provided logical bridges that have been crossed many times in media representations up to the present day. This has often been an entry point where observations have met longer-term data on changes in the climate. While it is difficult to access understanding about decadal climate shift through day-to-day observational trends, yet this remains a frequent 'way of knowing' about possible climate changes. Riffing off Mark Twain Stephen Schneider has commented, 'Weather is what you get; climate is what you expect ... weather is day-to-day fluctuations; climate is the long-term averages, the patterns and probability of extremes.' Journalist Bud Ward has added that 'weather helps us decide what to wear each day; climate influences the wardrobe we buy' (Russell, 2008).

Weather and climate are distinct but not mutually exclusive categories. Nonetheless, there is a tendency to take weather as evidence to support claims on a changing climate. But because of these overlaps – and distinctions – the propping up of weather as evidence either for *or* against climate change has proven to be a tricky practice. Ben Goldacre from the *Guardian* has commented that in this highly politicized atmosphere of climate science and politics, 'Any new weather event is currently explained away as yet another facet of global warming, but there has always been freak weather. Like most people, I find it hugely irritating when people draw too much from single events' (2008, 21). Curtis Brainard from *Columbia Journalism Review* has written, 'Short-term changes in the [weather] are irrelevant to the long-term trends in the [climate]. Yet every winter, the onset of cold inspires climate skeptics to once again attempt to "debunk" global warming and journalists to once again fall for the maneuver ... despite journalists' earnest and somewhat successful, efforts ... lingering confusion about the basics of climate science continues to plague public understanding' (2008).

Rooted in these histories, we can briefly ponder a few contemporary cases that emerged in media accounts which have illustrated the deployment of weather as evidence proving or dispelling anthropogenic climate change. For example, 'SNOWMAGEDDON' was the term first invoked on *NBC Nightly News* to describe the repeatedly heavy snowfall on the East Coast of the US in the winter of 2009–2010 (see Chapter 4 for more). In the context of negotiations for domestic Cap-and-Trade legislation in the US Congress at the time, this weather gave way to numerous articles linking to how this dispelled 'the myth of climate change'. In a story entitled 'Snow adds to political drift' in *The Wall Street Journal*, journalists Elizabeth Williamson and Neil King Jr wrote about how many political actors 'made hay over the contrast between the snow and the global-warming issue' (2010).

As another example, in the summer of 2010 Justin Gillis authored an article in the *New York Times* entitled 'In weather chaos, a case for global warming'. In it, Gillis wrote, 'far-flung disasters are revising the question of whether global warming is causing more weather extremes. The collective answer of the scientific community can be boiled down to a single word: probably' (2010, A1).

Such debate and discussion in the media has been fuelled by differing views on climate science between weathercasters and climate scientists themselves. Kris Wilson has attributed divergent views on links between weather and climate to differing conceptions and emphases placed on timescale as well as observational data. Moreover, Wilson explored how this disagreement has had significant implications for public understanding and engagement on climate change (2007). In a 2010 piece in the *New York Times* entitled 'Scientists and weathercasters at odds over climate change', journalist Leslie Kaufman wrote, 'The debate over global warming has created predictable adversaries, pitting environmentalists against industry and coal-state Democrats against coastal liberals. But it has also created tensions between two groups that might be expected to agree on the issue: climate scientists and meteorologists, especially those who serve as television weather forecasters' (2010, A16).

Twentieth-century media coverage of climate change

Rapid expansion of modern media communications continued into the twentieth century and set the stage for the impressive deployment of information via countless channels and outlets. This also gave rise to 'prestige' or 'quality' press, also known as 'elite' media, where journalistic professionalism as well as social and ethical responsibility were institutionalized, in contrast with partisan press (McQuail, 2005). Meanwhile, in North America circulation grew from one paper for every three households in 1870 to more than one paper for each household in 1910 (Starr, 2004). Along with these standards came the idealized journalistic standards of accuracy, accountability, independence, balance and checks on profit (Jones, 2009). Alex S. Jones argued that the primary responsibility of such modern media institutions was 'to be a democratic watchdog' (2009, 46).

However, corporate concentration, conglomeration and commercialization of mass media in the early 1900s carried conflicting impulses of expanding democratic speech and corporate capitalist pursuits of profit (Graber, 2000; Doyle, 2002). Many mass-media organs transformed into large-scale commercialized news apparatus (Starr, 2004). As these developments continued, the power of mass media became both amplified and more entrenched in society (McChesney, 1999).

Concurrently, US military interests developed and utilized media technologies and financially supported basic research in climate science with aims of achieving ongoing strategic goals and objectives. Besides the advantages of intra-military battlefield communications, propaganda campaigns were launched in order to weaken foreign enemies while whipping up domestic patriotism. Walter Lippmann famously wrote about how propaganda had the power to shape citizen decision-making, contributing to the 'manufacturing of consent' where common interests emerge from the 'complex unseen environment' (1922). Together, the twin military pursuits of media development and funding for climate science formed a 'military-climate industrial complex'.

Funding from bloated wartime military programmes was thus partly channelled into the progress of climate science research, effectively catalysing many scientific inquiries that significantly improved understanding of various aspects of climate science in the twentieth century. For example, in the 1950s Gilbert Plass drew on military funding to conduct research on atmospheric CO_2 and infrared radiation absorption. Plass worked at Johns Hopkins University and served as a consultant for the Office of Naval Research as well as Lockheed Aircraft Corporation (Weart, 2003). While this helped with the study of infrared absorption of heat-seeking missiles, it also added to a growing body of anthropogenic climate science research.

Also in the 1950s, funding from the US Navy and the US Atomic Energy Commission supported Hans Seuss and Roger Revelle's research on radiocarbon dating and isotope decay, to both examine fallout from nuclear bomb tests and trace the distinct isotopic signature of anthropogenic carbon emissions into the atmosphere. Through examinations of carbon cycling and carbon dioxide exchanges between the atmosphere and the oceans, Seuss determined that the oceans were acting as a massive sink, only partially counteracting an ongoing increase in atmospheric CO_2 levels (Hart and Victor, 1993; Corfee-Morlot *et al.*, 2007).

During this time, Charles David Keeling – a student of Revelle – began studying the interactions of atmospheric CO_2 and temperature. The initial stages of his research were paid for by funds from the US Atomic Energy Commission (after 1963, funding was continued through the United States National Science Foundation) (Fleming, 1998). This work – famously referred to as the 'Keeling Curve' – is now considered to be critical and foundational climate-change science research.

Over this period of time, mass-media coverage shifted from predominant attention paid to weather, food and climate to numerous articles that sought to describe the significance of this scientific research for society. For example, a *Chicago Tribune* article in 1913 endeavoured to explain the significance of the research of Svante Arrhenius. A passage read:

Svante Arrhenius, a Swedish Scientist, has contributed much to the theory of the beginning and ending of the world. According to him, the sun is dissipating and wasting inconceivable amounts of heat every year, and while its enormous energy may endure this loss for ages, the time must come when the sun will cool down and cover itself with a solid crust as our earth has done, and as the other planets have or will do some day. But no human being, he says, will be able to watch this death of the sun, for in spite of all man's desperate struggles and infinite inventions, all life will long have ceased on the earth for want of heat and life. Nor if people exist on any of the other wandering satellites of the sun will they be able to note its extinction, for they too will have failed to survive. But the end of the world by this means is far, far distant ...

While still scant, relative to the quantity of contemporary coverage of climate change, the spheres of climate science and mass media further came together in the 1930s. In 1932, the *New York Times* staff wrote, 'The earth must be inevitably changing its aspect and its climate. How the change is slowly taking place and what the result will be has been considered ...' (1932) Media coverage of early anthropogenic climate science began to appear as early as the 1950s. For instance, journalist Waldemar Kaempffert wrote in a 1956 *New York Times* article:

Today more carbon dioxide is being generated by man's technological processes than by volcanoes, geysers and hot springs. Every century man is increasing the carbon dioxide content of the atmosphere by 30 per cent – that is, at the rate of 1.1°C in a century. It may be a chance coincidence that the average temperature of the world since 1900 has risen by about this rate. But the possibility that man had a hand in the rise cannot be ignored.

This coverage became more prominent during the 'International Geophysical Year' of 1957. Journalist Robert C. Cowen wrote an article that appeared in the *Christian Science Monitor* called 'Are Men Changing the Earth's Weather?' (Cowen, 1957), which began:

Industrial activity is flooding the air with carbon dioxide gas. This gas acts like the glass in a greenhouse. It is changing the earth's heat balance. It could bring anything from an ice age to a tropical epoch … Every time you start a car, light a fire, or turn on a furnace you're joining the greatest weather 'experiment' men have ever launched. You are adding your bit to the tons of carbon dioxide sent constantly into the air as coal, oil and wood are burned at unprecedented rates.

In the subsequent three decades, mass-media coverage regarding climate change remained sparse, where climate science reports and meetings in the 1960s and 1970s, such as the National Center for Atmospheric Research (NCAR)-hosted conference 'Causes of Climate Change' in 1965, only generated occasional pieces. Yet more generally, literature that took up science and environment themes moved more visibly into public discourse and popular culture. For instance, as the 1950s began, Aldo Leopold's *Sand County Almanac* – published the year before – prompted many to consider environmental stewardship through his discussion of the 'land ethic'.

Moving into the 1960s, Rachel Carson's book *Silent Spring* raised public awareness of the environmental risk from pesticide exposure, and examined how chemical industry interests influenced the lack of environmental policy action. Moreover, Carson's analysis (focused on the disappearance of spring song birds due to fatal toxic exposure) has been credited for significantly shaping investigative environmental reporting and the profession of science journalism in the decades that followed (Kroll, 2001).

The 1969 moon landing as well as the first Earth Day in 1970 were key contributions that prompted further considerations of interactions at the human–environment interface. Furthermore, the global oil shocks in the 1970s began to draw attention to questions of energy security and the environment. Then US President Jimmy Carter called the energy crisis the 'moral equivalent of war' (quoted in Corfee-Morlot, 2007, 2763). During this time, scientific conferences exploring climate themes also increased. Bookending this decade, Stockholm, Sweden was the site of a 1971 conference entitled 'Study of Man's Impact on Climate', and in 1979 the World Meteorological Organization (WMO) organized the first 'World Climate Conference' in Geneva, Switzerland (Fleming, 1998).

The early 1980s began to see some increased coverage of climate science, focusing mainly on prominent and charismatic scientists such as the National Aeronautics and Space Administration's (NASA's) James Hansen and then NCAR's Stephen Schneider. For example, a front-page story at the *New York Times* in 1981 featured Hansen's recent *Science* study showing an increase in global mean temperatures along with a concurrent increase in atmospheric CO_2 emissions (Mazur and Lee, 1993). Meanwhile, international and domestic climate policy began to take shape in the mid 1980s, primarily through activities of the International Council of Scientific Unions, the United Nations Environment Program and the World Meteorological Organization.

In 1985, the Villach Conference convened in Austria to examine impacts of GHG emissions on the planet. Concurrently, academic research began to interrogate how media representations have fed back into ongoing formulations and considerations of environmental problems, issues and themes. For example, an investigation by Diana Liverman and D. J. Sherman examined portrayals of natural hazards in novels and films. This work was articulated in an edited volume by Jacquelin Burgess and John Gold examining intersections between media and culture across a number of environmental issues (1985). Furthermore, Dorothy Nelkin's book *Selling Science* was influential in examining reasons behind the media representations of science and technology (1987).

But it was in 1988 when climate science and governance flowed into full public view – by way of these numerous historical tributaries – through large-scale media attention (Carvalho and Burgess, 2005). Then, media coverage of climate change and global warming increased substantially in Western Europe and North America (Weingart *et al.*, 2000) (see Figure 2.1). Many factors contributed to this rise, and these can be further understood through the primary type or effect of each contribution.

First, there were *ecological/meteorological* events in the form of a North American heat wave and drought in the summer of 1988, as well as attention-grabbing forest fires in parts of Yellowstone National Park. These concomitant events were thought to sensitize many in the climate science and policy communities, as well as the media and public, to the issue of climate change. David Demeritt has asserted, 'The 1988 heat wave and drought in North America were arguably as influential in fostering public concern as any of the more formal scientific advice' (2001, 307).

Second, there were *political* issues that were emergent. For instance, then Prime Minister Margaret Thatcher spoke to the Royal Society in what became known as her 'green speech' on the dangers of climate change. In a rare address on the issue, she offered a warning regarding potential impacts due to climate change. She asserted, 'We may have unwittingly begun a massive experiment with the system of the planet itself' (Leggett, 2001, 10). Also, across the Atlantic Ocean, NASA scientist James Hansen forcefully warned Congress that global warming was a reality. He said on the Senate floor that he was '99 per cent certain' that warmer temperatures were caused by the burning of fossil fuels and that they were not solely a result of natural variation (Weisskopf, 1988). He also asserted that 'it is time to stop waffling so much and say that the evidence is pretty strong that the greenhouse effect is here' (Shabecoff, 1988, A1), while his testimony was offered on one of the hottest days of the year in North America. In the US, the impending presidential election also played a part, as campaign rhetoric became tinged with mentions of climate change and global warming. On the campaign trail that year, then-candidate George H.W. Bush acknowledged the seriousness of global warming and promised the administration would substantively address the issue. These political events garnered front-page coverage in the *Washington Post* and the *New York Times* among other publications at that time.

Third, *scientific* stories shaped media representational practices. Prominently, 1988 was the year in which the United Nations Environment Programme and the World Meteorological Organization (WMO) created the IPCC in Geneva, Switzerland. Also, the WMO held an international conference called 'Our Changing Atmosphere' in Toronto, Canada (Pearce, 1989). At this conference, 300 scientists and policymakers representing 46 countries convened, and from this meeting, participants called upon countries to reduce carbon dioxide emissions by 20 per cent or more by 2005 (Gupta, 2001).

Together, ecological, political and scientific factors intersected and dynamically brought the issue of climate change clearly onto the public arena (Wynne, 1994; Irwin and Wynne, 1996) (see Chapter 4 for more). At that time, narratives conformed to journalistic norms and informational predilections of the newspaper and television news media. According to Sheldon Ungar, 'What rendered 1988 so extra-ordinary was *concatenating* physical impacts *felt* by the person in the street'. (1992, 490)

Conclusions

While media coverage increased in the 1980s, research on the influence of media representations of climate and the environment burgeoned in the 1990s. These projects focused largely on practices and products in the Western world: North America, Europe and Australia/New Zealand. Scholarly work that sought to understand how meaning was constructed through media texts and discourses included important contributions by Jacquelin Burgess, Anders Hansen, Lee Wilkins and Craig Trumbo (Burgess, 1990; Hansen, 1991; Wilkins, 1993; Trumbo, 1996). In particular, Burgess put forward foundational conceptual work regarding the production and consumption of environmental meaning via the media, and set early guideposts for considering the emerging need to examine aspects of the intersections between mass media, science, environmental politics and civil society (1990). The majority of these studies examined print media coverage, mainly due to the influence of newspapers as agenda setters in mass media, but also as a consequence of data availability and access to newspaper archives. Some have also explored the role of television (e.g. Van Belle, 2000; Cottle, 2000; Smith, 2005; Boykoff, 2008b), but few have taken up questions surrounding radio (e.g. Harbison *et al.*, 2006).

The last decade of research has seen an expansion of approaches, methods and research questions explored under this umbrella of media and climate change. In the increasingly high-profile context of climate science and governance, more textured and nuanced considerations have emerged in analyses of media treatment of issues like how to govern the mitigation of GHG emissions from sources contributing to climate change, and how to construct and maintain initiatives to help vulnerable communities adapt to already unfolding climate impacts. The scope of these examinations has also expanded to analyses in many countries outside of the Western world.

For instance, a 2010 report by Tim Cronin and Levania Santoso examined media portrayals of climate change and REDD+ in the Indonesian context. They reasoned, 'Reducing emissions from defor-estation, forest degradation, and enhancing forest carbon stocks in developing countries (REDD+) has become a key area of debate in both global and national climate-change policy processes. Indonesia is the world's third largest emitter of carbon, with more than 80% of the country's emissions coming from land use change – primar-ily deforestation. This makes Indonesia's REDD+ policies not just nationally but also globally significant ... By examining the content of national media reports since the concept of REDD+ was first pro-posed ... this study has captured a snapshot of the events, frames, actors and perspectives that are driving REDD+ at the national level in Indonesia' (2010, 23). Through this work, the authors were able to more carefully delineate and analyze key claims-makers and the claims they made on REDD+ and other issues in climate politics in Indonesia. Through media analysis and interviews with Indonesian journalists covering the issues, the authors were able to effectively explore the cultural politics of climate change in Indonesia, by inter-rogating how and why particular media discourses gained traction while others did not (Cronin and Santoso, 2010).

In another case, innovative research by Simon Billett mapped out how nationally circulated English-language newspapers serving an elite Indian readership may have actually fortified rather than broken down barriers stemming from framing climate change along a 'risk–responsibility divide' during the study period of January 2002 through to June 2007. Billett's work has drawn out how there have been dif-ferences emergent in Indian and US press coverage of anthropogenic climate change over time: remarkably, 98 per cent of coverage in the sample set accurately attributed climate change to anthropogenic causes (see Chapter 6 for more on this issue). In so doing, Billett pos-ited that these tropes might seem to be useful domestically among the elite Indian readership, but they do not seem to ultimately aid progress over the chasm of ongoing North/South debates and discussions. Ultimately, Billett argued that the depoliticization of the scientific question of 'whether humans contribute to climate change' is supplanted by a strong normative and political frame around (Indian) risk and (Global North) responsibility (2010).

This chapter has sought to place contemporary media representations and expanding geographical locations of study in greater context through an exploration of intertwined historical 'roots and culture'. In so doing, it has endeavoured to set the stage for further considerations as to 'who speaks for climate' by way of mass media. This exploration of the trends in the amount of coverage still does not, however, centrally address questions involving the *content* and *context* of this coverage of climate change or global warming. These issues are taken up in the next chapters.

3 | *Fight semantic drift*
Confronting issue conflation

Few things are as much a part of our lives as the news ... it has become a sort of instant historical record of the pace, progress, problems and hopes of society.

(Bennett, 2002)

People typically do not start their day with a morning cup of coffee and the latest peer-reviewed journal article. Instead, citizens turn to mass media – television, newspapers, radio, internet and blogs – to link formal science and policy with their everyday lives. Members of the 'Fourth Estate' function as important interpreters of climate information: the public citizenry frequently learn about climate science, policy and politics from news and entertainment media. Studies across many decades have documented that consumer-citizens access understanding about science (and more specifically climate change) largely from the mass media (e.g. Nelkin, 1987; Antilla, 2010). In this context, central, fundamental and immediate challenges pervading media portrayals of climate change are those of fairness, accuracy and precision. While the previous chapters featured the quantity of news coverage on climate change and global warming, the next chapters take up issues involving content and *quality* of coverage.

In the high-stakes milieu of reporting, journalists, producers and editors as well as scientists, policymakers and non-nation-state actors must scrupulously and intently negotiate how climate becomes articulated. Whenever biophysical phenomena – such as changing precipitation patterns or changing ice-sheet dynamics – are captured and categorized through media portrayals or elsewhere, they undergo varying degrees of interpretation and are influenced by power and scalar factors (Jasanoff and Wynne, 1998). In this process, certain media 'storylines' gain salience (Hajer, 1993). Nonetheless, media reports have often conflated the vast and varied terrain – from climate science to governance, from consensus to debate – as unified and universalized issues.

These conflated representations can confuse rather than clarify: they can contribute to ongoing illusory, misleading and counterproductive debates within the public and policy communities on critical dimensions of the climate issue. To the extent that mass media have fused these distinct facets into climate gestalt, collective public discourses, as well as deliberations over alternatives for climate action, are poorly served. In this chapter, I pursue the conflation of 'claims' as well as 'claims-makers', along with treatment of 'uncertainty' in mass media.

Considering claims

There are facets of climate science and policy where agreement has become strong and convergent agreement dominates. Meanwhile, in other areas, contentious disagreement has garnered worthwhile debate and discussion. However, conflation of these diverse dimensions into one sweeping issue through media representations has contributed to confusion. Moreover, this has created a breeding ground for manipulation from outlier viewpoints to inadvertently or deliberately skew public discourse. Figure 3.1 is a four-panel schematic portraying the distribution of relevant expert-based agreement or disagreement on selected examples of climate science and governance issues. The bell curves illustrate the relative strength or weakness of such agreement.

First, consider panel A, 'Humans contribute to climate change'. In the last fifteen years, reports and findings have signalled a broad scientific consensus – despite lingering uncertainties regarding the *extent* of attribution – that human activity has significantly driven climate changes over the past two centuries, and that climate change since the Industrial Revolution has not merely been the result of natural fluctuations. As will be discussed further in Chapter 6, detection (of climate change) and attribution (to human activities) research has improved significantly over the last two decades of work (Karl and Trenberth, 2003; Tett *et al.*, 1999; Allen *et al.*, 2000b).

Noting this improved understanding, the UN Intergovernmental Panel on Climate Change (IPCC) has articulated this evidence-based view through multiple assessments of emergent peer-reviewed climate research and many stages of consensus-driven processes (Argrawala,

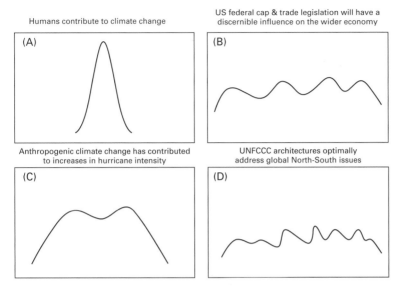

Figure 3.1: Media representations and the distribution of expert views in climate science and governance

This schematic is adapted from a *Nature Climate Reports* commentary by Boykoff (2008c) and comments by the *New York Times* journalist Andrew Revkin at the 2006 Society of Environmental Journalists annual conference. The bell curves illustrate the relative strength of agreement or disagreement on selected examples for environmental issues. Here, probability and strength of convergence are treated similarly. A long list of other examples could follow.

1998). A steady flow of IPCC reports since 1995 have represented 'critical discourse moments' that have solidified a narrative of consensus (Carvalho, 2005). Moreover, a managerial discourse has tethered institutional activities and actors to storylines that surround human contributions to climate change, and has reproduced itself (or has sought to do so) through policy-relevant research statements and decisions (Adger *et al.*, 2001). As a more recent example of such statements, the 2007 IPCC Fourth Assessment Report (AR4) from Working Group I (WGI) reported, 'Most of the observed increase in globally averaged temperatures since the mid 20th century is *very likely* due to the observed increase in anthropogenic greenhouse gas concentrations' (Solomon *et al.*, 2007, emphasis added). As I discuss below, the strength of convergence on particular issues has been quantified. In this case, 'very likely' has been a phrase deployed to also signify 'greater than 90% probability'.

In this particular aspect of climate change, statements coming out of the UN IPCC have clearly and consistently cohered with similar declarations from national science academies and other scientific groups. Organizations such as the American Geophysical Union (AGU), the National Oceanic and Atmospheric Administration (NOAA), the American Association for the Advancement of Science (AAAS) and the American Meteorological Society (AMS), among others, have converged on the detection and attribution findings that climate change is an issue that has human (anthropogenic) influences.

Despite this convergence, when mass media report on this issue, excessive attention has been paid to the tails in this schematic: outlier viewpoints at the ends of the distribution, rather than those under the bell curve that converge on agreement, have received amplified attention in media representations in particular country contexts such as the US and UK (Boykoff, 2007a; Boykoff and Mansfield, 2008). For instance, in 2003 the *Wilson Quarterly* featured a story entitled 'Global warming: both sides'. In research on scientific certainty argumentation methods, William Freudenburg discussed how embedded power and leveraged legitimacy have privileged constructions of 'non-problematicity', in this case with 'contrarian' claims that humans' role in climate change is negligible (2000).

Others have raised concern about 'alarmist' movements that push climate change discourse in the media beyond the parameters of what science can currently claim. This brand of outlier perspectives has been characterized in various ways such as 'global warming advocates', 'warmistas', 'panics', 'catastrophists' or 'climate fundamentalists' (Boykoff, 2009a; Hulme, 2009a). In a study commissioned by the Institute for Public Policy Research, Gill Ereaut and Nat Segnit warned about the dangers of alarmist tropes, writing, 'Its sensationalism and connection with the unreality of Hollywood films also distances people from the issue. In this awesome form, alarmism might even become secretly thrilling – effectively a form of "climate porn" ... undermining its ability to help bring about action' (2006, 7). Roger Pielke Jr has also warned that an alarmist discourse 'collapses under its own weight, because science does not compel action, and arguments that cannot be well supported by science will be found out' (2010, 198). Overall, these minority views – such as 'contrarian' or 'alarmist' discourses – have gained inordinate media traction, thereby perpetrating an information bias towards the perception of debate and disagreement (see Chapter 6 for more).

Second, panel B considers a schematic distribution of relevant expert-based views on the statement that 'US Federal Cap-and-Trade legislation will have a discernible influence on the wider economy'. As shown, a horizontal wavy line may most accurately depict the relative strength of agreement from 'positive effect' through 'no effect' to 'devastating effect'. In other words, there is a variety of legitimately divergent views on the potential effects that the implementation of Cap-and-Trade legislation may have on the wider US economy.

However, in research specifically on Senate Bill 2191 (the Lieberman–Warner Climate Security Act of 2008), Eric Pooley – former managing editor of *Fortune* and national editor of *Time* magazine – argued that mass media 'misrepresented the economic debate over Cap-and-Trade. It failed to recognize the emerging consensus among economists that Cap-and-Trade would have a marginal effect on economic growth and gave doomsday forecasts coequal status with nonpartisan ones. In other words...the press allowed opponents of climate action to replicate the false debate over climate science in the realm of climate economics' (2009, 4–5). Pooley conflated consensus from science to economics and mistakenly characterized a range of views more like panel A. However, closer examination reveals that this is a more challenging issue from which to derive a semblance of consensus.

Nonetheless, drawing from his results, Pooley argued that 'most of the reporting was bad in the painstakingly balanced way of so much daily journalism – two sides, no real meat...for most reporters covering this story, the default role was that of stenographer – presenting a nominally balanced view of the debate without questioning the validity of the arguments...the media's collective decision to play the stenographer role actually helped opponents of climate action stifle progress' (2009, 5). While he has been correct to point out the great need for further contextualizing stories, more critical engagement with the subject matter and enhanced deployment of fair and accurate journalistic reporting, in this case Pooley has reached beyond the relevant expert-based community views that inform this particular facet of climate governance. In so doing, this intervention has had the opposite effect: it has fed into, rather than alleviated, challenges that journalists face when they work to cover such a highly contentious and high-stakes story.

The insights we can draw from the distinctions between panels A and B carry extensively into other related climate issues where there are varying strengths of convergent agreement at present. More broadly, many science-policy issues – defined as 'decision-making related to the systematic pursuit of knowledge' (Pielke Jr, 2007, 79) – can usefully be considered through this lens. Examples include the rate of temperature change associated with climate change, the rate of sea-level rise or the heat capacity of greenhouse gases (GHGs). In addition, there remain a number of complex political questions regarding the most effective policy mechanisms (from a mandatory carbon tax to more voluntaristic approaches). Panels C and D illustrate further climate science and governance questions that have a range of perspectives, views and opinions. The bimodal distribution of panel C captures an issue being debated within the relevant expert community working on questions of hurricane intensity and anthropogenic climate change, such as findings by Chris Landsea contrasted with work by Kerry Emmanuel, Judy Curry and Greg Holland.

Overall, broad-brush treatment by mass media can both privilege or amplify marginal views as legitimate (panel A) and unduly dismiss legitimate claims (exemplified by panels B and D). Numerous factors – within the issues themselves as well as external contextual factors – contribute to the changing shape of these distributions over time. For instance, new scientific findings could contribute to further convergent agreement on an issue in climate science. Conversely, new findings could present rival hypotheses that would further distribute a spectrum of views across the schematic. In addition, an event such as widespread drought in Australia can change conditions through which these issues are understood and debated into the future.

Media portrayals of the details and nuances of expert views help journalists, scientists, policy actors and public citizens alike to better understand and appreciate these changing and contested contours of climate science policy. In contrast, issue conflation squanders opportunities to provide critical inputs for more informed decision-making regarding climate-change mitigation and adaptation alternatives.

Furthermore, such broad-brush media representations make mass media themselves relatively easy prey for the more nefarious and ideologically driven 'alarmists' or 'contrarians'. For example, the

2007 documentary *The Great Global Warming Swindle* combined many distinct issues into one great 'swindle' by misinterpreting research findings, editing interviewee comments and manipulating graphs to build a seemingly convincing argument that humans do not actually contribute to climate change. The film's narrator opined, 'As the frenzy of a man-made global warming grows shriller, many senior climate scientists say the actual scientific basis for the theory is crumbling.' Instead, director Martin Durkin and interviewees such as former British Chancellor of the Exchequer Nigel Lawson and physicist Nir Shaviv attributed the rise in global average temperatures to solar activity, ocean–atmosphere energy exchanges and volcanic activity.

The UK broadcast, watched by some 2.5 million viewers, provoked reactions from numerous climate scientists and policymakers, including prominent figures such as David Miliband, then the UK Secretary of State for the Environment, and Myles Allen of the University of Oxford. In the six weeks that followed, nearly 250 complaints were filed with the UK Office of Communications. In addition, a grievance was filed by a group of scientists against Channel Four, where the film originally aired. In the US, the Public Broadcasting System chose not to air the film. Director Martin Durkin later acknowledged many of the problems and inaccuracies. However, the grievance was denied in July 2008 and, by that stage, the seeds of public misunderstanding of the role of human activity in climate change had been sown through the inexact and hence misleading programme.

Considering claims-makers

As has been indicated above, efforts to make sense of complex climate science and governance through media representations involves decisions regarding who are 'experts' or 'authorities' to speak for climate. This is particularly challenging when covering climate change, where indicators of climate change may be difficult for most people to detect (Andreadis and Smith, 2007). Moreover, in the advent and increasingly widespread influence of new and social media, journalist Alissa Quart has warned of dangers of mistaken (or convenient) reliance on '*fauxperts*' instead of 'experts'. Such content-producing voices are amplified increasingly through new and social media, and are merely a Google search away from contemporary media

consumer-citizens. These ways of disseminating information inten-
sify possibilities of short-circuiting peer-reviewed literature, as well
as doing an 'end-run around established scientific norms' (McCright
and Dunlap, 2003, 359).

Chapter 2 touched on how weather patterns can be treated as
evidence for (and against) patterns of climate change. But with the
exception of those closely attuned to multi-decadal climate changes,
the challenges of translating observations to evidence create a need
for experts to make sense of the longer-term trends and patterns.

Over time, many researchers have sought to understand variegated
roles of authorities and experts via mass media in the public sphere.
For example, sociologist Arthur Edwards has worked through various
science-policy models – decisionist, technocratic, pragmatic – in order
to make sense of scientific expertise in society. He commented, 'The
media appear as an intermediary condensing the spontaneous communications taking place in the networks of daily life' (1999, 166).
There have been many ways devised to define an 'expert', from 'someone who has thought deeply on a subject' (Nordhaus, 1994, 46) to a
person who 'has status of authority in a subject by reason of special
training or knowledge' (Bray and von Storch, 1999, 441). As expertise relates to climate change, Thomas Lowe and Irene Lorenzoni have
combined these considerations to define them as 'individuals who,
having specialised in their particular area of work or research, had
extensive knowledge of wider climate-change issues demonstrated
through involvement in climate change-related projects and international publications' (2007, 133).

Richard Somerville pondered the role of climate scientists as experts
in an editorial in *Climatic Change* in 2006. He contrasted the treatment of climate 'expertise' by the public with the handling of expert
advice from medical sciences. He wrote:

We climate scientists are planetary physicians. We have learned many things
about climate, but we still have a lot to learn. Like the findings of media
science, our understanding of climate, although incomplete, is already
highly useful … The public has come to respect medical science, however,
and, although there will always be gullible people, most of us know there's
a difference between real experts and charlatans. Most people won't listen
to, or act on, medical advice from a quack who can talk plausibly about
medicine but who isn't really a physician. Everybody accepts this situation.
Even the least enlightened members of the US Congress don't hold hearings

to denounce modern medical science as a hoax. Yet, a few politicians and hard-core skeptics do attack climate science in exactly this way...medical science has achieved a measure of widespread respect that climate science can only envy. Journalists covering a medical discovery aren't usually suspicious of researchers and don't inevitably insist on hearing from "the opposing view". When reporting on research showing the need for people to eat sensibly and be physically active, the media do not frame the story of these scientific advances in terms of a debate or dispute. Journalists don't feel obliged to seek out medical contrarians "for balance." (2006, 1–3)

Somerville articulated a dimension of expertise through his take on how authorities 'speak for climate'. The way in which climate change is articulated, as well as how alternatives for climate action are considered, are products of claims and claims-makers. This has been unfolding for many decades. For instance, Myanna Lahsen has documented how influential US physicists sought to extend and maintain their authority and expertise on climate politics over the last thirty years (2008). However, this – along with ongoing conflation of climate change – has been particularly evident across the spectrum of news to entertainment media representations of climate change. Broad-brush treatments of claims-makers, and the claims they make, are readily found throughout the contemporary media landscape.

For example, Lou Dobbs – former host of *CNN*'s *Lou Dobbs Tonight* – ran a segment called 'Climate Change Battle'. He introduced the debate by saying, 'A renewed battle this week over global warming...whether it even exists at issue. Joining me now [are] two of the best experts on climate change: John Coleman, he's one of the founders of the Weather Channel. He says global warming is nothing more than a conspiracy. Good to have you with us. Henry Pollack – he says there are many examples of global warming, and it's for real. Good to have you with us'. In the segment, Dobbs distilled a range of distinct climate science and governance questions as to whether climate change is 'real' or whether it is a 'conspiracy'. Moreover, Dobbs propped up the expertise and authority of weathercaster John Coleman against that of geophysicist Henry Pollack, thereby putting their claims and counter-claims regarding climate science on a par with one another. High levels of public trust in weathercasters (see Chapter 2) provided some contextual backing to this juxtaposition as well.

Another example arose through coverage of Cap-and-Trade legislation in the US Congress. *Politico* journalist Erika Lovely, covering legislative debates, began a 2008 article, 'Climate-change skeptics on Capitol Hill are quietly watching a growing accumulation of global cooling science and other findings that could signal that the science behind global warming may still be too shaky to warrant Cap-and-Trade legislation.'

First, Lovely amplified the 'global cooling' claims of one source – Josef D'Aleo – with convergent agreement that the global average temperature has increased over the last century. Second, the author collapsed a 'debate' over this issue with reasons behind Congressional debate on whether Cap-and-Trade is an effective as well as a feasible policy mechanism to combat climate change. Through these problems with the article among many others, the *Politico* story overlooked possible questions of the veracity of the various claims as well as expertise of the claims-makers, along with issues of climate science, policy and politics involved (Lovely, 2008).

To the extent that claims are picked up on and flatly reported, and that claims-makers are frequently placed on equal footing irrespective of expertise, individuals (and organizations) have become empowered to speak with authority through mass media. Furthered by amplified media attention, these tendencies have skewed policymaker and public understanding of the issues, stakes involved and spectrum of possible actions to take.

Clearly, the role of the journalist is not that of a parrot. There are critical choices about how to represent various aspects of climate science and policy, and these depend on available information, perspective, interpretation and context as well as contextual social, political, cultural economic and environmental factors (Boykoff, 2007b). Nonetheless, all aspects of climate change should not be treated equally. Furthermore, legitimate disagreement and dissent have clear value in shaping understanding, so it remains a shifting set of challenges to represent these disagreements accurately, fairly and responsibly. These issues are further complicated through the difficulties involved in portraying various dimensions of climate (un)certainty.

Considering uncertainty

A continuing challenge to communicating about climate change has been how to accurately and fairly represent the contours of uncertainty. Meanwhile, uncertainty has been a salient theme in media coverage of climate science and governance over the last three decades (Weingart *et al.*, 2000; Zehr, 2000). Peter Taylor and Fred Buttel have pointed out how various dimensions of uncertainty in complex global environmental issues – like climate change – are particularly susceptible to misrepresentation and manipulation (1992). Other scholars have also pointed out that as scientific understanding improves, rather than settling questions, it often unearths new and more questions to be answered. Moreover, *greater* scientific understanding actually can contribute to *more* complicated policy decision-making by offering up a greater supply of knowledge from which to develop and argue varying interpretations of that science (Sarewitz, 2004).

In the 1990s, conceptual work sought to define and delineate aspects of uncertainty in the context of global change. In a seminal 1992 contribution, Brian Wynne worked to disaggregate these broadbrush considerations of risk and uncertainty in order to more capably consider open and more complex human–environment interactions. Wynne unpacked these considerations in the context of what Silvio Funtowicz and Jerry Ravetz characterized during this time as 'postnormal science' where 'facts are uncertain, values in dispute, stakes high and decisions urgent' (1993, 739). Wynne described 'four kinds of uncertainty' in this way:

(1) 'risk' – where we know the odds, system behaviour and outcomes can be defined as well as quantified through probabilities
(2) 'uncertainty' – where system parameters are known, but not the odds or probability distributions
(3) 'ignorance' – risks that escape recognition
(4) 'indeterminacy' – this intersects with the previous three kinds and captures elements of the conditionality of knowledge and other contextual scientific, social and political factors

While this characterization might at first glance seem overly abstract, this well-known utterance from former US Secretary of Defense Donald Rumsfeld helped to succinctly encapsulate these distinctions. In February 2002 – regarding US military risk and uncertainty – Rumsfeld commented, 'As we know, there are known knowns. There are things we know we know. We also know there are known unknowns. That is to say there are some things we do not know. But there are also unknown unknowns, the ones we don't know we don't know.' These Rumsfeldian distinctions break down quite usefully along the categories defined by Brian Wynne and illustrate the interacting features of the fourth grouping. While wary of rolling out this hackneyed quotation, its frequent reference through mass media and in the public arena demonstrates the potential for more textured treatment of 'uncertainty' as its dimensions relate to climate change.

Uncertainty remains an inherent feature of contemporary scientific inquiry and policy as well as everyday decision-making. At the interface of climate science, policy and media, uncertainty often garners a great deal of attention and is a battlefield for meaning. Regarding scientific uncertainty, Henry Pollack has considered this the challenge of 'translating error bars into ordinary language' (2003, 77). Media representations of uncertainty have the potential to inform a set of alternatives for individual as well as collective action on climate change. However, media portrayals also have the potential to distract (e.g. Revkin, 2010a) as well as impede substantive actions to reduce GHG emissions (Zehr, 2000), as the reduction of uncertainty has long been framed as a prerequisite for political and policy progress.

For example, in 1989 then US Senator Al Gore was widely quoted as saying, 'More research and better research and better targeted research is absolutely essential if we are to eliminate the remaining areas of uncertainty and build the broader and stronger political consensus' (quoted in Pielke Jr and Sarewitz, 2002, 27). As another example, an *International Herald Tribune* article covered ExxonMobil Corporation CEO Rex Tillerson's comments at a 2007 oil industry gathering where he commented that, 'My understanding is there's not a clear 100 percent conclusion drawn [regarding human contributions to climate change]. Nobody can conclusively 100 percent know how this is going to play out' (Krauss and Mouawad, 2007). These examples do not mean to suggest that improvements in scientific knowledge are not viable and important pathways to address uncertainty concerns; however, these illustrations do shed light on the fact that reduction of scientific uncertainty is not the sole and requisite way forward. Moreover, improving scientific certainty does not automatically prompt 'proper' policy and political climate actions.

In numerous cases, media portrayals have overly amplified uncertainties. In others, Peter Weingart and colleagues have actually argued that 'the media...tend to translate hypotheses into certainties' (2000, 262). In fact, Ulrika Olausson has argued – through analyses of the Swedish newspapers *Dagens Nyheter, Aftonbladet* and *Nerikes Allehanda* – that media may systematically underplay uncertainty as such representations can demobilize engagement. While she acknowledged that the findings may play out very differently in cultural contexts outside Sweden, Olausson claimed that this 'reluctance' is a consequence of conscious or unconscious efforts to avoid 'undermin[ing] the demand for collective action' (2009, 433).

These findings have made for a provocative argument. However, media misrepresentation of uncertainty must be held in consideration with larger institutional and contextual factors that give rise to both inadvertent and deliberate oversimplification, reductionism and omissions of uncertainty. Overall, amplification or diminution of uncertainty has troubled communications across this interface and has confused many important aspects of climate science and governance. Moreover, it has been an issue plagued by universalizing media treatments.

To begin to illustrate these intersecting elements, in 2008 there appeared a piece in *USA Today* by Doyle Rice called, 'Climate now shifting on a continental scale – study: migration patterns adjust, plants bloom early'. The news 'hook' was research findings from *Nature* documenting a range of physical and biological shifts in response to changes in the climate. Rice reported on early arrivals of migratory birds to Europe and declines in Antarctic penguin population as evidence for these connections. However, the article then followed (2008, B11):

'It was a real challenge to separate the influence of human-caused temperature increases from natural climate variations or other confounding factors, such as land-use changes or pollution,' says study co-author David Karoly, a climate scientist at the University of Melbourne in Victoria, Australia. Scientists reported in the study, however, that 'these temperature increases at continental scales cannot be explained by natural climate variations alone'. But Pat Michaels, a senior fellow in environmental studies at the Cato Institute in Washington, DC, says the research 'is a retrospective study, with very little to say prospectively, given the unevenness of global warming'. Michaels says that there has been no warming since 1997 and that a recent study, also published in *Nature*, found that global warming isn't likely to get started again for at least another 10 years. 'I think the problem with this study is not in matching the past with the changes but in projecting the future.'

To the frustration of scientists involved in the *Nature* study, Rice conflated a number of distinct scientific issues when assembling the article. In so doing, he called numerous facets of climate science into question, thereby raising the spectre of uncertainty over well-established findings in climate science. Therefore, this piece enabled Pat Michaels to raise blanket questions of likelihood and certainty, thus fundamentally calling into question whether the climate is changing at all (Woodside, 2009).

James Schlesinger penned the *Washington Post* opinion piece entitled 'Climate Change: The Science Isn't Settled', which provides another illustration of the misrepresentation of uncertainty through the media (2003). Schlesinger was Director of the US Central Intelligence Agency and Secretary of Defense under Presidents Nixon and Ford, then Secretary of Energy under President Carter. Also, among other roles he was a member of the Board of Directors for Peabody Energy and Coal. In this opinion piece, he de-emphasized the influences of anthropogenic climate change through this focus on 'unsettled' science, while he re-framed uncertainty arising from biophysical complexity as scientific confusion and incompetence. To conclude, Schlesinger called for greater humility and effectively turned the 'no regrets' policies inside out as he insisted that climate policy was best suited to a wait-and-see approach. This opinion piece – which misrepresented uncertainty among other errors – was communicated through this prominent media outlet, thereby serving to further obfuscate rather than illuminate considerations of climate action.

Part of the challenge here is that many of these sorts of characterizations of uncertainty in mass media have been drawn from risk assessments that assume well-defined, well-structured, primarily technical, closed systems. Examples might include efforts to reduce uncertainty regarding risks of leakage from nuclear plants or uncertainties associated with risks involving a range of transportation innovations. This way of approaching uncertainty may also stem from commonly held, more reductionist views that uncertainties are 'due to incomplete definition of an essentially determinate cause–effect system … they suggest that the route to better control of risks is more intense scientific knowledge of that system, to narrow the supposed uncertainties and gain more precise definition of it' (Wynne, 1992, 116). Mike Hulme has described how this has guided climate science-policy considerations for many years through 'simple linear' or 'bipolar' framing that 'either the scientific evidence is strong enough for action or else it is too weak for action' (2010).

However, another part of the challenge is that over time there have been many deliberate efforts to raise the broad perception of uncertainty – regarding basic science as well as implications of policy action. Strategies have ranged from deceptive disinformation campaigns and initiatives to subtle scientific certainty argumentation methods (Freudenburg *et al.*, 2008). Numerous undertakings to amplify uncertainty have sought to destabilize public support for climate mitigation and adaptation endeavours (see Chapter 7 for more).

For example, in 1998 the *New York Times* published a leaked draft report of a proposal compiled by industry opponents of climate mitigation action. Industry players from big oil companies, conservative policy research organizations and trade associations were reported to have met in the American Petroleum Institute's Washington office to assemble a plan that 'would be directed at science writers, editors, columnists and television network correspondents, using as many as twenty "respected climate scientists" recruited expressly to inject credible science and scientific accountability into the global climate debate, thereby raising questions about and undercutting the "prevailing scientific wisdom"'. The document revealed a 'campaign to recruit a cadre of scientists who share the industry's views of climate science and to train them in public relations so they can help convince journalists, politicians and the public that the risk of global warming is *too uncertain* to justify' (Cushman, 1998, 1, emphasis added). Indicating their recognition of the power of mass media, the group planned to measure success 'by counting, among other things, the percentage of news articles that raise questions about climate science and the number of radio talk show appearances by scientists questioning the prevailing views' (Cushman, 1998, 1). In this case, the media were the target for such actions as well as the vehicle through which the plans were leaked to the public.

There are many further cases where such movements have targeted the power of media to amplify certain views, and where mass media have exposed initiatives to manipulate public perception of climate change (Hoggan and Littlemore, 2009). As another example, a memo from US Republican strategist Frank Luntz was leaked to the press in 2003 (Burkeman, 2003). This memo focused on 'Winning the global warming debate' and emphasized key messages that Republicans should convey to the public via mass media. Among them, the memo outlined, 'Voters believe there is *no consensus* about global warming within the scientific community … Therefore, *you need to continue to make the lack of scientific certainty a primary issue in the debate* … the scientific debate is closing (against us) but not yet closed. There is still a window of opportunity to challenge the science' (Luntz, 2003, 142, italics in original).

Yet another example of policy and carbon-based industry relations' attempt to highlight uncertainties in climate science was reported through the mass media two years later. Documents regarding the United States Climate Science Program drafts in 2002 and 2003 were leaked to the press, showing edits by White House Council on Environmental Quality (CEQ) Chief of Staff Phillip Cooney that were made after they had undergone multiple drafts of peer review from experts in climate science. His edits subtly changed the wording and tone in many passages in the draft, thus raising uncertainty and debate. For instance, Cooney inserted the words 'significant and fundamental' before the word 'uncertainties', thereby further emphasizing the articulation of uncertainty in the document.

The *New York Times* journalist Andrew Revkin noted that they 'tend[ed] to produce an air of doubt about findings that most climate experts say are robust' (2005a, A1). Notably, Cooney has no background in science, nor was he considered an 'expert' in the areas of climate science that he was editing. Instead, Cooney had worked as a lobbyist for the American Petroleum Institute on climate issues before his time at the CEQ (Revkin, 2005a). Two days after these edits were leaked, Cooney resigned from the CEQ; three days after that, Cooney was hired as a consultant for ExxonMobil Corporation (Revkin, 2005b). Overall, these actions were seen as clear violations of scientific integrity to suit carbon-based industry interests (Hebert, 2005).

Considering these patterns of inadvertent as well as deliberate (mis) representations of media (un)certainty, journalist Ross Gelbspan has opined, 'If the public relations specialists of the oil and coal industries are criminals against humanity, the US press has played the role of unwitting accomplice' (Huck, 2006). The perception of uncertain climate science via media representations has also permeated the policy arena in numerous ways. In the US, policymakers such as James Inhofe have received extensive media coverage for their contrarian comments

on climate change. Inhofe (Republican, Oklahoma) – former Chair of
the Senate Environment and Public Works Committee – sent a 'Truth
Commission' to the UN COP15 talks in Copenhagen in 2009 to dis-
pel 'the myth of climate change' and has also famously said, 'could
it be that man-made global warming is the greatest hoax ever perpetrated on the American people? It sure sounds like it' (Inhofe, 2003;
Bowen, 2004a).

The various mobilizations of 'uncertainty' – and misappropriations
therein – have long played a critical part in ways of making climate
change meaningful in civil society. Among communities facing these
challenges, over the last decades, members of the IPCC have grappled with the difficulties of placing uncertainty associated with their
research into a familiar context.

Following the UN IPCC Second Assessment Report (SAR), Stephen
Schneider and Richard Moss took up an effort to assess uncertainty,
'using expert judgement'. They sought to reduce both inadvertent and
deliberate misinterpretations by formally introducing quantitative and
qualitative confidence intervals. They aimed to deploy these appraisals in order to effectively translate scientific certainty/uncertainty in
issues with sufficient evidence to do so, thereby improving communications between the scientific community and the media, policy
actors and civil society. Through numerous deliberations, meetings,
discussions and debates over the course of three years, Schneider and
Moss developed a scale that paired qualitative descriptions of likelihood and corresponding quantitative probability ranges (Schneider,
2009). Invoking the term 'very likely' then became translated to a
clear probability of 'greater than 90 per cent confidence', while
'likely' signified 'between 67 and 90 per cent confidence'. Over time
these scales – prominent in the Third and Fourth IPCC Assessment
Reports – have been seen as a significant step towards clarifying the
nuances of uncertainty in mass media and mitigating against its mis-
use in policy and political deliberations.

Suffice it to say that mass media workers have struggled to adequately capture these nuanced and complex distinctions over time.
While disaggregating the dimensions of uncertainty can help, contextualizing reports of (un)certainty is also important. Research by Julia
Corbett and Jessica Durfee examined coverage of climate change with
a focus on uncertainty (2004). Through an experimental design of
three newspaper story treatments – controversy, context and control

(context or controversy) – they found that greater contextualization within climate science stories helped to mitigate against controversy stirred up through uncertainty. So reader perceptions, and by extension 'public understanding', were found to be affected by the subtle characteristics of context.

Language and translation

Mass-media conflation of claims, claims-makers and uncertainty has been wrapped up in inherent and general challenges of translation. Within language resides the power to effectively (mis)communicate. However, differences in language use between science, policy, media and civil society can unavoidably impede efforts to make climate change – or any other issue – meaningful in society. In this way, important research, effective arguments and interesting insights can suffocate under a wet blanket of jargon.

Starting from the interpretation of climate through science, such a process has often involved highly specialized language to translate its complex and nuanced dimensions. However, this has often alienated people who aren't part of these specialized scientific communities – the overwhelming majority of the general public. In other words, jargon-laden lexicon has struggled to translate smoothly into the crisp, unequivocal commentary that is valued in the press, policy community and civil society. As Andrew Weaver has put it, 'for the average person, the scientific jargon emanating from [scientists'] mouths translates into gobbledygook' (2008, 29). Considered in this way, responsibilities for media conflation cannot be placed on journalists, producers and editors themselves.

Instead, these responsibilities can be partly attributed to long-standing differences between the 'Two Cultures' first explained by C.P. Snow in the 1950s. For example, in peer-reviewed scientific journal articles, the professional culture of science trains authors to build the case of the research and then place key findings in the results and discussion sections; in professional media reports, journalistic norms instruct reporters to lead with the most important conclusions and discoveries (see Chapter 5 for more).

In other words, information generation fundamentally differs in each of these communities. Malcolm Hughes has said, 'We scientists in most cases will emphasize the condition clauses in any sentence because if you are close to the issue, you are aware of the scientific uncertainties in any statement that you make. The culture of the university and scientific societies is to hedge everything...we are a little too unwilling to say things as we see (them)' (quoted in Boykoff, 2007b, 483). Furthermore, Judy Curry, Peter Webster and Greg Holland have commented, 'For a scientist whose reputation is largely invested in peer-reviewed publications and the citations thereof, there is little professional payoff for getting involved in debates that mix science and politics. Scientists becoming involved in policy debates and with the media may put their scientific reputations at risk in this process' (2006, 1035).

Another element at work can be the pressure from one's scientific peer communities to not overextend their media outreach beyond their own specialized research programmes. From a journalist's perspective, Robert Wyss has written, 'Call it what you want, from professional jealousy to shyness, but many have been critical of scientists who took a very public role in dealing with the press. Such professional pressure made it less likely that scientists would stick their necks out and agree to be quoted' (2008, 73).

Consequently, many scientists have been unwilling to invest their time in reaching beyond their academic circles to communicate the relevance and importance of their work. Many scientists have simply undervalued the importance of communication efforts in relation to other professional duties and responsibilities. Yet such unwillingness has detrimental impacts on public understanding when those recoiling from media engagement are the relevant expert communities who are most capable of providing useful and informed commentary.

Moreover, it is much easier to be burned by a misquote or mis-characterization than it is to build consistent and positive relations with mass media. For example, journalist James Painter commented that in the aftermath of 'Climategate', scientists were 'diving under their desks' to avoid mass-media contact. Against this trend, journalists need quotes to meet their unforgiving deadlines. Without consistent access to expert climate scientists, they are forced to find them elsewhere. This pressure has had an inevitable agenda-setting effect. Journalist Dale Willman, a veteran correspondent and field producer with *CNN*, *CBS News* and *National Public Radio*, has commented, 'in terms of agenda-setting ... the media don't tell people what to think, but they tell them what to think *about*' (quoted in Boykoff, 2009a, 444).

Former *New York Times* Science Editor Cornelia Dean has said, 'The scientific community needs to speak out more. It needs to acknowledge that scientists have an affirmative obligation as citizens to take part in the public debate in the country, and on the whole they have not done that ... they often blame the media for not being prepared to go out and say things that they – who have the knowledge base – will not say in public' (quoted in Boykoff, 2007b, 484). In the high-stakes issue of climate change, the realm of 'pure science' has been a working fallacy onto which scientists mistakenly cling (Pielke Jr, 2007).

However, it must be acknowledged that in fact some scientists might best be left out of the media spotlight, as their inability to communicate can cause frustration rather than help improve public understanding. The US-based satirical newspaper *The Onion* captured this in an article, 'Actual expert too boring for TV', where they began:

Dr Gary Canton, a professor of applied nuclear physics and energy-development technologies at MIT and a leading expert in American nuclear-power applications, was rejected by MSNBC producers for being 'too boring for TV' Monday. 'We could deal with Dr Canton being so short,' said Cal Salters, a segment producer at MSNBC. 'And we could've made him up so he didn't look like he spends all day in front of a computer. We even considered cutting away to stock footage so our audience didn't have to look at him for too long. But when it turned out that listening to him is about as interesting as picking the lint off his lapels – well, there was nothing we could do about that'. (2005, 1)

Yet, scientific findings usually require translation into more colloquial terms in order for them to be comprehensible and valued in communications and decision-making. In his book *Don't Be Such a Scientist*, Randy Olson offered numerous ways for scientists to improve their communication skills. Among them, he called for scientists to improve their storytelling and to develop the art of 'concision' in communication. Olson described concision as 'conveying a great deal of information using the fewest possible steps or words or images or whatever the mode of communications is ... [it] is a thing of beauty that can project infinite complexity' (2009, 116).

Frankly, it is unavoidably challenging to accurately break down years of iterative research into media- and public-friendly morsels. Most scientists need not look far – to colleagues or a mirror – to realize that climate scientists have often shied away from media interactions, thus leaving sourcing for stories to other communities for interpretation. The possibilities for inaccurate amplification or diminution of representation arise when these spaces are ceded from relevant experts to other non-nation-state actors (NNSAs) – such as environmental non-governmental organizations (ENGOs) to carbon-based industry spokespeople.

In other words, the 'battlefield' of communicating and understanding climate change is not well served by scientists reluctant to acknowledge and act on what is an integral piece of one's contemporary responsibility: interacting with mass media and the public. Long-time journalist Robert Cowen has said, 'An obligation of the scientist is to interact with the public and to have a seat at the policy table ... it has come front and center in scientist's education and professional life, even if they don't like to admit it' (quoted in Boykoff, 2007b, 482). This has fed into the tendency of mass-media conflation.

Conclusions

While media interventions seek to enhance understanding of complex and dynamic human–environment interactions, vague and decontextualized reporting instead can enhance bewilderment. Through media conflation of distinct claims, claims-makers and uncertainty, systematic media conflation has been detrimental for public understanding and engagement. By collapsing distinctions from evidence-based science to policy opinions, and by overlooking places where there is convergent agreement or divergent views within expert communities, public understanding has suffered. For readers and news consumers in a hurry, these shortcomings – while detected in certain pockets of mass media and overcome by others – have likely been accepted at face value by large segments of civil society.

For example, in 2007 US *National Public Radio* aired an Oxford-style panel debate by 'Intelligence Squared' based on the statement 'Global Warming Is Not A Crisis'. The debate was based on two sets of nested questions:

First of all, on the science of it. Does science really have the ability to tell us with a good degree of reliability what is going to happen to our climate over a hundred-year period? And secondly, the economics. This all leads in effect to public policies that say we should invest money now for benefits in the future. Well, that always poses the traditional questions of, well, what are the costs? What are the benefits? What are the risks of inactions?

Arguing 'for' the motion were author Michael Crichton and Professors Richard S. Lindzen and Philip Stott. Arguing 'against' the motion were Drs Brenda Ekwurzel and Gavin Schmidt along with Professor Richard Somerville. Before the show began, the stated distribution of audience views was that 30% said global warming was *not* a crisis while 57% opined that it *was* a crisis. However, after the debate the distribution shifted to 46% stating that global warming was *not* a crisis, while 42% then viewed that it still was.

Overall, the framing of the show was fatally problematic on three main fronts: first, the show made a conflated claim that 'global warming was not a crisis' into which it placed a basket of distinct science and policy issues with very different distributions of expert views (see Figure 3.1). Second, to argue against the motion that 'global warming was not a crisis' meant that panellists Ekwurzel, Schmidt and Somerville were forced to argue an awkward double-negative to the live studio and listening radio audiences: that global warming was *not not* a crisis. Third, this structure forced panellists and audience members to argue and vote on this flawed premise. In the end, although it was good theatre, the actors involved as well as the claims made during the radio programme did a disservice to effective communications on the nuance of climate science and governance.

Much as storylines are fuelled within science and policy, these last chapters have shown how the mass media play an important role in the 'theater' of discursive constructions (Hajer, 1995). There have been some signals that organizations have acknowledged the need to more clearly and effectively address issue conflation in order to more capably communicate the range of potential agreement and disagreement in relevant expert communities of researchers. For example, in 2010 the Royal Society of London published a paper called 'Climate change: a summary of the science', in which they distinguished between areas of climate science policy where there has been 'wide agreement', 'continuing debate' and issues 'not well understood' (2010). Disagreement and dissension certainly have value in reshaping understanding. However, when these are not effectively placed *in context* with the larger currents of scientific views – from convergence to contention – public understanding of these issues suffers.

Context helps sort out marginalized views from counter-claims worthy of consideration on various aspects of climate change. The *New York Times* journalist Andrew Revkin has referred to reporting without context as 'whiplash journalism'. He has written that, 'the media seem either to overplay a sense of imminent calamity or to ignore the issue altogether because it is not black and white or on a time scale that feels like news. This approach leaves society like a ship at anchor swinging cyclically with the tide and not going anywhere. What is lost in the swings of media coverage is a century of study and evidence...' (2007, 141–142). As a result, it becomes more (rather than less) challenging for citizens and policy actors to make sense of these issues, influencing their everyday lives and livelihoods.

There are many reasons why media accounts have failed to provide greater distinction in these aspects of climate change. Among them, processes behind the building and challenging of dominant discourses take place simultaneously on multiple scales. Large-scale social, political and economic factors influence everyday individual journalistic decisions, such as how to focus or contextualize a story with tight deadlines. These issues intersect with processes such as journalistic norms and values, to further shape news content. This chapter has focused on some key challenges facing mass media: representations have struggled to cover varied dimensions of uncertainty and they have often collapsed varied issues within the umbrella term of 'climate change'. The next chapters now explore how media representational practices 'frame' various aspects of climate change in varying contexts and conditions.

4 | *Placing climate complexity in context*

Climate change has never been a front-burner issue, and it's the ultimate nightmare to communicate: you don't see carbon in the air the way you see smokestack emissions. It's global not local. The effects evolve over the long, long run.

Peter Applebome (2010)

Clearly, science and politics have influenced media coverage of climate change. Conversely, media representations have also shaped ongoing scientific and political considerations, decisions and activities. In other words, mass media have influenced who has a say and how. This chapter puts coverage of the complexities of climate science and governance into context, and interrogates *how* and *why* conditioning factors have contributed to media representations of climate change.

The practices of journalism take shape through relationships of power, where knowledge and meaning arise through discursive struggle (Hall, 1988). In professional journalism, power is partly expressed by the artefact of the media story itself (Foucault, 1975; 1984). Media actors generate stories within the opportunities and constraints of rich histories of professionalized journalism (Starr, 2004). Such mobilizations are complex and often subtle. Moreover, wider discourses shape power relations within journalism: socio-political and economic factors have given rise to distinct norms and values, and these influence ongoing journalistic practices (Bennett, 2002). In fact, as Chapter 5 will elaborate, discontinuities can arise in media coverage of climate change through the very professional journalistic norms and values that have developed to safeguard against potential abuses of asymmetrical power.

Over time, positivist conceptions of communication have characterized media portrayals of climate change as a link in a chain of one-way communications of science-as-tool-to-inform-policy (e.g. Gross, 1994; Roberts, 2004). Competing conceptions of these interactions – a view to which this volume adheres – instead sees media representations as emerging through a web of dynamic processes, conditions and factors.

Harry Collins and Robert Evans have delineated these competing perspectives in three 'waves' (Collins and Evans, 2002). The first wave of interactions is that of a 'deficit model' approach. This perspective posits that poor choices and actions are attributed to 'deficits' of knowledge and information necessary to make the 'correct' choice. Further, any lack of public and policy engagement with climate issues is attributed to deficiencies in knowledge of science. For example, well-known National Center for Atmospheric Research (NCAR) scientist Kevin Trenberth has carefully examined the science–media–policy interface. When pondering 'what can be done' to improve public and policy decision-making on climate change, Trenberth has called for building better climate-observation systems and better media coverage to facilitate decision-making based on improved science (Trenberth 2008).

Such approaches are often associated with norms and ideals of science as an open and objective practice. This was first described by Robert K. Merton in the 1940s through the goals of communalism, universalism, disinterest and organized scepticism (and the acronym CUDOS). Since the 1950s, this view has been critiqued in a variety of ways. Critics have pointed out that this model has been too simple a characterization of the dynamic and non-linear interactions between science and governance. For instance, Naomi Oreskes has remarked, 'When trying to communicate broadly – to the public or the press – scientists follow a deficit model that presumes that their audiences are ignorant and need to be "supplied" with good, factual information... however, the model has failed' (quoted in Boykoff, 2009b, 2). Nonetheless, in the policy and public spheres, there have been residual impulses that have emanated from this deficit model view. These have included a stated reliance on 'sound' science in order to make decisions, as well as pursuits to eliminate uncertainty as a precondition for action (see Chapter 3 for more).

The second wave of engagement was considered as the wave of 'democracy'. This 'wave' marked more non-nation-state actor (NNSA) participation in the processes of science (or 'upstream engagement') – or democratization – as societies grappled with new-found global risks. In the 1990s, Ulrich Beck examined the democratization of the interface of science and society, particularly in his book *Risk Society* (Beck, 1992). There he challenged views of techno-optimism, and posited that there are common 'bads' in our shared society as well as common 'goods'. Beck pointed out that techno-economic development itself could actually *increase* problems in practice rather than solve them.

Collins and Evans then called the third wave a 'normative theory of expertise'. They considered this to be similar to the second wave in terms of the democratizing commitments. But, this wave marked more nuanced mapping of institutional boundaries between formalized spaces of science–governance and the informal public arena. This then noted the more variegated roles of expertise and authority. In the case of climate change, this advancement marked further clarification as to which groups and institutions might be 'authorized' to speak on behalf of climate. This approach focused largely on how scientific ways of knowing were taken up, negotiated and influenced by societal pressures and trends. This social constructivist position therefore more capably interrogates how power and scale constructs, reflects and reveals heterogeneous and complex phenomena such as language, knowledge and discourse (Lahsen, 2005).

Science is often privileged as the dominant way through which climate change is thought to become meaningful. This can be attributed in part to the residual influences of Enlightenment thinking, as well as partly to how long-term trends that emerge as evidence of climate change are difficult to access through day-to-day observational trends – such as the changing weather – for those who are not closely tuned to decadal climate shifts. However, scientific understanding of climate change is embedded within a matrix of cultural, social, political and economic processes that make climate change meaningful in our everyday lives (O'Connor, 1999). This matrix has also been described by Bruno Latour through complex formulations where facts–values interact with nature–society (2004). In articulating various climate issues by way of media portrayals, it is clear that 'rational' scientific 'ways of knowing' do not exist exclusively from other pathways to knowledge creation. In other words, scientific 'ways of knowing' are not independent of politics and culture, but are co-produced by scientists embedded in society (Jasanoff, 1996).

At the end of the day, exposure to more information can help us to understand the world around us and enhance decision-making on climate issues. But Susanne Moser has cautioned, 'providing information and filling knowledge gaps is at best necessary but rarely sufficient to create active behavioural engagement' (2009, 165). In capturing this dimension, Brian Wynne has also proclaimed, 'So the deficit model is dead – Long live the deficit model!' (2008, 23).

Clearly, there are information gaps in climate communications that can be improved. In the African context, journalist Patrick Luganda – chair of the Network of Climate Journalists in the Horn of Africa – concluded, 'We need an educated public with improved abilities to make better decisions on climate choices.' In the US context, William Ruckelshaus – the first Environmental Protection Agency (EPA) Administrator – has argued, 'If the public aren't adequately informed [about climate change], it's difficult for them to make demands on government, even when it's in their own interest' (quoted in Boykoff, 2008d, 39). Yet, consistent with this expanded 'third wave', information exchange takes place within a complex matrix of interactions and influences.

To get at views of climate change, it is important to consider these multiple ways of organizing the world around them (Kahneman *et al.*, 1982; Harvey, 2010). In other words, experiential, visceral, emotional and interactive interpretations of climate change are also vital (see Chapter 7 for more). Considered through a more textured 'third wave' of science in society, public understanding and engagement is informed by rational inquiry as well as personal values, political perspectives, perceptions of one's relation with nature/environment and ethical/moral considerations. This expanded view helps to better comprehend pathways to understanding and engagement, and helps recognize what Mike Hulme has referred to as the often overlooked 'limits of laboratory science' (2009b).

Contextual influences on media representations of climate change

Dynamic interactions of multiple scales and dimensions of power critically contribute to how climate change is portrayed in the media. Mass-media representations arise through large-scale (or *macro*) relations, such as decision-making in a capitalist or state-controlled political economy, and individual-level (or *micro*) processes such as everyday journalistic practices.

Climate journalism around the world is fraught with capacity challenges to collectively cover complex and dynamic stories at the human–environment interface. Recent years have seen significant reductions in media ecosystem services. Journalists, producers and editors striving for fair and accurate reporting have been getting swamped by these contemporary and large-scale political and economic pressures (Boykoff, 2007b).

Influencing factors like state-run or corporate media ownership, as well as control, shape media coverage differently in countries and contexts around the world. While the main principle of democratic news production has been that media organizations then serve as a check on the state, in practice it has been argued that corporate-controlled media have acted systematically in the service of state power (Curran, 2002). Nonetheless, media organizations in Western countries have continued to consolidate power and resources, particularly over the last three decades.

Over time, numerous researchers have explored how economic pressures and ownership structures have impacted news production (Herman and Chomsky, 1988; Bagdikian, 2004). Robert McChesney has posited that profit motivations, 'can go a long way to providing a context (and a trajectory) for understanding the nature of media content' (1999, 31). Furthermore, Anabela Carvalho has commented, 'factors like ownership and the wider political economy of the media can provide significant contributions … as well as the press's relations with established interests and the social distribution of power' (2005, 21). Arguments for greater diversity, pluralism and support for non-profit and 'independent' media models – in this atmosphere of mergers and more concentrated corporate control – have been explained by Gillian Doyle as, 'about sustaining representation within a given society for different political viewpoints and forms of cultural expression' (2002, 14).

Meanwhile, modern multi-national media organizations have continued to consolidate and/or close. Indicators of these trends – particularly in the newspaper industry – appear nearly every day. For examples in recent years, in 2008 *CNN* slashed their entire science, technology and environment reporting unit; in 2009 the *Seattle Post-Intelligencer* discontinued their print run while the *Rocky Mountain News* shuttered their doors altogether; and the *Los Angeles Times* has cut their newsroom staff in half in the last dozen years. In the US, it has been estimated that approximately 25 per cent of the news industry's workforce has been cut since 2001 (Pew Research Center, 2009b; Boykoff, 2009a). Concurrently, the number of newspapers that featured weekly science sections atrophied, losing nearly two-thirds in the past two decades (Pew Research Center, 2009b; Carroll, 2006).

These economic developments – and cut-backs therein – have made it as difficult as ever for news professionals to cover climate change. Decreased mass-media budgets for investigative journalism have adversely affected communications of scientific information where complex scientific material has often been oversimplified in media reports (Anderson, 1997; McChesney, 1999). *Guardian* environmental journalist Paul Brown has commented, 'The amount of resources in travel and time the reporter is allowed to use to chase the story has diminished. All over Europe and America staffs are being cut and budgets for getting out of the office slashed' (quoted in Boykoff, 2009b, 5).

In the name of efficiency, reporters have increasingly covered a vast range of news beats under tighter deadlines, making it as difficult as ever to satisfactorily portray the complexities of climate change amidst numerous demands. Moreover, content producers in publishing organizations that have survived newsroom cuts and shortfalls have faced increased multi-platform demands (video, audio and text along with blogs, Twitter, Facebook, YouTube postings etc.). For example, the *New York Times* journalist Andrew Revkin attributed his 'worst misstep' in his many decades of reporting to the tightening time demands he faced towards the end of his tenure at the *New York Times* (Ward, 2009). Revkin has referred to this succinctly as the 'tyranny of time and space'.

These numerous political and economic challenges have proven to be detrimental for communication of climate change. *Columbia Journalism Review's* Alissa Quart has posited, 'When journalists are generalists, they rely, often uncritically, on outside experts for specialized things. They are famously able to immerse themselves in a fresh subject and report back. But they carry with them their ignorance of the area's debates and politics' (2010, 18). From a scientist's perspective, Malcolm Hughes has commented, 'There is a huge gulf in the nature of the questions and concerns that come from journalists working very broadly' (quoted in Boykoff, 2007b, 483).

In the Global South, these contemporary challenges perpetuate chronic problems in covering climate change (see Chapter 8 for more). In most places, journalists have lacked the capacity and training to cover the intricacies of climate science and policy, as well as lacking access to clear, timely and understandable climate-related resources and images (Shanahan, 2009). For instance, a Honduran reporter commented, 'I would love to ... work only on nature issues ... but the press does not give me the opportunity' (Harbison *et al.*, 2006, 9). Rod Harbison and colleagues have observed that lack of journalist training for specialized environmental reporting has decreased the number of climate-change stories in these countries (2006). This has been evident in Figure 1.1 as well.

However, organizations are adapting to these changing conditions in innovative ways. For example, the group Climate Central – founded in 2008 – is a collective of scientists and journalists who provide specialist reporting on climate change for a range of traditional and new media sources. Also, the web-based magazine *Grist* – founded in 1999 – has been very influential through its innovative partnerships with traditional news sources like the *Washington Post*, and has developed a following of 800,000 readers (Spencer, 2010). Both organizations have found their success through a non-profit organizational structure and strong foundation support. Such an approach – increasingly taken by other news groups like The Center for Public Integrity in Washington, DC and the iNewsNetwork based in Boulder, Colorado (part of the national Investigative News Network Coalition) – is seen as a potential way forward for environmental journalism in the twenty-first century, in place of the faltering for-profit industry structure (Halpert, 2009). Over the last decade there have been dozens of other new and emerging organizations popping up under this non-profit model across the globe.

These issues begin to work across scales from macro-level political economic factors to micro-level processes and pressures. Amongst these cross-cutting issues are notions of how larger ideological cultures shape news content and the news agenda. A clear example is found in the US, where the cable television news channel *MSNBC* is often tied to the ideological left, while *Fox News* is associated with movements from the ideological right. These relationships can be subtle, evidenced by what issues may get traction on particular channels and how. But they can also be quite explicit, such as the close coverage of early US Tea Party demonstrations by numerous *Fox News* programmes.

Anabela Carvalho has examined how ideological cultures have influenced media reporting on climate change in the UK. Through analyses of *The Guardian* (and *Observer*), *The Independent* (and *Independent on Sunday*) and *The Times* (and *Sunday Times*) from 1985 to 2001, she found that the left-leaning *Guardian* and *Independent* provided more coverage of market regulation, the precautionary principle and climate mitigation than their right-of-centre counterpart *The Times*. Furthermore, *The Times* 'advocated business-as-usual using the lack of definitive proof as justification for the continuation of [status quo] policies and practices' (2007, 238).

Another illustration can be found through the words of well-known *Sun* commentator Jeremy Clarkson. The UK-based Clarkson has also been one of the hosts of the popular BBC programme 'Top Gear' (Robinson, 2008). In his columns in the *Sun*, Clarkson has utilized variants of ideological frameworks to present government regulations on climate emissions as unpopular and threats to individual freedom. For instance, in a piece on a new gasoline tax on automobiles, Clarkson reasoned:

It seems likely that, from November, the amount you pay for car tax will be based on the amount of carbon dioxide your car produces. This is not sensible … I've just had tea with my daughter who spent the entire time telling me that trees need carbon dioxide to live. And she's five. She was therefore a little perplexed when I explained the new plan … 'But what about the trees?' she wailed. 'It's not fair.' Quite right, it isn't … Let me put it this way. If carbon dioxide really is such a bad thing, and the Government really is worried about its effects, then how come they are deliberately introducing measures to slow cars down? Surely, the best thing you can do is get the motorist to his destination, and parked, as quickly as possible, because that way his engine will be running for the shortest possible time. In fact, they should go further. People caught speeding should be given bonus points on their licence and car tax discount for helping to prolong the life of the planet. My daughter thinks this is a great idea. But then she would because, of course, she's five. Our rulers, sadly, aren't that grown-up. (2000, 25)

In commentaries, segments and articles like this, content producers deploy discourses that appear to be focused on techno-centred administration of nature. However, such pieces are subtly infused with socio-economic, public–private and freedom-constraint tropes that activate ideological cultures and perspectives. Sometimes under the guise of irony and cynicism, such comments also then effectively cohere with and sustain particular political-economic interests such as a penchant for market-led and anti-regulatory management of the environment. Overall, these ideological factors shape who is empowered to speak for the climate, and how various climate science and governance issues are treated in the media.

Contextual influences extend to how local weather events can have agenda-setting influences (see Chapter 2 for more). Whether from journalists assembling the stories themselves or from editors prioritizing climate stories on warmer days, a study by James Shanahan and Jennifer Good found a relationship between high temperatures and higher word counts for stories on climate change. Specifically, they looked at coverage in the *New York Times* and the *Washington Post*, as well as temperature data from the US National Climatic Data Center from 1987 through to 1995, and found a positive correlation between local temperature and coverage of climate change in the *New York Times* (2000). While a pattern was detected, the authors still acknowledged that, 'local temperature is not the most important determinant of attention to climate issues; more likely it is political events and scientific studies that attract the majority of the coverage' (2000, 293).

This was also illustrated through media representations of repeated heavy snowfalls on the East Coast of the US during the winter of 2009–2010, during a time when the US Congress were deliberating the Cap-and-Trade bill. An article from the *New York Times* – titled 'Climate fight is heating up in deep freeze' – linked the record snowfall to the ongoing climate legislation and debates therein. Featured in the front-page story was US Senator James Inhofe (Republican, Oklahoma), 'a leading climate skeptic in Congress (who) built a six-foot-tall igloo on Capitol Hill and put a cardboard sign on top that read "Al Gore's New Home". The extreme weather, Inhofe said by e-mail, reinforced doubts about scientists' conclusion that global warming was "unequivocal" and most likely caused by human activity' (Broder, 2010a, 1). The story then shifted to a response by Joseph Romm, 'a climate-change expert and former Energy Department official who writes about climate issues at the liberal Center for American Progress'. In the article, Romm plainly called such claims 'nonsense'. However, Romm's comments were picked up in the continued story on page A18, leading readers and analysts to wonder what editors considered was the most appropriate 'front-page thought'. These claims feed journalistic pressures to serve up attention-grabbing, dramatic personal conflicts (see Chapter 5 for more), thereby drawing attention towards decontextualized individual claims-making. Concurrent coverage in the *Daily Mail* in the UK went with the news hook, 'Donald Trump has called for Al Gore to be stripped of the Nobel Peace Prize he was awarded for campaigning on climate change', saying, 'record-breaking snow storms proved that the former US Vice-President was wrong on global warming...' (Daily Mail Reporter, 2010).

These examples demonstrate how spatial dimensions – by way of varied national and cultural contexts – feed into differentiated interactions between media representations and policy prioritization (Burgess, 2005). In fact, divergent climate policy stances emerge from dynamic and complex mosaics of public trust in authority and structures of media institutions as well as architectures of decision-making (Lorenzoni and Pidgeon, 2006). Sheila Jasanoff has attributed differences to the divergent architectures of governance (2005). She commented, 'If you have an adversarial system [like in the US], then the science will get picked apart... In Europe, it's not a winner-take-all system' (Thacker, 2006). In terms of media representations, the UK press itself is known for being more adversarial, while the US press has been seen to be more deferential to their sources. Leonard Doyle, foreign editor of *The Independent*, has called US mass media 'too trusting of the media establishment hand that feeds them' (Columbia Journalism Review, 2004, 49). However, Michael Getler – ombudsman at the *Washington Post* – has argued that 'European readers, in contrast to Americans, are much more accustomed to, and accepting of, newspapers with political leanings' (Columbia Journalism Review, 2004, 45). In combination, these influences have become manifest in divergent representations of US and UK roles in international negotiations, from foot-dragger to climate champion (Boykoff and Rajan, 2007).

These issues also further bridge into individual-level and temporal issues – beyond journalists' deadlines – that can hamper relations between scientists, policy actors, media workers and civil society. One key factor here is the varying conception of timescale in their professionalized cultures. In climate science, new insights are typically gained through longer-term iterative endeavours such as field research, modelling and peer-review processes. In climate policy, political cycles, negotiations and mobilization of constituencies generally function in short- to medium-term timescales. In journalism, 'breaking news', efficiency and profitability often pressure journalists to work on short-term timescales.

Other factors regarding timescale issues are differences in norms of knowledge production. While norms and rituals in each community all similarly seek to improve on the relevant corpus of knowledge, the expressions of this focus turn out to be quite divergent. The peer-review process in academia drives *how* (and what) assertions, results and conclusions reach print (see Chapter 3 for more). Subject to multiple stages of reviews by peers and editors considered experts in the particular field(s) of inquiry, these reviewers assess the quality of the arguments, analyses and findings in a negotiated space typically before a given study finds its way into print. These rituals and norms do not remove conflict from print, but rather constitute protections to mitigate against untested, out-of-context and inaccurate entries into the ongoing and unfolding scientific discourse. While imperfect, this process has endeavoured to impose safeguards and standards on contributions to the ongoing production of scientific knowledge.

In journalism, while reporters and editors undergo associated negotiations in the pre-print stage, professionalized journalistic norms and standards instead *propel* conflict into print (see Boykoff and Boykoff, 2007 for more). In negotiations between journalists and their editors and publishers, the 'MEGO factor', as *New York Times* journalist Andrew Revkin has put it, is always in consideration – 'my eyes glaze over' (2007, 149).

Attention-grabbing and exciting new topics gain primacy over dry and abstruse stories and may fortify established concepts. This does not suggest that these trends are mutually exclusive, or that potential contributions are scrutinized any less by experts in the field of journalism. Instead, it means that through the differing norms of knowledge production, claims unexamined by relevant expert peer communities then find visibility through media representations at times when such attention may later prove to be unwarranted. In short, these are questions of the veracity and timing of the proverbial genie.

Furthermore, in climate science – and more broadly, academia – most reward systems are structured such that little is gained professionally through increased 'non-academic' pursuits such as media outreach. Geophysicist Henry Pollack has written, '[T]here is an underlying feeling that in an academic career, advancement is retarded by spending time in non-academic endeavors' (2003, 75). At the same time, much can be risked in terms of being misquoted about the implications of one's research. As a result, 'many researchers are hesitant even to speak to the popular press, for fear of having their carefully chosen words twisted beyond recognition' (Nature, 2009, 260). In media and policy communities, there are more immediate needs for 'climate stories', and these disparate priorities lead to communication breakdowns.

However, some argue that trends are changing. For instance, research by Hans Peter Peters and colleagues – surveying over 1300 researchers across the US, Germany, Japan, France and the UK – found that scientists' interactions with journalists across all the countries were actually more productive and positive than anecdotal stories of woe might suggest (2008). While the study did not focus specifically on climate change, the researchers found that 'scientists most involved in these interactions tend to be scientifically productive, have leadership roles, and – although they consider concerns as well as perceived benefits – that they perceive the interactions to have more positive than negative outcomes' (2008, 205). These findings may indicate that academic researchers are increasingly recognizing that media interactions are central to their responsibilities rather than a distraction from them. Nonetheless, ongoing pressures of publishing and teaching still limit potential for more consistent media interactions and outreach activities. The facts remain that at the end of the day – or at academic tenure and promotion decisions – media interactions and outreach get ranked routinely below many other pressures (Mooney and Kirshenbaum, 2009).

Academics who choose to become content producers themselves and communicate directly to media consumers through 'blogging' have found benefits of increased visibility and social status, as well as funding (Allen, 2008). However, they can also take the risks through heavy time investment as well as potential criticism from academic peers and the general public. Among academic bloggers, NASA scientist – and *Real Climate* blogger – Gavin Schmidt has argued, 'Scientists know much more about their field than is ever published in peer-reviewed journals. Blogs can be a good medium with which to disseminate this tacit knowledge' (2008, 208). Nonetheless, blogging among the academic community remains a rare enterprise. In a 2009 commentary, *Nature* editors conceded that, 'Sadly, these activities live on the fringe of the scientific enterprise. Blogging will not help, and could even hurt, a young researcher's chances of tenure. Many of their elders still look down on colleagues who blog, believing that research should be communicated only through conventional channels such as peer-review and publication' (2009, 260).

Also among these micro-level factors are journalistic norms, such as objectivity, fairness, accuracy and balanced reporting; issues that are taken up in detail in Chapter 5. These multi-scale and multi-dimensional complex and iterative processes contribute to systemic and institutional power and context (Foucault, 1975; Stone, 1980). To examine how these and other multi-scale interacting factors come together in practice, we can look to the example of representations of climate change in the UK tabloid press. This case study provides an opportunity to explore questions of socio-economic class and audience reception, which are additionally important contextualizing factors shaping media representations of climate change.

Wat about Di Workin' Claas?: climate change in the UK tabloid press

With regard to climate change, through the 1970s the UK was often called 'the dirty man of Europe' due to its reputation as a country with low priorities for environmental stewardship (Cass, 2007, 40). Then, in the 1980s British Prime Minister Margaret Thatcher ushered in neoliberal initiatives of deregulation and privatization. In so doing, she also reduced the power of unions, such as those in the coal industry. These decisions facilitated eventual movements from heavy reliance on coal for energy, which served to help lower UK greenhouse gas (GHG) emissions in the 1990s and 2000s (Pielke Jr, 2010), but the policy reforms also had socio-economic implications as they hurt working-class interests.

These class relations have comprised a strong thread through UK historical accounts of public support for various policy measures. Therefore, assessments of class issues in the UK provide opportunities to better understand wider issues of public awareness and climate change. To gauge climate and energy narratives threading through working-class interests, power and the public sphere, it has been instructive to appraise discursive themes in publications that cater to this socio-economic segment of society. 'Tabloids' have typically been considered 'working-class' publications in the UK. Around the world and among different segments of civil society, the segment of mass media referred to as 'tabloids' can carry with it quite different meanings. Among some camps, this term stirs populist sentiments; in others, it is code for low-brow journalism. However, tabloid media typically share three features in common:

(1) *breadth*, where domestic stories as well as scandal and conflict earn greater attention than stories on international politics and economy (Connell, 1998; Rooney, 2000);
(2) *(lack of) depth*, where surface-level, simplistic and sensationalist topics like entertainment, sports and personal lives are salient (Djupsund and Carlson, 1998); and
(3) *tenor*, where opinion and commentary as well as informal rhetoric drive reporting and coverage (thus de-emphasizing 'objective' or 'straight' reporting) (van Zoonen, 1998)

Through time, political-economic pressures have contributed significantly to these characteristics. Aforementioned capacity constraints are acute and specialist 'environment' and 'science' training is sparse. Instead, tabloid outlets rely on reporters to 'work holistically' and to be 'jacks of all trades' (Deuze, 2005, 877). Despite these challenges and trends, Figure 4.1 – depicting coverage from 2000 through to 2010 – shows that climate change has been an issue increasingly covered in the UK tabloid press.

Most analyses of media portrayals of climate change have largely focused on 'prestige-press', 'broadsheet' or 'quality' newspapers. The rationale behind this has been that 'quality' press sources have had a reputation for traditionally higher-quality reporting, and that they have more frequently employed specialist reporters on science and environment news beats (Doyle, 2002). Moreover, these sources were reasoned to be primary influences on policy discourse and decision-making at national and international levels (Carvalho and Burgess, 2005; Boykoff, 2007b). However, these approaches have suffered from a massive blind spot in analyses, where large segments of the population are simply reading other newspapers – the tabloids.

Therefore, in 2007, along with University of Oxford researcher Maria Mansfield, I undertook a study of UK daily tabloid media

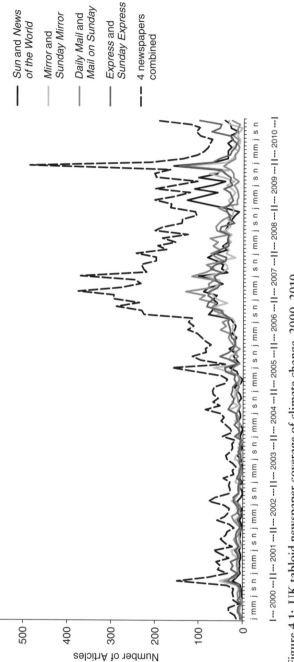

Figure 4.1: UK tabloid newspaper coverage of climate change, 2000–2010

coverage of climate change in four 'popular' and 'working-class' newspapers in the UK – the *Sun*, *Daily Mail*, the *Mirror* and *Express*, along with their respective Sunday counterparts – *News of the World*, the *Mail on Sunday*, the *Sunday Mirror* and *Sunday Express*. We examined articles on 'climate change' or 'global warming' over a seven-year period (2000–2006), and I combined this with two-dozen semi-structured interviews of journalists and editors from these newspapers. Average daily circulations in each of the tabloid newspapers have been as much as ten times higher than their counterparts in UK broadsheet newspaper readership. Also, tabloid papers are more traditionally 'shared' in public spaces such as trains and workplaces, thus pushing some estimates of daily readership to double that of circulation figures (Newspaper Marketing Agency, 2010).

Furthermore, the demographics of tabloid and broadsheet press readership are important. The classification scheme of the National Readership Survey (NRS) social grades reveals clear socio-economic differences between broadsheet and tabloid newspaper readership. These NRS data show that over half of the broadsheet press readership are 'upper middle class' or 'middle class', while the majority of tabloid readership occupy the category of 'working class'. For example, 63 per cent of *The Times* readers are categorized as 'middle class' or wealthier, while just 11 per cent of *Sun* readers fit into that category. While readership patterns are clearly not dictated by socio-economic status, habits are formed and perpetuated in this heterogeneous group of readers through complex factors and feedback processes that are part economic (e.g. the price for tabloids is lower than broadsheets), and part cultural (e.g. identities shape what are 'working class' newspapers, which then further fuel readership habits) (Newton, 1999).

Four distinct increases in coverage can be seen. The first rise – in November and December of 2000 – was mainly due to considerable coverage of the intense flooding in the northeast of England, with particular devastation centred in Yorkshire. Moreover, COP6 was taking place in The Hague at the same time as this flooding, and this earned considerable coverage as well. The second rise came in June and July of 2005. Articles here focused primarily on European Union Emissions Trading Scheme proposal debates held at the time, and the Group of Eight (G8) Summit in Gleneagles, Scotland. The G8 summit prompted headlines such as 'Blair salvages deal as G8 leaders set aside their doubts' and 'Blair wrings concessions out of the US'.

The third distinct increase was from September through to November 2006, because of four intertwined events: first, the film *An Inconvenient Truth* featuring Al Gore was released in the UK in mid September; second, in late September Virgin Group Ltd chief Richard Branson made a multi-billion-dollar 'donation' to renewable energy initiatives and biofuel research that garnered much tabloid attention; third, in October Sir Nicholas Stern released the 'Stern Review', which generated intense media coverage in the following weeks; and fourth, these events fed into continued abundant news coverage on climate change by way of attention paid to COP12 in November. The fourth district increase at the end of 2009 was connected to coverage surrounding COP15 in Copenhagen, Denmark, as well as the UEA CRU email hacking scandal dubbed 'Climategate' (see Chapter 2 for more).

Employing the tools of Critical Discourse Analysis (CDA), this project examined the 'framing' of climate stories in this socio-economic, spatial and temporal context. CDA considers texts as they are situated in context (van Dijk, 1988), pays attention to how the constitution of certain discursive frames privileges (and marginalizes) particular ways of knowing, as well as how they structure interactions (Fairclough, 1995). Anabela Carvalho has pointed out that CDA 'allows for a richer examination of the resource used in any type of text for producing meaning. It shares with framing analysis an interest in the variable social construction of the world but puts a stronger emphasis on language and on the relation between discourse and particular social, political, and cultural contexts' (2007, 227). Thus, CDA accounts for how meanings are partially fixed as well as negotiated as they are constructed in the texts over time (Laclau and Mouffe, 2001). This approach captures how textual representations contribute to discursive narratives that – while anchored to social, economic and cultural norms – dynamically shape ongoing considerations and actions (Phillips and Hardy, 2002).

In the study, CDA enabled nuanced and textured assessments that could capture subtle factors as well as the explicit ones that shape representational practices in context. The work examined context while paying attention to forms and content of the texts (such as headlines, framing techniques, salience of elements, ideological stances, tone and tenor and relationships between clusters of messages) (Carvalho, 2008). The project also analyzed the tone of tabloid headlines in each article. This was conducted because headlines provided an opportunity to examine relationships between journalists (who typically write the stories) and their editors (who typically write the headlines). Moreover, tabloid newspaper readers – and readers in general – typically scan headlines rather than reading each article in a newspaper in its entirety (Dahlgren and Sparks, 1992; McManus, 2000).

Through this approach, Figure 4.2 shows that emphases were consistently placed on political-economic frames, as well as ecological/ meteorological stories. Regarding political-economic frames, there was frequent reporting on the actions and claims of political actors. As a representative example of political-economic articles, a *Mirror* article by Oonagh Blackman covered the 2006 release of the Stern Review. Entitled, 'Climate is threat to economy', it began, 'Chaos from climate change could trigger the worst ever global recession, an economist fears. [Stern] believes floods, storms and natural disasters may cause a downturn that will surpass the Wall Street Crash and the Great Depression' (2006, 12). Meteorological/ecological frames were dominated by stories on weather events and biodiversity.

Fewer stories focused on conservation and protection, but many covered the movements of charismatic megafauna as they related to climate change. For example, concerns regarding the changing feeding ranges of shark species – and their threat to humans – prompted stories such as 'Jaws…off Hartlepool' in the *Daily Mail* by Dan Parkinson (2005). Culture and society frames then accounted for a fifth of stories and science themes comprised about a tenth of articles during that time period.

Of note, among the least utilized frames were those of 'justice and risk'. This trend in framing UK tabloid news articles notes muted treatment of unequal structural, political or institutional conditions. Jane Hamilton from the *Sun* has said, 'The key is relevancy…we cover the issues that most immediately affect our readers, and most in our readership are working class. They are not as interested in theoretical science papers at an academic conference' (quoted in Boykoff, 2008a, 559).

However, considering the readership trends of lower socio-economic demographics in these UK tabloid newspapers, these sources have been well positioned to offer readers a meaningful and relevant critical assessment of differentiated impacts from climate change. Instead, these data show that across all the tabloid sources, journalists, producers, editors

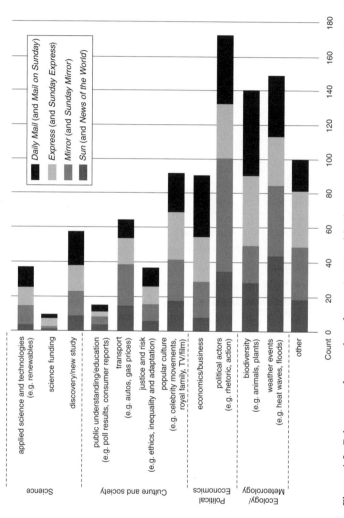

Figure 4.2: Primary and secondary frames in UK tabloid newspaper headlines and texts, 2000–2006 These show the distribution of news frames on climate change from 2000–2006; reproduced with permission from *Political Geography*.

and publishers focused instead on the rhetoric and actions of individual political actors or storm events at the expense of attention paid to questions such as the ethics surrounding uneven abilities to cope with climate change. So, rather than frames and analyses of climate 'justice and risk' that may be relevant to UK tabloid readership, this study has instead found a prevalence of discourses that do not address – much less confront – existing power relations and inequalities.

Amid great nuance and complexity regarding class position and associated perspectives on a range of political, economic, cultural, societal and environmental issues, it is useful to think through socio-economic class as a contextual factor shaping media representations of climate change. Considering class issues and UK tabloid news coverage, *Mirror* journalist Mike Swan said, 'We are very conscious of our readers' lives...something like [carbon] taxes on flights are going to hit our readers a lot harder than broadsheet readers' (quoted in Boykoff, 2008a, 565).

By drawing attention to these silences through tools of CDA, this study illuminated a number of intersecting contextual factors, in particular, which contribute to these larger patterns. Among them, larger political-economic forces have contributed to a preference to cover uncomplicated stories that do not require considerable investigation, and this is especially the case for tabloid journalists facing acute challenges of tight deadlines and limited column inches (Boykoff, 2008a). Emanating from contextual factors such as these, the texts in this case study demonstrate how media representations are negotiated texts, by way of dynamic and complex contextual factors.

Conclusions

ABC News reporter Bill Blakemore has commented, 'The job of a professional journalist is to give the audience information that is a good thing for them to know' (Russell, 2008). However, there are many vexing conditioning factors that make this challenging for media actors to achieve. Path dependence through histories of professionalized journalism, journalistic norms and values, as well as power relations, have shaped the production of news stories (Starr, 2004). These dynamic and multi-scale influences are interrelated and difficult to disentangle. This chapter has explored how media portrayals are infused with cultural, social, environmental and political-economic elements, as well as how media professionals must mindfully navigate through hazardous terrain in order to fairly and accurately represent various dimensions of climate science and governance (Ward, 2008).

These elements intersect with biophysical processes of climate change themselves. The *New York Times* journalist Andrew Revkin has called climate change a 'classic incremental story', which makes it particularly challenging to cover *in the context of* these numerous and multi-scale pressures (2007). Moreover, historian John McPhee expressed another dimension to the challenges of communicating long-term climate changes when he wrote, '[T]he human mind may not have evolved enough to be able to comprehend deep time' (McPhee, 1998).

Valuable research from political ecology has contested the assertion that nature is considered the passive backdrop for discursive and material human activities (Blaikie and Brookfield, 1987). For example, common assessments by experts in climate science have interpreted biophysical processes through a focus on changes in the *mean* of particular climate characteristics over time; thus, prognostications for future climate changes are widely considered through these mean global atmospheric temperature readings. In the Intergovernmental Panel on Climate Change's (IPCC's) Third Assessment Report, climate scientists placed the likely global mean temperature increase in the range of 2.5°F (1.4°C) to 10.4°F (5.8°C) by 2100. This and other similar estimates of mean temperature change have been picked up by mass media and have been included in numerous news reports on climate change over time. However, through a focus on changes in global *averages*, this way of 'speaking for climate' runs a risk in climate policy decision-making by minimizing considerations of potential non-linear and abrupt climate changes (Mastrandrea and Schneider, 2004).

While attention was paid in the UK tabloid press to weather events – as expressions of climate changes – doing so without providing context missed critical opportunities to 'advance the climate story'. In addition, mass-media coverage of nature's agency in response to human influences has often been subsumed by socio-political and economic concerns, such as how certain GHG reduction efforts may restrict economic activities. By articulating climate change in this way, greater stress is placed on the danger of climate policy on trade and the economy than on consideration of how trade and the economy may detrimentally affect the global climate. As the next chapter elaborates, journalists often focus reporting on events, thereby underemphasizing these 'creeping' stories as well as the contexts within which they take place (Dunwoody and Griffin, 1993). As the example of UK tabloid press has also shown, the tools of CDA have helped researchers to better understand the many challenges involved in media representations of climate complexities.

Thus, analyses of *how* and *why* media represent climate change through articles, segments and spots demonstrate that differences are not random or simple. Rather, media representations are derived through complex and non-linear relationships between scientists, policy actors and the public that are often mediated by journalists' news stories. Furthermore, they are systemic and occur through complex socio-political and economic reasons rooted in power relations, as well as through innate biophysical characteristics that shape various 'ways of knowing' over time. This chapter has sought to take steps to unpack and examine important co-produced forces that innately undergird this problem (Jasanoff, 2004; Demeritt, 2001).

Multi-scalar processes of power shape how mass media depict climate change. Representations can 'fix' interpretive categories in order to help explain and describe complex environmental processes (Robbins, 2001). This process involves an inevitable series of choices to cover certain events within a larger current of dynamic activities, and it is a mechanism for privileging certain interpretations and 'ways of knowing' over others. Through the web of contextual factors described above, the stream of events in our shared lives gets converted into finite news stories. Thus, constructions of meaning and discourse on climate change are derived through combined structural and agential components, and are often represented through mass media to the general public.

The process of media representation involves an inevitable series of choices to portray certain events, issues or pieces of information within a larger current of dynamic activities. Resulting images, texts and stories compete for attention and thus permeate ongoing interactions between science, policy, media and the public in varied ways. Furthermore, these interactions spill back onto ongoing media representations. Through these selection and feedback processes, mass media give voice to climate itself by articulating aspects of the phenomenon in particular ways, via claims-makers or authorized speakers.

Moreover, as discussed in Chapter 1, various actors – both individuals and collectively – seek to access and utilize mass-media sources in order to shape perceptions of various climate issues contingent on their perspectives and interests (Nisbet and Mooney, 2007). According to Tim Forsyth, examinations of the complexities of framings and discourse in context provide an opportunity to question 'how, when, and by whom such terms were developed as a substitute for reality' (Forsyth, 2003). Media representations also then contribute – among a host of factors – to setting agendas for considerations within environmental issues and cultural politics.

Media portrayals simply do not translate scientific truths or truth claims, nor do they fill knowledge gaps for citizens and policy actors to make 'the right choices' (Demeritt, 2006; Boykoff, 2007b). Numerous factors contribute to how we negotiate the range of evidence and claims about climate change, as well as evaluate experts and claims-makers. A given media message, text, image or clip has the potential to galvanize and inspire an individual, group or community, while that same message might irk or paralyze others. Although tricky, putting the complexities of climate science and governance into context is critically important for successfully communicating climate change and for achieving greater connectivity between communities of science, policy, media and the public citizenry.

5 | Climate stories
How journalistic norms shape
media content

The previous two chapters mapped out elements shaping how mass media have represented complexity and nuance. It is critically important to look at how both the issues themselves as well as the surrounding contextual factors shape media representations of climate change. This expanded assessment of the networks or webs within which these issues emerge helps to then more capably appraise how and why certain climate issues find traction. Large-scale social, political and economic factors (such as shrinking newsrooms and fewer specialist journalists covering environmental issues) influence everyday individual journalistic decisions (such as how to focus or frame a story with limited time to press as well as a finite number of column inches).

Together, constructions of meaning – negotiated in the spaces of cultural politics – are shaped by structural and institutional as well as cultural and psychological factors, operating simultaneously at multiple scales. These issues intersect with journalistic norms and values. Over the last century, there have been numerous examinations of how journalistic 'norms' and 'values' influence story narratives (e.g. Galtung and Ruge, 1965; Wilkins, 1993). However, fewer studies have linked this work with how mass media have portrayed issues of climate science, policy and politics.

Michael Getler – ombudsman at *The Washington Post* – has argued that 'what is most crucial for news organizations, and what is most useful to the public, is news that is delivered in a manner that is beyond reproach journalistically. Readers understand, and can factor in, government or special-interest spin. But they can smell reportorial opinion and bias a mile away and that is guaranteed to distract from the power of the news' (Columbia Journalism Review, 2004, 45). Getler's comment strikes a hopeful chord. However, this chapter discusses how reporters, producers, editors and publishers who are enmeshed in systematized and professionalized journalistic norms can struggle – both consciously and unconsciously – to actually produce

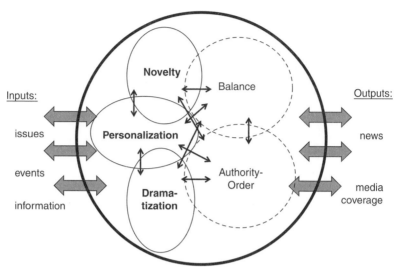

Figure 5.1: Interacting journalistic norms
The public arena of mass-media production, where journalistic norms interact; reproduced with permission from *Geoforum*.

fair and accurate climate narratives. In so doing, this chapter works through the messy, complex and multi-faceted 'spaces of sub-politics' (Foucault, 1980) (see Chapters 1 and 8 for more). So, this chapter places an analytical gaze on how interacting journalistic norms shape what become 'climate stories'.

Journalistic norms and values

Contextual factors interact with the deployment of journalistic norms and values. Pacific University professor Jules Boykoff and I have described these as personalization, dramatization, novelty, authority-order bias and balance (see Figure 5.1). These norms significantly influence both the selection of what are 'climate stories' and the content of news stories. Moreover, they shape who 'speaks for climate' and how.

First, we can consider the journalistic norm of 'personalization'. The inclination to personalize stories means coverage focuses on 'charismatic humanoids', struggling in the negotiated spaces of cultural politics and the environment. W. Lance Bennett has described personalization as 'the tendency to downplay the big social, economic, or political picture in favor of the human trials tragedies, and triumphs that sit at the surface of events' (2002, 45). The personalized story subscribes to the notion that 'climate stories' are driven primarily by individuals rather than group dynamics or social processes (Gans, 1979). In this way, there is a tendency to highlight competition between personalities and stories focus on individual claims-makers while de-emphasizing issues of power, context and process. Thus micro-level issues – such as pitched battles between personalities – take precedence over macro-scale issues. As Kathleen Quinn – former Op-ed Editor at the *New York Times* – described an aspect of it, 'let's face it, newspaper editors prefer bullies' (1992, 29).

Figures 5.2 and 5.3 show arbitrary time splices of the terms used in posts from prominent and influential new bloggers. From 14 September 2010 and 1 November 2010 respectively, these 'word clouds' capture varying attention paid to themes, events and people. Six blogs were sampled, such as Marc Morano's *Climate Depot* and *Climate Progress* from the Center for American Progress. These blogs were selected based on relative influence, readership numbers and diversity of ideological perspectives. In Figure 5.2, issues of 'energy', and 'climate' remain consistently frequent, but names like Oxburgh, Koch, McCain and Monkton can also provide news hooks for blog postings. In Figure 5.3, some of the blogs – such as *Real Climate* and *Watts Up with That* – appear quite focused on the issues themselves, while others – such as *DeSmogBlog* and *Climate Audit* – remain focused on individuals like Koch, Briffa, Russell and Jones.

While individuals remain the most commonly perceived site of agency, the common deployment of this journalistic norm makes logical sense. However, considering representations of public engagement, challenges arise when the gaze on the individual claims-makers subsumes deeper structural or institutional questions. In her book on consumption and the environment, Jo Littler commented that the political-economic and societal dimensions can often be lost when coverage is overly focused on atomized alternatives for action (2009). In the case of climate change, the highly personalized news resulting from the employment of this norm can distract media consumer-citizens from more textured analysis of climate science and governance.

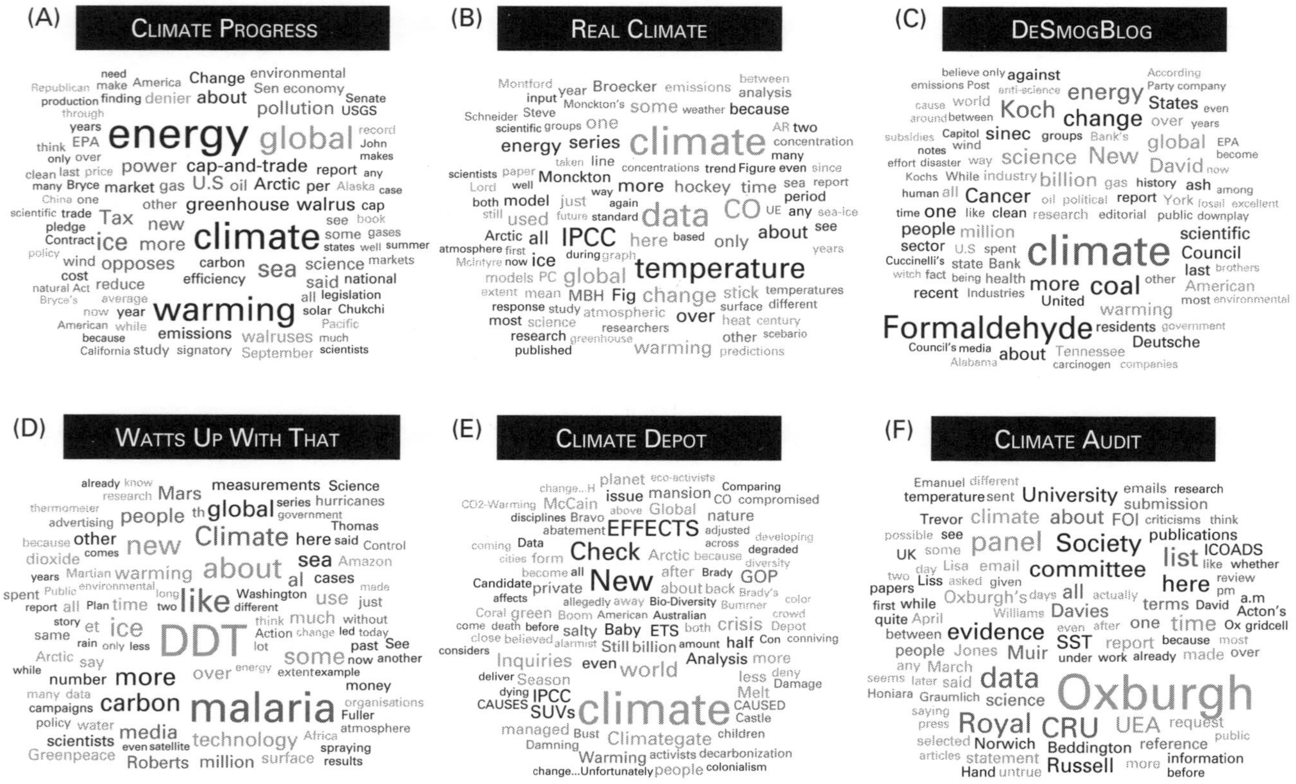

Figure 5.2: New media coverage of climate change, 14 September 2010

This figure extracts word frequencies from the previous twenty posts on each blog, where the size of the term signifies the frequency of the term's usage. These 'word clouds' were generated using the online web tool worditout.com. These blogs were chosen through their high readership as gauged by Technorati Top Green blogs http and through their familiarity with the influence of these blogs in the public sphere.

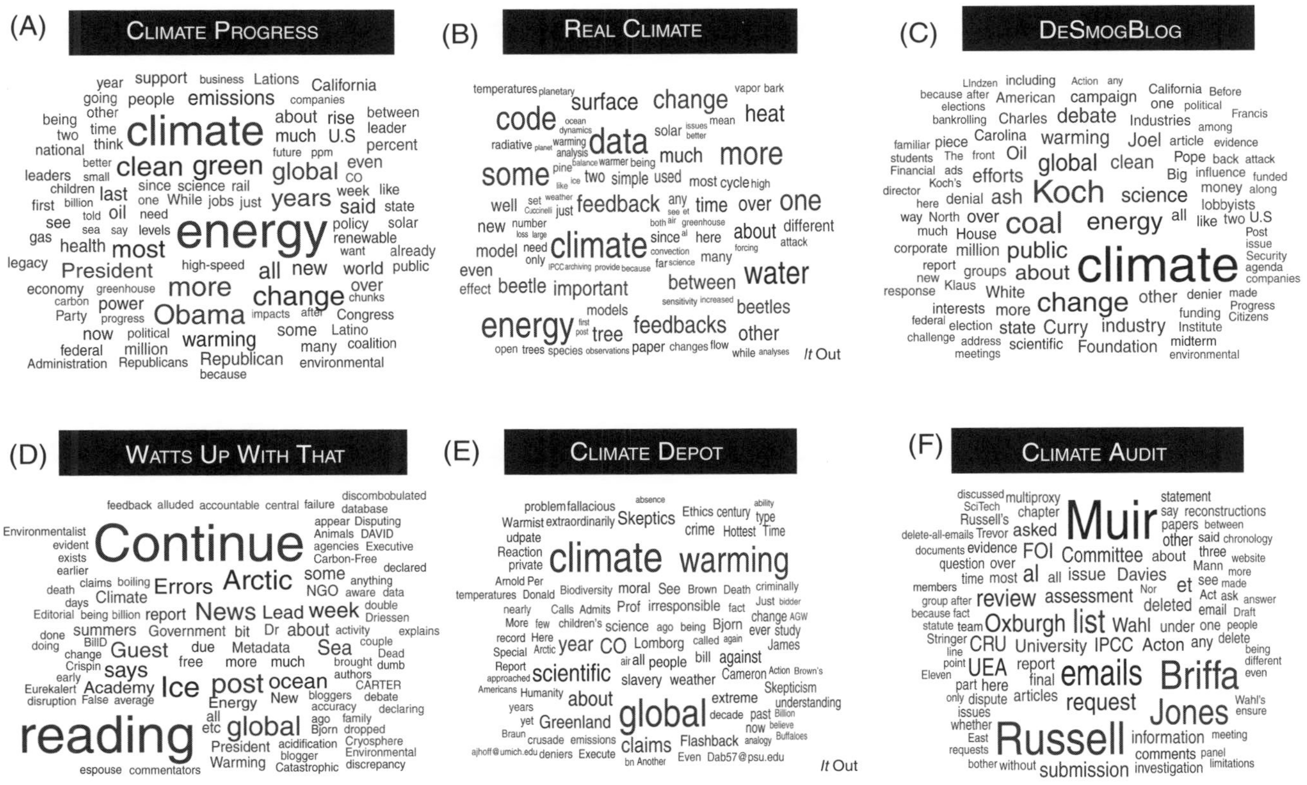

Figure 5.3: New media coverage of climate change, 1 November 2010

This figure extracts word frequencies from the previous twenty posts on each blog, where the size of the term signifies the frequency of the term's usage. These 'word clouds' were generated using the online web tool worditout.com. These blogs were chosen through their high readership as gauged by Technorati Top Green blogs http and through familiarity with the influence of these blogs in the public sphere.

For instance, during coverage of COP15, popular *Fox News* programme 'The O'Reilly Factor' pitted the comments of former US Vice-President Al Gore against those of former US Alaska Governor Sarah Palin, with the segment title 'The Climate Feud' (O'Reilly, 2009). Sarah Palin's authority to speak on the climate derived from an opinion piece she wrote in the *Washington Post* the day before. In that piece, she confused and conflated weather and climate among other issues, where she opined, 'While we recognize the occurrence of these natural, cyclical environmental trends, we can't say with assurance that man's activities cause weather changes. We can say, however, that any potential benefits of proposed emissions reduction policies are far outweighed by their economic costs' (Palin, 2009). These error-laden claims apparently passed editorial correction by the weight of her importance and personality-driven arguments. This example also illustrates the gulf that can emerge between accuracy and effectiveness (see Chapter 8 for more on this).

'Dramatization' is a second journalistic norm or value that contributes to media representations of climate change. Again turning to W. Lance Bennett, he has described this tendency for dramatization as a process that accentuates 'crisis over continuity, the present over the past or future, conflicts' (Bennett, 2002, 46). Through the deployment of this norm, stories focus on the immediate and spectacular, often then displacing subtle, enduring and more chronic issues in the public arena (Wilkins and Patterson, 1987).

As a result, narratives, events, studies or developments that do not contain clear elements of controversy and provocation may be deemed less newsworthy than a tantalizing and dramatic climate story (Ungar, 2000). In the UK context, Gill Ereaut and Nat Segnit have argued that this predilection to present climate science and governance issues in a dramatized form then leads to commonly 'sensationalized' and dramatic reporting. They have commented that these pressures have fed into 'alarmist' reporting on climate change and 'a form of "climate porn"' (2006, 14). Stephen Hilgartner and Charles Bosk have written, 'Drama is the source of energy that gives social problems life and sustains their growth' (1988, 62).

The journalistic preference for 'novelty' is a third value that interacts with these norms of personalization and dramatization (Wilkins and Patterson, 1991; Gans, 1979). Commonly, journalists mention the need for a novel news hook in order to translate an event into a 'climate story'. Across multiple media platforms, Herbert Gans has asserted there is a 'repetition taboo' where 'fresh' stories are favoured over persistent and pervasive issues (1979, 169). The power of this penchant for novelty in reporting is lifeblood that pumps through the veins of collective processes of media representational practices, from the individual journalist up through the editorial staff and through the capillaries of media organizations.

Holly Stocking and Jennifer Leonard have characterized this in terms of 'It ain't news unless it's new'. They have argued that this media thirst for novelty 'allows persistent, and growing, environmental problems to slide out of sight if there is nothing "new" to report' (1990, 40). Yet ironically, these news hooks are often novel ways of portraying or depicting already existing things, in the context of ongoing storylines and historicized or pre-existing norms and pressures. Hence, this is a perceived need rather than absolute novelty that contributes to story formation. Yet because of the perceived need for a 'news peg', certain stories are deemed suitable while others are not (Wilkins, 1993; Wilkins and Patterson, 1987). When portraying climate change through mass media, Kris Wilson has noted, 'The underlying causes and long-term consequences are often overlooked in the day-to-day grind to find a new angle by deadline' (2000, 207).

This need for 'new' stories therefore combines with other newsroom pressures as well, such as working to represent interesting and important dimensions of climate science and governance within a finite 'news hole' and fast-moving news cycle. *Guardian* journalist Paul Brown has commented, 'Journalists work in a highly competitive environment. The stories environmental specialists produce have to compete for space in their papers or on radio and television with football, crime, education, war and terrorism. It takes skill, hard work and ingenuity to get newsdesks interested in climate change against all the other competition for space and air time. For a relatively slow-burning topic, journalists need a constant stream of new and interesting developments to keep the subject alive' (quoted in Boykoff, 2009b, 1).

Hurricane Katrina, which made landfall in August 2005 along the Gulf Coast of the US, provides an example of an event that generated many dramatic, personalized and novel climate stories. Despite various facets of uncertainty that remain regarding links between hurricane intensity and frequency and climate change (see Chapter 3), this biophysical and socio-political event generated a great deal of coverage as it tapped into multiple external influences (see Chapter 4) and mobilized these journalistic norms.

Questions such as what were the causes of such destruction, who was responsible and what needed to be done – particularly in New Orleans, Louisiana – supplied many inroads for media coverage. For instance, Jurgen Trittin – Minister of the Environment in Germany – commented, 'The American president has closed his eyes to the economic and human damage that natural catastrophes such as Katrina – in other words, disasters caused by a lack of climate protection measures – can visit on his country' (Bernstein, 2005, D5). The unprecedented impacts of the storm and the multiple layers of political, economic, environmental, social and cultural consequences generated voluminous 'climate stories' across all segments of mass media.

Furthermore, the pursuits of these issues as they related to the hurricane then called on a range of actors – from experts to everyday people – to make sense of these issues. In this reporting frenzy, media often portrayed claims and claims-makers irrespective of their validity. Moreover, at the level of the story, duelling authority figures and personalities such as then-Director of the Federal Emergency Management Agency (FEMA) Michael Brown, New Orleans Mayor Ray Nagin and members of the Bush administration provided news hooks aplenty.

Consistent with more general coverage of hurricanes and climate change that Judy Curry and colleagues have noted, media representations focused on conflict and debate (2006). Furthermore, many stories bridged to discussions about climate governance. In the US, Juliet Eilperin reported in the *Washington Post*, 'Katrina's destructiveness has given a sharp new edge to the ongoing debate over whether the United States should do more to curb greenhouse gas emissions linked to global warming' (2005, A16). Overall, the intense devastation of human livelihoods and ecosystems, as well as the toll on human lives, made for overwhelmingly dramatic, personalized and novel portrayals on television, newspaper, radio and the internet. But through these norms and values, this 'wave' of coverage of the event appeared to downplay more comprehensive and textured analysis of associated and enduring questions of climate science and governance. In other words, these pressures can lead to 'episodic' climate coverage, where stories lack needed contextualization (Allan *et al.*, 2000). Shanto Iyengar has shown that these kinds of representations have often impeded more comprehensive understanding and awareness of critical political, economic, environmental, cultural and societal issues in the public sphere (1991).

Related to novelty, personalization and dramatization, 'authority-order' is a fourth journalistic norm that significantly influences the production of stories on climate change. Through this value, media workers seek to consult and quote 'actors' and figures such as political leaders, high-profile scientists, government officials, environmental non-governmental organization (ENGO) figureheads and titans of carbon-based industry in order to find voices and perspectives that authoritatively 'speak for climate'. Often embedded in this journalistic value is a desire to make sense of the complexities of climate science and governance questions being pursued, and therefore a perceived need to turn to leadership or expertise to provide order to an otherwise confusing and complex world (Gans, 1979). Effects of this journalistic norm remain apparent, but become less straightforward in the face of overtly clashing authorities.

To briefly illustrate, Thaddeus Herrick from the *Wall Street Journal* wrote, 'For much of his 30-year career, oceanographer Lloyd Keigwin yearned to publish something groundbreaking, a paper that would win him the recognition of his fellow marine geologists. His wish came true in 1996 with his pioneering research on ocean temperatures and climate, which gave scientists a glimpse of natural warming and cooling patterns in the recent past. But his data made an even bigger splash with global-warming sceptics – including oil giant ExxonMobil Corporation – who cited his work on Web sites and other venues as evidence that natural climate change, rather than human activity, is causing the Earth to warm' (2001, B1). In this piece, Herrick's heavy reliance on these statements of authority came at the cost of providing greater context on the issues covered. As another example, an *NBC Nightly News* report began a piece on climate change by covering a statement by then-US President George Bush stating that warming might be due to anthropogenic causes. However, the news story then counterbalanced Bush's statement with comments from commentator Rush Limbaugh (Hager, 2002). Despite the fact that the story began through coverage of Bush's policy position aligning momentarily with the relevant expert climate science community, the story in effect engendered conflict through these authority-laden counterweights.

Complex issues of public trust in authority also feed into this value in media coverage (Lorenzoni and Pidgeon, 2006; Pidgeon and

Gregory, 2004). Research such as that conducted by James Painter on media coverage of COP15 has shown that through media coverage of climate change, there is often significant reliance upon voices of authority. He found that the overwhelming majority of those quoted at this time were authorities from the IPCC and UN Framework Convention on Climate Change (UNFCCC), as well as international organizations like WMO and national organizations such as the UK Met Office (2010). Of course, events and issues are often inherently dominated by authority figures who, in an idealized conception, work for the public order. Thus, the appearance of elite figures on news stories is the sole result of journalist adherence to the 'authority-order' norm. However, overreliance on this norm – in combination with other journalistic values – can come at the sacrifice of giving voice to a wider range of perspectives on the complexities of climate science and governance. In light of the previous discussion of expertise and authority (see Chapter 3), this is certainly a challenging push-pull for media content producers.

These considerations lead to the fifth journalistic norm, that of 'balance'. 'Balanced reporting' is a value that often appears to fulfil pursuits of objectivity (Cunningham, 2003). Robert Entman has defined balanced reporting as the practice where journalists 'present the views of legitimate spokespersons of the conflicting sides in any significant dispute, and provide both sides with roughly equal attention' (1989, 30). Balance can also provide a 'validity check' for reporters who are on deadline and have neither the time nor scientific understanding to verify the legitimacy of various truth claims when covering complex issues in climate science and governance (Dunwoody and Peters, 1992). However, in their book *Merchants of Doubt*, Naomi Oreskes and Erik Conway have importantly pointed out the basic notion that, 'In an active scientific debate, there can be many sides' (2010, 214).

Chapter 3 touched on how the deployment of this norm has the power to swiftly, accurately and fairly represent the relevant range of views on sub-issues within climate science and policy, depending on the particular climate story being covered. However, with some issues such as anthropogenic climate change, a non-discerning application of this norm can serve to perpetuate informational biases in news reporting (see Chapter 6 for more on this). Through these related processes and practices of journalism, minority viewpoints have gained inordinate attention in the media landscape, and therefore have had their voices amplified when providing outlier perspectives on climate change. For example, a *Los Angeles Times* article entitled 'Studies Point to Human Role in Warming' contributed to this notion of a lively 'debate'. Article author Usha Lee McFarling wrote, 'The issue of climate change has been a topic of intense scientific and political debate for the past decade. Today, there is agreement that the Earth's air and oceans are warming, but disagreement over whether that warming is the result of natural cycles, such as those that regulate the planet's periodic ice ages, or caused by industrial pollutants from automobiles and smokestacks' (2001, A1).

The development and widespread reliance on this norm can partly be attributed to the influence of the 1949 'Fairness Doctrine' in the US. This law stated that all sources licensed by the Federal Communications Commission had to present contrasting viewpoints on controversial issues of public importance. It did not require 'equal' time per se; rather, it required the representation of contrasting viewpoints on critical contemporary issues in the public arena. Although US President Ronald Reagan officially discontinued this rule in 1987, its influence still cascaded throughout the principles of 'good', 'responsible' and 'professional' journalism. Todd Gitlin has commented that this 'set up the sort of balances that journalists routinely equate[d] with "good stories"' (1980, 90). The next chapter takes up the deployment of this journalistic norm of balanced reporting in more empirical detail (see Chapter 6).

Lost in translation? Representing climate in US media

To concretize how these journalistic norms and values work in combination over time, it is useful to briefly explore climate-change coverage on US television and in newspapers over the last few decades. Accounts such as Eric Pooley's 2010 book *The Climate War* and Jeremy Leggett's (2001) book *Carbon Wars* have well-documented US climate science-policy decision-making in the public arena during this time. Certainly this brief foray does not do justice to the many facets, as well as emergent (and submerged) discourses and themes that unfolded during this period. Nonetheless, such an exercise remains instructive in order to overlay analyses of US media representations of climate science and governance over this time to further explicate these spaces of cultural politics.

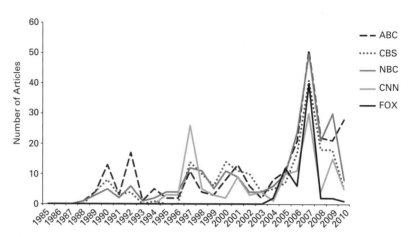

Figure 5.4: US television coverage of climate change, 1985–2010
This figure tracks the ebbs and flows of US television coverage of 'climate change' or 'global warming' from 1985 to 2010. These data include *ABC World News Tonight*, *CBS Evening News* and *NBC Nightly News* from 1985. *CNN* data begin in 1995 while *Fox News* data start from 2004.

Chapter 2 outlined how climate stories burst into the public arena in the late 1980s through concatenate and intersecting *political, scientific* and *ecological/meteorological* themes. Figure 5.4 shows US television news coverage of climate change or global warming from 1985 through to 2010. The trends here are generally consistent with ebbs and flows demonstrated in US newspaper coverage during this time as well (Boykoff, 2007a).

Following on from increase in coverage in the late 1980s, mass-media accounts portrayed early climate politics mainly by way of prominent personalities and authorities. For instance, numerous media representations in 1988 captured strong rhetoric regarding the challenge of climate change by then US Presidential candidate George H. W. Bush. In particular, Bush promised to 'fight the greenhouse effect with the White House effect' (Peterson, 1989, A1). Also in that year, two US Senate bills were introduced on the heels of James Hansen's attention-getting testimony (see Chapter 2 for more).

Moreover, coverage focused on emergent scientific claims that humans have been contributing to contemporary changes in the climate. Two articles from US newspapers illustrate this development. A *Los Angeles Times* article reported that 'Interest in global warming has exploded in Congress, the news media and among world organizations, rapidly taking the topic from the laboratory to the living room' (Dolan and Lawrence, 1988, A1). Journalist Philip Shabecoff from the *New York Times* noted 'mounting evidence that carbon dioxide from the burning of fossil fuels and other industrial gases are accumulating in the atmosphere, where they trap heat from the sun like a greenhouse. Many scientists predict that the greenhouse effect will cause the earth's temperature to rise within a century to levels unreached in human experience' (1988, A8). Mass media continued to cover reports on the science of climate change in the subsequent years. In August 1990, the IPCC released its First Assessment Report, and in November 1990 at the World Climate Conference, an IPCC technical report was reviewed and more than 700 scientists released the Scientists' Declaration.

However, moving into the 1990s there emerged numerous climate sceptics and contrarians who began to challenge claims from these texts. Prominently, the Global Climate Coalition (GCC) was assembled in late 1989 by a consortium of carbon-based industry interests – ExxonMobil, Ford, General Motors, American Petroleum Institute, British Petroleum and Royal Dutch Shell (Hoggan and Littlemore, 2009). Among their activities, the GCC publicly questioned the validity of science that evidenced humans' role in climate change as well as the wisdom of policy proposals that sought to address the changing climate (McCright and Dunlap, 2010). These emergent conditions fed into news stories, particularly placing the conflict involved in debates at centre stage.

This was illustrated in television news through a March 1990 *NBC Nightly News* report, where Tom Brokaw stated, 'for all the alarm about global warming, there's a major new study questioning whether it is happening ... certain to trigger even more debate over whether temperatures in fact are on the rise on planet Earth' (Brokaw, 1990). Another example appeared in an April 1990 *ABC World News Tonight* segment that emphasized 'scientists [are] still debating whether it's even happening', and featured portions from such a debate that had just taken place on *ABC's This Week with David Brinkley* between Patrick Michaels and Michael Oppenheimer (Delasky, 1990).

Such coverage of climate science also extended into media representations of ongoing politicking in Washington, DC. Personalization, drama and authority-order norms in particular mobilized numerous segments and articles focusing on political negotiations on climate change at the domestic and international levels. The *Washington Post* article called 'Environmentalists Try to Cut Sununu Down to Size' began:

John H. Sununu has made so many environmental headlines lately that his critics named a newsletter after him yesterday. Called 'Sununews' and illustrated with a caricature of him wielding a chainsaw, the newsletter issued by the National Wildlife Federation promises to publish 'each time Mr Sununu pulls out his chief-of-staff chainsaw and cuts down progress toward strong environmental policy.' In a more serious tone, the federation and seven other environmental groups sent a letter to President Bush complaining that Sununu intervened in three actions that led to 'policy statements by your administration, which not only adversely affected the environment but also broke pledges you have made to the American public'. (Weisskopf, 1990, A21)

ABC World News Tonight also focused on the personality of John Sununu and his concern about climate policies that rely on 'scientific data he doesn't trust'. Their piece quoted his dismissive comments on the science of anthropogenic climate change. Sununu declared, 'There's a little tendency by some of the faceless bureaucrats in the environmental side to try and create a policy in this country that cuts off our use of coal, oil and natural gas' (Compton, 1990). The *CBS Evening News* perpetuated this trope through coverage of President George H. W. Bush's speech at that time. President Bush vowed to 'continue efforts to improve our understanding of climate change [and] to seek hard data ...' (Andrews, 1990)

This personalization also fuelled these media narratives on climate change over the years that followed. US news media coverage continued to rise into 1992. In this year, a great deal of coverage was focused on the novelty and drama of the mid-year UN Conference on Environment and Development (or Earth Summit). The subject of climate change was central to this summit meeting, with the unveiling of the UNFCCC. For instance, while deploying journalistic norms like dramatization and balance, a segment during the *NBC Nightly News* sought to outline the salient themes surrounding the associated climate science and politics. Reporter Robert Bozell stated, 'All sorts of precise scientific observations – including studies of ancient glaciers – reveal that most of the Earth is getting warmer. The big question is whether the temperature change is due to natural trends or is the result of the greenhouse effect, a warming of the Earth from increased carbon dioxide in the atmosphere ... from the burning of gasoline, coal and other fossil fuels' (1992).

More generally, as coverage increased substantially in this year, the Earth Summit fulfilled the journalistic 'hook' of novelty. Whether US President George Bush would attend the Rio conference was a central feature of this larger landscape of media attention. *The Washington Post* journalist Michael Weisskopf wrote:

Yesterday, after a White House meeting with UN Secretary General Boutros Boutros-Ghali, Bush called the treaty a 'historic step' and announced his plans to go to Rio for an unspecified period of time. The announcement ended what officials acknowledge was an artful game of diplomatic 'chicken.' Bush was under pressure by world leaders to lend the luster of his office to the most ambitious environmental conference ever held. He refused to agree to attend, however, until the US position on global warming prevailed, saying April 21, 'I'm not going to go to the Rio conference and make a bad deal or be a party to a bad deal'. (1992, A3)

Over this period, coverage that tracked and documented the to-and-fro movements of various US political authorities and individuals staking claims about both climate science and governance was predominant.

However, climate-change coverage then decreased in the mid 1990s. Contributing contextual factors included the 1994 Republican takeover of Congress, and a 'concomitant rightward shift in the national political culture' which served to diffuse policymaker and public urgency for climate action (McCright and Dunlap, 2003, 366). Furthermore, in 1995 a group representing carbon-based industry interests undertook a $13 million campaign, named the 'Global Climate Information Project'. This effort sought to undercut the consensus regarding anthropogenic climate change as well as calls for concerted international climate action (Johansen, 2002). These contrarian interventions fuelled a perception of 'non-problematicity' as well as de-prioritizing climate mitigation and adaptation action (see Chapter 3 for more).

Yet, there was still plenty of climate science as well as ongoing political posturing to report on. Most prominent among these reports is the IPCC Second Assessment Report (SAR), released in late 1995. Among its findings and appraisals, the SAR stated that, 'Future unexpected, large and rapid climate system changes (as have occurred in the past) are by their nature difficult to predict. This implies that future climate changes may also involve "surprises"' (Houghton *et al.*, 1995). In terms of climate governance, in 1995 the first Conference of Parties meeting (COP1) took place in Berlin, Germany. There, participating countries agreed to the terms of the 'Berlin Mandate', which provided a foundation for what was to become the terms of the Kyoto Protocol. However, these events garnered little coverage in US mass media. These scientific findings and political actions during the 'slow' years of climate-change coverage demonstrated that if the first-order journalistic norms of dramatization, personalization and novelty were not met, the chances for extensive, in-depth coverage of this environmental problem diminished.

But 1997 saw another rise in US newspaper and television media coverage of climate change. This was, in large part, attributed to conflict, novelty and drama that emerged from COP3, in Kyoto, Japan. Coverage of the lead-up to the event included a 95–0 US Senate resolution against US participation in the Kyoto Treaty, as well as a carbon-based-industry-funded $13 million TV ad campaign that further maligned the treaty. These sorts of attention-grabbing actions provided dramatic, personalized and novel climate stories (Gelbspan, 1998). Nebraska Senator Chuck Hagel asserted, 'There is no way, if the President signs this [treaty] that the vote in the United States Senate will be even close. We will kill this bill' (Bennet, 1997, A1).

Among the political, scientific and meteorological/ecological factors shaping US mass-media coverage at the turn of the decade was the release of the IPCC Third Assessment Report (Houghton *et al.*, 2001). Also, in 2001 the newly-elected President George W. Bush abandoned hopes of sending the Kyoto Protocol to the Senate for possible ratification and reversed a campaign pledge to seek major reductions in US power-plant carbon dioxide emissions. White House spokesman Ari Fleischer explained these Bush stances by saying, 'The president has been unequivocal ... It's a question of what we can do based on sound science and a balanced approach as a nation to take action against global warming' (Fleischer, 2001).

The sheer novelty and authority of the President taking an unequivocal stance against the Kyoto Protocol and domestic reductions made them newsworthy. In addition, the personalization, drama and conflict generated by responses of criticism further garnered coverage. For example, the *Washington Post* story by Dana Milbank and Keith Richburg ran with the headline 'Bush, EU clash over climate policy: Europeans plan to pursue Kyoto curbs despite US stance' (2001, A1). These norms also came to the fore at this time when the Bush administration ousted the head of the IPCC, Robert Watson, in favour of Indian economist and engineer, Rajendra Pachauri. The Bush administration deemed Watson's interests for climate governance to be at odds with US GHG emissions reduction priorities and proposals (Revkin, 2002). Furthermore, John Fialka from the *Wall Street Journal* reported that officials from ExxonMobil Corporation called him 'a minion of former Vice-President Al Gore' and therefore sought to remove him from the IPCC Chairmanship (2002, C18).

Another noticeable increase in television and newspaper coverage of climate change was detected around 2004. Heavily politicized moves from the increasingly isolated Bush administration earned press coverage along with other concatenating events. For instance, in May *CBS Evening News* carried a piece on the film *The Day After Tomorrow*, which drew on the intermingling of entertainment and science-policy struggles. In the introduction to the segment, anchorperson Dan Rather opined, 'In a never-ending debate over global warming, the latest battle lines run from Washington to Hollywood … a sci-fi flick is the catalyst for a fight over science facts.' The news segment then cut between movie clips and statements by Robert F. Kennedy, Jr and President George W. Bush, mobilizing journalistic norms of personalization and drama. The *CBS Evening News* piece continued with a portion of a 2003 (in)famous speech by Oklahoma Senator James Inhofe on the Senate floor, where he spoke of the possibility of anthropogenic climate change as being potentially 'the greatest hoax ever perpetrated on the American people' (Bowen, 2004a).

Such focus on pitched battles and debates came at the expense of providing larger context of climate science. As another example, *CBS Evening News* framed the anthropogenic climate-change issue as one of mere political opinion. In this segment, reporter Jerry Bowen leaned heavily on numerous journalistic norms and values when he commented flatly, 'President Bush insists scientists can't definitively link man-made carbon dioxide emissions to a warming planet.' The segment then quoted climate contrarian Sherwood Idso saying that, 'it is just coincidental that the Industrial Revolution has come along at the same time and is putting all this extra CO_2 into the air'. Bowen counter-posed these positions – utilizing the journalistic norm of balance – when he then continued, 'But the President's own panel on climate change issued [a] report this year acknowledging the human impact on warming, a view shared by the majority of the world's scientists' (Bowen, 2004b).

Moving into 2006, climate policy rhetoric ahead of mid-term US congressional and State-level elections connected with domestically focused media coverage of multi-scale climate governance. What had not been a particularly legible voting issue in previous elections had become a rallying point for politicians in State elections as well as for Democrats regaining control of both houses of US Congress at that time. For instance, Arnold Schwarzenegger gained widespread recognition for signing into law a California bill to cap GHG emissions from industry, and this helped his re-election campaign (Finnegan, 2006). Moreover, Democratic control of the Senate meant that Barbara Boxer (Democrat, California) replaced James Inhofe (Republican, Oklahoma) as Chair of the Senate Committee on Environment and Public Works. In contrast to Inhofe's sceptical stance on climate science and governance, Boxer called global warming 'the greatest challenge of our generation' (Simon, 2006, A12).

Moreover, the mid-year release of the film *An Inconvenient Truth* catalysed heavy media coverage. US media accounts of the film release spanned the News, Business, Entertainment and Style sections, thus pushing climate change from an environmental issue to one garnering the attention of a wide range of interests and permeating many political, economic, social and 'celebrity' issues. This upsurge continued through to the end of 2006, with heavy coverage of the late October release of the UK 'Stern Review' on the economic costs (and benefits) of climate mitigation, as well as the COP12 meeting in Nairobi, Kenya that followed. This conference discussed implementation of the first phase of the Kyoto Protocol as well as possibilities for participation from key 'developing' countries, such as China and India.

These narratives provided strong doses of journalism-friendly content for ongoing media representations of climate change. This peak in coverage continued into the first half of 2007, through news hooks related to ongoing domestic US climate politics and through the release of the Fourth Assessment Report from the IPCC. In addition, highly fluctuating oil prices and high gasoline prices at the pump provided many news hooks into various dimensions of the climate issue. As was discussed in Chapter 1, a stagnation that followed 2007 in US as well as global coverage of climate change and global warming could be attributed to more attention paid in the finite news hole to the economic recession, among other contextual issues. However, as was discussed in Chapter 2, the increases in media coverage seen in 2009 can be largely attributed to movement associated with COP15 (see Chapters 1 and 2 for more).

Tracking US media treatment of climate change and global warming over these two decades elucidates how these journalistic norms can help to provide traction for concatenate and intersecting *political*, *scientific* and *ecological/meteorological* climate themes. Such an accounting can also help demonstrate how these journalistic values are not expressed in isolation from one another; rather, they are both consciously and unconsciously deployed in the dynamic arena of larger political, economic, social, environmental and cultural conditions. The patterns revealed in the mobilizations of these journalistic norms cohere with dominant market-based and utilitarian approaches to discussing the spectrum of possible mitigation and adaptation action on climate change.

This has also been associated with a shift called 'responsibilisation', where climate change becomes the responsibility of the individual *in place of* governments or regulators who might influence policy decision-making by altering rules relating to GHG emissions-related production and distribution issues. While such trends may appear to open up space for the development of more (pro)activist stances, this individualization tends to atomize social, economic and environmental movements for change. Tim Luke has argued that such trends are consistent with larger movements in a 'new green order' where commodified and highly individualized solutions actually are seen to move citizens further from considering their role in requisite collective institutional shifts towards decarbonization (1999). He has also warned that such ways of viewing one's engagement with environmental challenges remain 'too entwined in the reproduction of most existing power relations and global market exchange' (2008, 1811). While 'low-carbon' or meat-free diets, the purchasing of hybrid cars or the installation of fluorescent lightbulbs can be seen as individual pro-climate behaviour, these acts of more sustainable consumption choice are argued to be feeble engagements in the face of the scale of the challenge.

Moreover, in the case of representations of climate change, Robert Brulle has argued that an excessive mass-media focus merely on the debaters and their claims, 'works against the large-scale public engagement necessary to enact the far-reaching changes needed to meaningfully address global warming' (2010, 94). Looking at how new and social media have represented climate change, one can detect the challenges involved in excessive focus on the individual at the expense of attention paid to the issues themselves as well as larger political and social forces.

Conclusions

In the context of multi-scale pressures and processes, this chapter has sought to more centrally explore how first-order and second-order journalistic norms and values shape *how* and *why* certain facets of the global warming issue become 'news' and others do not. Climate-change issues, events and developments that climb to the top of the mass-media agenda may not do so merely for intrinsic characteristics and reasons. They also become articles, segments and clips by way of journalistic norms as well as concatenate contextual factors.

So, journalistic decision-making can involve the mobilization of norms as well as negotiations with editors and producers in the news-room. Together with other contributing political, economic, social and cultural factors, they shape what becomes a 'story'. For example, a 2008 article by Richard Luscombe in *The Observer* stemmed from the news hook that shark attacks had increased in the early months of that year. He quoted shark expert Dr George Burgess, who said, 'The one thing that's affecting shark attacks more than anything else is human activity. As the population continues to rise, so does the number of people in the water for recreation. And as long as we have an increase in human hours in the water, we will have an increase in shark bites.'

This appeared to be a straightforward story. However, further along in the piece, Luscombe offered this speculative and throw-away comment: 'Another contributory factor to the location of shark attacks could be global warming and rising sea temperatures' (2008, 34). While this was not central to explanations for increased shark attacks, a copy-editor swiftly picked it up and titled the story 'Surge in fatal shark attacks blamed on global warming'. As Chapter 4 noted, it is important to also analyze headlines and their relation to stories on climate and the environment (e.g. Einsiedel and Coughlin, 1993; McManus, 2000; Boykoff, 2008a).

With the editor's misguided headline, Richard Luscombe possibly thought the frustrating swerve in the central story narrative would have ended. However, a short story ran in the sister newspaper *The Guardian* ten months later entitled 'Sharks go hungry as tourists stay home'. As it turned out, the months following the first story saw a dramatically reduced number of attacks, and 2008 actually had fewer attacks overall – fifty-nine – compared to the previous year – seventy-one in 2007. Shark expert Dr George Burgess was again quoted, citing the economic contraction and decline in shark numbers from overfishing as possible reasons for this decrease.

To casual readers who may have made a connection between shark attacks and global warming from earlier media portrayals, this updated trend may have residually influenced scepticism about climate change. In other words, it is quite possible that a passing reading of this progression would suggest to media consumers that global warming may not be as urgent and acute an issue as one may have previously thought. While these could be dismissed as trivial linkages, these are precisely the sorts of subtle semiotics at work in everyday life that swirl – and mix with values and belief systems – to congeal into personal perspectives and priorities on climate change. Thus, inadvertently, journalists' norms as well as interactions with their editors are important to wider media representations and public understanding on climate change.

This chapter has concentrated attention on the professionalized journalistic behaviours – held together with the glue of norms – that construct meaning and representations. It is clear that these journalistic norms are tools to help translate and make meaningful oft-complex and abstruse issues in climate science and policy for consumer-citizens. But there are dangers lurking here and uncritical deference to these journalistic standards has far-reaching effects. Pete Spotts – journalist for the *Christian Science Monitor* – commented, 'If one is simply adhering to the standards of journalism then (discontinuities) can happen by default' (quoted in Boykoff, 2007b, 484–485). But Stephen Schneider replied, 'I don't think we are asking more of journalists than they can deliver, but we may be asking more of narrow corporate media than they can deliver' (quoted in Boykoff, 2007b, 485).

Critically exploring how journalistic norms operate – amid a complex web of influences – helps to understand how these factors combine with other multi-scale pressures and processes to influence ongoing climate science and governance discourses. The next chapter focuses on the particular workings of the norm of 'balanced reporting', and its misapplication over time in coverage of human contributions to climate change.

6 | *Signals and noise*
Covering human contributions to climate change

Due to the unprecedented scale of influences that humans have had on the global climate and environment, Paul Crutzen famously dubbed this contemporary time the 'Anthropocene Era' (2002). For billions of years, radiative forcing – producing changes in the climate – has occurred in response to energy imbalances. Atmospheric temperature change is the most evident form of climate forcing (Wigley, 1999). However, an effect of the energy harnessed through carbon-based industrial development has been GHG emissions and anthropogenic climate change.

The term 'anthropogenic' comes from the Greek root 'anthropos', meaning 'human'. Anthropogenic climate change is also often referred to as the 'enhanced greenhouse effect'. Anthropogenic sources include fossil-fuel burning (primarily coal, gas and oil) and land-use change. Current heavy reliance on carbon-based sources for energy in industry and society has led to significant human contributions to climate change, noted in particular through increases in temperature as well as sea-level rise.

The task of separating and distinguishing anthropogenic forcing from natural variability has been a critical scientific challenge. But over time, signal (anthropogenic) to noise (natural) schemes have been derived and enhanced (e.g. Tett *et al.*, 1999). As was discussed in Chapter 3, the past twenty years of research have seen tremendous advances in detection and attribution research (Karl and Trenberth, 2003; Allen *et al.*, 2000). Consistently, through many independent and peer-reviewed research endeavours, human activities have been found to account for the majority of global warming since the Industrial Revolution (e.g. Crowley, 2000). As a result, there has emerged convergent agreement in the climate science community that human activity – rather than natural fluctuation – has accounted for a significant portion of climate changes over the past two centuries.

This storyline of consensus regarding anthropogenic climate change has evolved; this can be evidenced through high-profile articulations by the Intergovernmental Panel on Climate Change (IPCC) and other scientific bodies. These top-level assessments have emerged from the aggregation of numerous peer-reviewed climate studies and reports (Argrawala, 1998). In the case of anthropogenic climate change, IPCC statements have achieved greater clarity and detail regarding this human 'fingerprint'. The IPCC Second Assessment Report made this detection and attribution work clear through the statement that, 'The balance of evidence suggests that there is a discernible human influence on the global climate' (Houghton *et al.*, 1995, 4). This convergent view then strengthened further in the years that followed. Prominently, the Third Assessment Report in 2001 contained the statement that, 'There is new and stronger evidence that most of the warming observed over the last 50 years is attributable to human activities' (Houghton *et al.*, 2001, 10). At that time, US National Oceanic and Atmospheric Administration administrator D. James Baker, commented that, 'There's a better scientific consensus on this than on any issue I know – except maybe Newton's second law of dynamics ... ' (Warrick, 1997, A1).

This consensus was made even more detailed and explicit in the 2007 IPCC Fourth Assessment Report statement that, 'Most of the observed increase in globally averaged temperatures since the mid-20th century is *very likely* due to the observed increase in anthropogenic greenhouse gas concentrations' (Solomon *et al.*, 2007). Fielding over 30,000 comments from experts and governments, this multi-stage peer-review and consensus-building process represented a clear view of the state of scientific understanding of climate change, corroborated by numerous statements from national science academies and other scientific organizations.

Truth translated?

While it is challenging to appropriately characterize and delineate general views in a broadly construed expert community, the intergovernmental collaboration of top climate scientists from around the world in the form of the IPCC has presented a unique opportunity to do so. This group has drawn their authority from peer-reviewed scientific findings and from their identification as 'experts' by their peer communities (Adger *et al.*, 2001). Thus, the IPCC has emerged as an organization that authoritatively interacts with national and international policy discussions and debates through policy-relevant research statements and decisions.

In 2004, a study by Naomi Oreskes sought to appraise the distribution of expert views on anthropogenic climate change by way of assessing the relevant scientific literature on the topic. This study found unanimous agreement across the nearly 1,000 peer-reviewed research papers regarding the presence of a human 'signal' (2004a). In this analysis of work from 1993 to 2003, Oreskes found that three-quarters accepted the consensus view that humans contribute to climate change, while the remaining quarter of the papers took no position. In the widely cited and landmark *Science* essay called, 'The Scientific Consensus on Climate Change', Oreskes concluded, 'Politicians, economists, journalists, and others may have the impressions of confusion, disagreement, or discord among climate scientists, but that impression is incorrect' (2004a, 1686).

But is the establishment of convergent agreement an effective proxy for 'truth' translated? How should this scientific way of knowing about the changing climate form the basis for policy priorities and everyday actions? These remain difficult and open questions. Scholar Steve Rayner has grappled with these challenges:

For good or ill, we live in an era when science is culturally privileged as the ultimate source of authority in relation to decision-making. The notion that science can compel public policy leads to an emphasis on the differences of viewpoint and interpretation within the scientific community. From one point of view, public exposure to scientific disagreement is a good thing. We know that science is not capable of delivering the kinds of final authority that is often ascribed to it. Opening up to the public the conditional, and even disputatious nature of scientific inquiry, in principle, may be a way of counteracting society's currently excessive reliance on technical assessment and the displacement of explicit values-based arguments from public life. However, when this occurs without the benefit of a *clear understanding* of the importance of the substantial areas where scientists *do* agree, the effect can undermine public confidence. (2006, 6, emphasis added)

As mentioned in Chapter 3, there are many other topics in climate science and governance – such as the rate of temperature change and whether Cap-and-Dividend mechanisms are optimal climate-mitigation policy tools – where there can be a widely distributed range of expert views. However, Steve Rayner's comment here can prompt further consideration regarding how 'clear understanding' in science – scientific consensus on anthropogenic climate change – has been represented. Such considerations can also open up explorations of what possible effects this has on policy and public awareness as prioritization. While acknowledging that this scientific consensus on anthropogenic climate change is not the 'truth' translated, this 'policy-relevant' information provides a critical input to national and international climate policy. Such solidified discourse has helped to shape institutional considerations of policy alternatives and their accompanying discursive frames and narratives in mass media (Hajer, 1995).

Approaching issues in this way thus helps to unpack and interrogate *how* meanings are made and maintained, and what historical and biophysical contingencies shape our perceived opportunities and alternatives for climate action. Thus, media interpretations of climate change are not simply a mirror of reality, but rather shape these realities.

Moreover, these portrayals are not merely the 'truth' translated, but instead are depictions of many 'regimes' of truth that, in the words of Stephanie Rutherford, 'circumscribe how the world is apprehended' (2007, 300). Seen in this way, media coverage of climate change is not just a collection of news articles and clips produced by journalists and producers; rather, media coverage signifies key frames derived through complex and non-linear relationships between scientists, policy actors and the public, often by way of the news story.

Bias as balance?

While viewing IPCC deliberations as imperfect and IPCC reports as heterogeneous constructs of facts and values, the convergent agreement on human contributions to climate change within relevant expert science communities makes it therefore possible to empirically consider to what extent this has been portrayed accurately as consensus, or inaccurately as contention.

As was mentioned in the previous chapter, the journalistic norm of balance can be a very important tool in the toolkit for working journalists. Brent Cunningham has noted how this norm has often effectively and appropriately guided how many news stories are framed and covered, providing a valuable 'fairness check' for reporters

(2003). In an intensely competitive contemporary news environment, reliance on this norm can also be preferred when journalists do not have time or deep scientific knowledge resources in order to verify the legitimacy of competing claims (Gamson and Modigliani, 1989; Dunwoody and Peters, 1992). Consequently, this journalistic norm becomes a useful and quick way to seek out a variety of perspectives, conduct newsgathering and storytelling practices as deemed responsible by the profession and file a piece on time.

As was mentioned in the previous chapter, balance has been defined as a tool that seeks to dispassionately 'present the views of legitimate spokespersons of the conflicting sides in any significant dispute, and provide both sides with roughly equal attention' (Entman, 1989, 30). Similarly, Herbert Gans has written that 'balance is usually achieved by identifying the dominant, most widespread, or most vocal positions, then presenting "both sides"' (1979, 175). Complexities emerge through the operationalization of this norm. For example, challenges arise when grappling with the introduction of new and complex ideas into the discourse. These ideas take more time to explain than old ideas that support the status quo, so in this sense, equal time falls in favour of people proffering easily digestible, not ideologically contrary, viewpoints. Amidst these many time pressures, this norm can then become a 'surrogate for validity checks' (Dunwoody and Peters, 1992, 2010).

Through these processes and practices, at times the deployment of the journalistic norm of balanced reporting can depart from the goals and objectives of fairness and accuracy. When it comes to coverage of anthropogenic climate change, balanced reporting has the potential to actually be a form of informational bias. W. Lance Bennett has pointed out that informational biases 'make news hard to use as a guide to citizen action because they obscure the big picture in which daily events take place' (Bennett, 2002, 44). This informational bias refers to the 'joint product of internalized professional values and of newsgathering routines' (Entman, 1989, 48), thus leading to distorted news. Herbert Gans has noted that while 'objective or absolute non-distortion is impossible', the notion of 'bias as distortion' remains important for consideration (1979, 304). Information bias is therefore correctly seen as a relational and historical product of the ongoing interactions between mass-media workers, scientists, politicians and citizens.

Over the last few decades, scholars, policy actors and media actors working in climate science and governance had sensed that information bias may have cropped up when media have covered this issue of human contributions to climate change. For example, in 1993 Stephen Schneider stated, 'It is difficult for the media to do what sometimes I wish they would: back off their concept of "balance" in favour of the concept of "perspective"' (1993, 173). In 2001, he was more emphatic: 'The public is often so confused by … the media's dutiful reporting of polarized extreme views (or their attempts to "balance" the conclusions of a 500-scientist assessment with a few outlier Ph.D.s who say "It ain't so!") that political leaders ask groups such as the US National Research Council or the IPCC to help society sort out where current consensus really lies' (2001, 339).

However, there had not been work done to reach beyond the spaces of anecdote and assumption to empirically analyze these intersections in media representation of climate change. This juxtaposition of the tendency to provide 'balanced' coverage of any given issue with the convergent agreement that humans play a role in modern climate change has provided an opportunity to address some key and fundamental questions, such as: while there has been agreement in the relevant expert scientific community that human actions are contributing to global warming, has this consensus been portrayed accurately in mass media? Or, has the journalistic norm of balanced reporting – representing 'both' sides of the story – been a mediating variable that skewed and distorted global warming coverage? In other words, was coverage of global warming 'balanced', and therefore actually perpetrating an informational bias?

In 2002, Pacific University professor Jules Boykoff and I examined to what extent anthropogenic climate change was represented as consensus or as contention in major US newspapers up to that time. This study analysed how the *New York Times*, the *Washington Post*, the *Los Angeles Times* and the *Wall Street Journal* covered this issue. A dataset of approximately 3,500 news articles was compiled through searches with the key terms 'climate change' or 'global warming' in articles from these sources from 1988 to 2002. The sample set then drew on about 20 per cent of the total population for analysis. Over this period of time, over four in ten of the articles appeared in the *New York Times*, and nearly three in ten in the *Washington Post*, while about 25 per cent appeared in the *Los Angeles Times*, with

5 per cent in the *Wall Street Journal*. The focus was placed on these newspapers due to their high daily average circulations as well as their influence on smaller newsrooms across the country over this period of time. These newspapers were considered as 'first-tier' or 'prestige-press' news sources, and each had some of the highest average daily circulations in the country (Audit Bureau of Circulations 2010).

Previous research also identified these sources as major influences on policy discourse and decision-making at national and international levels (McChesney 1999), with policy actors routinely monitoring these sources for salient aspects of contemporary public discourse, including climate science. Moreover, beyond direct reach to their readers, these publications have also influenced news coverage of other, 'second-tier,' or smaller newspapers across the country, because: (a) reporters, editors and publishers have frequently consulted these sources for decisional cues on what is 'newsworthy', and (b) stories from these outlets have often been repurposed or printed verbatim in regional, state and local newspapers. Moreover, these newspapers have set the agenda for science stories then picked up by wire services such as the *Associated Press*, and smaller press services that comprise part of this larger news organization (Antilla, 2005). Thus, news coverage in these papers has provided opportunities to track the dominant news frames in the public arena associated with anthropogenic climate change.

Similarly, in 2004 I examined US television news segments on anthropogenic climate change on evening newscasts. The study assembled a dataset of nearly 300 segments that appeared on *ABC World News Tonight*, *CBS Evening News*, *NBC Nightly News*, *CNN WorldView*, *CNN Wolf Blitzer Reports* and *CNN NewsNight* from 1995 to 2004. The sample set examined about half of the total population for analysis. Each network evening news programmes comprised just over a quarter of the sample set each, while the *CNN* broadcasts made up about two in ten segments in the sample. At the time of the study, *Fox News* programmes and archives were not available for analysis. These programmes were similarly selected because of their agenda-setting influence and high levels of viewership across the US. At the time of the study, on average nearly 30 million viewers watched these newscasts each evening (PEJ, 2006).

The unit of analysis was the news article/segment and analyses took place within the particular piece (intra-text) as well as examining relations between articles/segments (inter-textual). Both newspapers and television samples were compiled by selecting every fifth or second article/segment respectively, as they appeared chronologically. A content analysis coding scheme was developed to assess how anthropogenic climate change was portrayed in each article/segment. Codes were assigned to correspond to assessment of articles/segments that (1) presented the viewpoint that anthropogenic global warming (distinct from natural variations) accounts for *all* climate changes, (2) presented multiple viewpoints, but emphasized that anthropogenic contributions, distinct from yet still in combination with natural variation, significantly contribute to climate changes (most accurately communicating the dominant view from climate science), (3) gave 'a balanced account' surrounding existence and non-existence of anthropogenic climate change, and (4) presented multiple viewpoints but emphasized the claim that anthropogenic component contributes *negligently* to changes in the climate.

Category one captured what Chapter 3 has characterized as 'alarmist' views: those portrayals that overlooked possible natural contributions to climate change by characterizing contemporary climate change as entirely human-caused. Category two was considered accurate coverage. The third category – 'balanced reporting' – accounted for coverage that provided roughly equal attention and emphasis on competing viewpoints on anthropogenic climate change; however, not necessarily equal time and space (Entman, 1989; Dunwoody and Peters, 1992). The fourth category captured dominant attention paid to 'contrarian', 'sceptical' accounts and commentaries. In other words, these are representations that emphasized the view that humans do not contribute to climate change, despite the convergent agreement within the climate science community that there has been a human signal in modern climate change.

The coding was determined not simply by tallying up comments or frequencies of words or phrases. Importance was placed on labelling of those quoted, terminology, framing techniques, salience of elements in the text, tone and tenor, and relationships between clusters of messages. This more interpretative approach effectively accounted for subtle factors shaping representational practices.

Across the fourteen years analyzed in the newspapers study, over half of the coverage (53%) was found to best fit in the third category of 'balanced reporting'. In other words, these articles gave 'roughly equal attention' to the view that humans contributed to global warming and the view that humans' role in climate change was negligible. Accurate coverage comprised just over a third of the coverage (35%), while the two ends of the coding scheme generated about 6% of coverage each. Over the nine years of the television study, nearly seven in ten segments provided 'balanced' coverage regarding anthropogenic climate change vis-à-vis natural variation (70%), while just over a quarter of the news clips accurately represented the scientific consensus (28%), and just 3% of the sample depicted anthropogenic climate change as a negligent factor in overall changes in the climate.

Each study then assessed whether this divergent reporting from the previously mentioned consensus on anthropogenic climate change was significant. Z-score analyses – which compare ratios – tested whether reporting that diverges from accurate coverage of anthropogenic climate change met established criteria for significance. In newspapers, the study found the convergence in climate science regarding anthropogenic climate change significantly depicted instead as conflict and contention from 1990 through to the end of the study period in 2002. In television, the significant divergence was detected from 1995 through to the end of the study in 2004. In sum, this period of time was largely seen to be a 'lost decade' of US traditional media coverage of anthropogenic climate change.

Consequently, Jules Boykoff and I referred to the informational bias perpetrated through the journalistic norm of balanced reporting in shorthand, as 'bias as balance'. Focusing on the content of coverage, media depictions consistently framed discussions of anthropogenic climate science as contentious. The questions then became, what was going on during this time? *How* and *why* were there such discrepancies? *How* and *why* did media represent this evolving consensus that humans contribute to climate change in an informationally biased way? Why was there a shift in 1990?

Political-economic factors as well as social and cultural influences (discussed in the previous chapters) permeated and influenced US mass-media coverage over time. In this context, numerous articles and segments in the dataset specifically illustrated how the deployment of the journalistic norm of balanced reporting contributed inadvertently to an informational bias.

In 1988 and 1989, the vast majority of coverage emphasized anthropogenic contributions to global warming, thereby mirroring

the scientific discourse of the time. The relative novelty of the phenomenon may help explain this trend, but surrounding US political and
electoral considerations at that time were also important (see Chapter
5 for more). However, by 1990, coverage had shifted to significantly
'balanced' accounts. This shift was explained by the increasingly complex politicization of the global warming issue (Trumbo, 1996), as
well as a coalescence of a small group of influential spokespeople and
scientists who emerged in the news to refute these findings (Gelbspan,
1998; Leggett, 2001). In 1990 government officials, often armed with
the findings of this 'scepticism' and 'contrarianism', became the most
cited source in prestige-press articles, surpassing scientists who were
the most cited sources before that time (Wilkins, 1993). Moreover,
numerous US politicians often called for more research on global
warming as a necessary precursor to taking action.

So, from that time forward, balance became a common feature of
the journalistic terrain. For example, Rudy Abramson from the *Los
Angeles Times* article reported, 'The ability to study climatic patterns
has been critical to the debate over the phenomenon called "global
warming". Some scientists believe – and some ice core studies seem
to indicate – that humanity's production of carbon dioxide is leading
to a potentially dangerous overheating of the planet. But sceptics con-
tend there is no evidence the warming exceeds the climate's natural
variations' (1992, A1).

As another example during this time, Rick Atkinson from the
Washington Post authored a piece entitled, 'Reaching a Consensus
Is the Hot Topic at Global Climate Conference'. After quoting the
president of the Maldives calling for urgent action to combat sea-level
rise, Atkinson wrote, 'On the other hand, some skeptical meteorologists and analysts assert that global warming reflects a natural cycle
of temperature fluctuation and cannot be decisively tied to human
actions.' He then closed with this statement from astrophysicist Piers
Corbyn: 'As far as we are concerned, there's no evidence for global
warming, and by the year 2000 the man-made greenhouse theory
will probably be regarded as the biggest scientific gaffe of the century'
(Atkinson, 1995, A10).

Moving into the twenty-first century, an *NBC Evening News*
segment in 2003 called 'Clearing the Air' focused on 'Bush administration claims that [the EPA draft 'Report on the Environment']
didn't contain sound science' (Gregory, 2003). Because of Bush

administration tinkering with the language of the document regarding anthropogenic climate change, the Environmental Protection Agency (EPA) ultimately deleted the entire section on climate change because they felt that such manipulation inaccurately represented the consensus science. The story spotlighted EPA (science) and White House (policy) conflict, and lesser attention was paid to what the suppressed consensus statement was. Rather than a focus on the convergent views regarding anthropogenic climate science that drove the draft report assessments, the correspondent David Gregory instead drew attention to disagreement. He commented that there was 'too much uncertainty about the causes of global warming science to draw conclusions for this report'. Another representative piece from *CNN* in 2006 aired a speech by US President George W. Bush in which he commented, 'I have said consistently that global warming is a problem. There is a debate over whether it is man-made or naturally caused' (2006). This statement was aired without reference to the larger context of scientific consensus on this issue of human contributions to climate change. It therefore further fuelled an atmosphere of confusion and conflict.

Together, these selected examples illustrate how US television and newspaper coverage in the sample set contributed to a storyline of increased uncertainty and debate. In the aggregate, the two studies drew attention to the fact that adherence to the norm of balanced reporting had led to informationally biased coverage of climate change. Tracing these influences has helped to explain how US media have depicted conflict rather than coherence regarding scientific explanations of anthropogenic climate change over time. Moreover, informational bias, hidden behind the veil of journalistic balance, was also found to have the potential to make both discursive and real political space for the US government to shirk responsibility and delay action regarding global warming over these periods of study.

Stephen Zehr commented in an influential paper that the intense focus on uncertainty 'implied that there were many unanswered questions' (2000, 92). So, despite general agreement in the scientific community regarding the existence of anthropogenic influences on global warming, coverage seemed to indicate a significant split within the expert scientific community.

In the 2006 documentary film *An Inconvenient Truth*, Al Gore discussed the findings from my US newspaper study with Jules Boykoff, juxtaposing the 'bias as balance' with Naomi Oreskes's findings from *Science* in that same year. Also in 2006, *New York Times* columnist Paul Krugman wrote about the study in the context of carbon-based industry efforts to confuse the public about human contributions to climate change. In discussing his film soon after its US release, Al Gore said to Terry Gross on *National Public Radio's* 'Fresh Air', 'this slide [containing these newspaper findings along with findings from Oreskes's 2004 study] is probably the one slide that has evoked more post-presentation commentary ... than any other'.

Recognition for the usefulness of the newspaper study was gratifying. Yet, these comments in 2006 suggested that this 'bias-as-balance' phenomenon had continued through the present time, while the actual study period ended in 2002. While it was encouraging that our research seemed to illuminate ongoing discussions of the role of media in public (mis)understanding, I found it curious that our research ending in 2002 was held up four years later as evidence of an ongoing problem. The question remained: what happened since the end of the study period?

In the intervening years, many scientists, journalists and policy researchers I had interviewed in my research had actually commented that they felt this 'balanced' coverage of anthropogenic climate change was no longer so pervasive in the US. As a result, I felt compelled to examine this empirically, and therefore conducted follow-up work where I examined coverage in these US newspapers from 2003 to 2006. I endeavoured to find out if the journalistic norm of balance continued to contribute to informationally biased reporting in these key countries, or if we were instead now flogging a dead norm.

The dataset for the study was composed of newspaper articles from the *Los Angeles Times*, the *New York Times*, *USA Today*, the *Wall Street Journal* and the *Washington Post*. *USA Today* was added to the follow-up study as it has emerged as an influential newspaper in intervening years. Circulation had outpaced the other sources, with average daily circulations at about 2.5 million copies (Audit Bureau of Circulations, 2010). The sample set and coding schemes were developed in coordination with the earlier research designs mentioned above. In total, approximately 2,500 articles on climate change were published in these newspapers between 2003 and 2006. Through selection of every sixth article as it appeared chronologically, news articles consisted of 27% from the *Los Angeles Times*, 33% from the

New York Times, 7% from *USA Today*, 12% from the *Wall Street Journal* and 21% from the *Washington Post*.

I also took this as an opportunity to do comparative research with coverage in the UK. So I concurrently analyzed coverage in UK 'quality press' – *The Independent* (and *Independent on Sunday*), *The Times* (and *Sunday Times*) and the *Guardian* (and *Observer*).

Results from these analyses showed that the portion of US coverage providing 'balanced accounts' of anthropogenic climate change decreased over the period from as much as one-third of coverage in 2003 down to just over 3 per cent of coverage in 2006. Statistical tests of difference – as those described above – found that US media representations of anthropogenic climate change diverged significantly from the scientific consensus in 2003 and 2004, but that this was no longer significant in 2005 and 2006. Meanwhile, the examination of UK newspapers sampled approximately 1,100 articles – 35% from the *Guardian* (and the *Observer*), 36% from *The Independent* (and *Independent on Sunday*) and 29% from the *Times* (and Sunday *Times*) – found the percentage of divergent coverage was just around 1% across all newspapers and all years. In 2003, 2% of coverage was 'balanced', while this percentage was around 1% in 2004 and 2005, and 0.4% in 2006. During this time, reporting that anthropogenic contributions to climate change are significant – in line with scientific consensus – comprised 98% to 99% of total coverage during these years.

However, I also undertook a study of 'working-class' UK tabloid newspapers – the *Mirror* (and *Sunday Mirror*), the *Express*, the *Sun* (and *News of the World*) and the *Daily Mail* (and *Mail on Sunday*) – over the period 2000 to 2006. In addition to the descriptions of the audience demographics and analyses mentioned in Chapter 4, I examined coverage of anthropogenic climate change in nearly 1,000 articles. The research findings were distinct from the previous analysis of UK 'quality' press: in tabloid representations, all sources were found to have conveyed significantly divergent coverage from the scientific consensus that humans contribute to climate change across all the years of study.

Illustrations of comments and reports persistently divergent from the convergent agreement abounded. As a succinct illustration of the utilization of the journalistic norm of 'balance', a 2002 passage from the *Express* read, 'The world is warming but whether due to natural climate fluctuations or to man-made effects is unclear' (Disney,

2002, 13). As another example, journalist Ivor Key wrote, 'Over the past century, the average surface temperature of the Earth has risen by about one degree Fahrenheit and the rate of warming has accelerated in the past 25 years. This, say scientists, is a significant amount, considering that the world is only five to nine degrees warmer than it was in the last ice age about 20,000 years ago. Experts are still arguing about whether this is a natural phenomenon, or the effect of industrial societies releasing heat-trapping gasses into the atmosphere' (2000, 25).

However, almost one-third of this divergent coverage was attributed to the view that human contributions are negligible. Such a stance was amplified in numerous articles through 'contrarian' accounts and comments. For instance, a commentary in the *Mail on Sunday* stated, "In the closed minds of the Green lobby, the theory that manmade pollution is causing global warming is an unquestioned and unquestionable article of faith. In fact there are many reputable scientists who dispute it. It seems that the most significant global warming is caused by the hotheads who are anxious to believe their own propaganda' (2002, 24). In another case, the *Sun* commentator Jeremy Clarkson responded to a 2004 study documenting methane emissions from cattle by writing, 'This confirms what I've been saying for years – cars do not cause global warming. Now we learn that all along it was bloody sheep and cows…' (2004, 25).

As third representative illustration over this study period, Peter Hitchens commented in the *Mail on Sunday*, 'The Green Thought Police will be after me for daring to say this, but nobody actually knows if global warming is caused by human activity' (2006, 25). Thus, quantitative content analyses of the UK tabloid press found that combined influences of contrarianism and the utilization of the journalistic norm of balance have jointly contributed to informationally biased coverage of anthropogenic climate change. Such a difference between UK 'quality' and 'tabloid' press accounts has been attributed to differences in how the notion of climate change has been considered by UK citizens as a primarily elite concern (Boykoff, 2008a). These ongoing patterns have been both fuelled and reflected by UK tabloid press coverage, through synchronization with generalized neoliberal approaches to climate governance and by the perceived information needs of their working-class readership (see Chapter 4 for more).

Overall, results from these analyses revealed spatially and socio-economically differentiated coverage in UK and US sources over the study periods. But findings also pointed to an evolutionary shift in US newspaper coverage in 2005 from explicitly 'balanced' accounts to reporting that more closely reflected the scientific consensus on attribution for climate change (Boykoff and Boykoff, 2004; Carvalho, 2005). Why might this shift in US reporting have taken place? The contributing influences can be usefully considered in three primary ways: *political, scientific* and *ecological/meteorological* (Boykoff and Boykoff, 2007).

First, primarily *political* movements in climate rhetoric and policy promises comprised a substantial amount of coverage. Reporting of the Gleneagles G8 Summit comprised one prominent example of this phenomenon. Ahead of the Summit on his home soil, Prime Minister Tony Blair voiced strong climate policy rhetoric, seeing this meeting as an opportunity to leave a positive 'legacy' of committed policy action (Lean, 2005, 18). Moreover, en route to the meeting, George W. Bush made an unusually clear statement regarding anthropogenic climate change, declaring that, 'I recognize that the surface of the Earth is warmer and that an increase in greenhouse gases caused by humans is contributing to the problem' (VandeHei, 2005, A14). The Blair and Bush statements fed into tremendous US media speculation about the potential for a shift in the Bush administration's stance on climate policy. A communiqué coming out of the meeting also acknowledged human contribution to climate change and included the signature of President Bush, despite his previous equivocations on the subject.

This coverage was also primed by pronouncements at the State level that increased the pressure for US federal action, including the widely reported executive order by Arnold Schwarzenegger calling for an 80 per cent reduction in Californian GHG emissions by 2050. This prompted headlines across all the major US newspapers, such as 'California sets emission goals that are stiffer than US plan' in the *Wall Street Journal* (Ball, 2005), and 'Gov. vows attack on global warming' in the *Los Angeles Times* (Bustillo, 2005). Such an atmosphere of US and international politics – as well as coverage therein – stood in contrast to these spaces in the preceding years.

These political factors intersected with *scientific* activities that contributed to this critical discourse moment. Generating particular media attention was news leaked to the *New York Times* regarding drafts of the report by the US Climate Change Science Program (mentioned in Chapter 3). Moreover, a joint statement by eleven international science bodies was released just as news unfolded about Cooney's editing of the climate science documents. It was also significant that this statement included the science bodies of Brazil, China and India (Joint Science Academies Statement, 2005), and media coverage noted how this bridged some of the tensions between Global North and South on responsibility for emissions and reductions.

Third, *ecological/meteorological* events in 2005 further contributed to this shift. The most dramatic – as discussed in Chapter 5 – among numerous extreme weather events in that year was Hurricane Katrina. This storm made landfall on the US Gulf Coast, devastating large parts of New Orleans. While Chapter 3 discussed how scientific research has continued to debate the extent of connections between climate change and hurricane intensity and frequency, Katrina prompted widespread speculation and discussion in climate policy and public circles, as well as many media reports on the potential link between human activities, future storm events and climate change.

These three sets of factors fed into this critical shift in media representational practices regarding anthropogenic climate change. These moments not only shaped ongoing coverage of discourse on human-induced climate change, but they also fed back into ongoing interactions at the science–policy interface. These media shifts were articulated in media accounts themselves, most prominently by Dan Vergano in *USA Today*. The story's headline on the front page of *USA Today* proclaimed: 'The debate is over: globe is warming'. In the front-page story, he wrote, 'Don't look now, but the ground has shifted on global warming. After decades of debate over whether the planet is heating and, if so, whose fault it is, divergent groups are joining hands with little fanfare to deal with a problem they say people can no longer avoid' (2005, A1). Two days later, an editorial from the same newspaper began, 'Yes, the globe is warming, even if Bush denies it' (2005, 10A).

This particular set of reports in *USA Today* was significant for two central reasons. First, this was because of the influence of the source. During this time, *USA Today* had become the most widely circulated daily US newspaper (Audit Bureau of Circulations, 2010). Along with other top newspaper and television outlets, this newspaper – through a range of format, content and distribution strategies – had been shown to have contributed to discourses shaping ongoing climate governance in the US as well as internationally (Boykoff, 2007a). Second, this reporting shined a light onto ongoing contentious climate politics at the US federal level, where the George W. Bush administration was viewed to take on a climate science and policy stance at odds with many supporting science and governance bodies such as the US National Academy of Sciences. Vergano's lucid piece went on to win the 2006 David Perlman Award for Excellence in Journalism from the American Geophysical Union, while many scientists and policy actors – who over time had felt that their research findings, comments and statements have often been misrepresented by a range of mass-media outlets – felt this marked a watershed moment towards more accurate climate-change reporting (Boykoff, 2007a).

There have been pockets of dissent regarding this detected shift, arguing that this reduction in 'balanced' coverage marks a form of censorship of alternative views. For example, a special report of the Business & Media Institute – a group proclaiming to 'Advance the Culture of Free Enterprise in America' – was issued in 2008 entitled, 'Global Warming Censored: how the major networks silence the debate on climate change'. Central to their arguments was the assertion that news consumers 'are being sent only one message', calling for increased media attention for 'alternative opinions' (Seymour and Gainor, 2008). As discussed in Chapter 3, the report conflated a range of issues – from whether humans contribute to climate change to whether it is a 'catastrophe' – and also reduced evidence-based scientific pursuits to those of 'opinion'. Considered in this way, viewing the more recent developments in media representations of anthropogenic climate change as an enhanced way of approaching balance as accuracy, this sort of claim appears tenuous, and at times disingenuous.

Why were these results similar in some cases and distinct in others as media sources moved across these spaces? As very general comparisons, US and UK contexts share several similarities. For the better part of two centuries, influential policy actors in the UK and US have shared a commitment to capitalist–neoliberal development frameworks, utilitarian views of environmental services and exploitative interactions with nature. Equally, in both countries, entrenched technological optimism and an aversion to precautionary action in the absence of conclusive scientific evidence have also influenced the wider regulatory architectures of environmental policy (Boykoff and Rajan, 2007). Finally, over time, modern media communications have expanded their reach and influence, forming increasingly powerful social, political, economic and cultural institutions in both countries (Starr, 2004).

However, the differences across these socio-economic and national contexts can be attributed in part to their diverse domestic political environments. This notion centres on key political, economic and cultural variants that influence reporting. Prominent among these are differentiated regulatory and societal networks and institutions that have shaped varied carbon-based industry decision-making behaviour and practices; similarly, carbon-based industry interests have shaped divergent federal climate policy priorities and actions (Pulver, 2007). In the UK, the Liberal Democratic, Labour and Conservative parties have all taken up forceful climate policy rhetoric. Meanwhile, resistance to international climate policy implementation in the US has primarily been the province of the Republican Party. For instance, the conservative vanguard that won a Republican majority in the House of Representatives in the 2010 mid-term elections comprises many actors who have taken a sceptical stance on the connection between GHG emissions and climate change. As journalist Ronald Brownstein in the *National Journal* put it, many 'have declared the science either inconclusive or dead wrong, often in vitriolic terms' (2010).

Also, as has been discussed earlier, ideologically driven climate contrarianism has been often associated with the political right in the US, whereas it has not been such a politically identifiable group elsewhere (Dunlap, 2008). Moreover, despite the fact that carbon-based industry interests have exerted considerable influence over climate policy in both countries, associated scientists and policy actors who have questioned the significance of human contributions – often dubbed 'climate contrarians' – have been primarily housed in US universities, think tanks and lobbying organizations (McCright, 2007).

US movements from the political right – such as the Tea Party movement – have voiced scepticism about a range of climate issues, from whether humans play a role to whether it is worth addressing through emissions-reduction policy initiatives. As described by journalist John Broder in the *New York Times*, this stance has been seen as an 'article of faith'. This has also been evidenced by polling data that show 'more than half of Tea Party supporters said that global warming would have no serious effect at any time in the future, while only 15 per cent of other Americans share that view' (2010b, A1). US-based non-nation-state organizations such as the Heartland Institute have held numerous meetings to promote contrarian views on climate science and policy. For instance, in 2009, they held a three-day gathering in Chicago with the theme: 'Is global warming a crisis? Is Cap-and-Trade dead? You decide.' The groups heavily promoted the event through efforts such as a full-page advertisement in *USA Today* and radio adverts on *Fox Radio News*. So, while it has been a politically divisive issue in the US, this has not been the case in dominant UK politics and policy amongst the elite class.

Conclusions

Convergent agreement within expert climate science communities that humans contribute to climate change has evolved over the past century of climate research. The clear consensus on this aspect of climate change has enabled the empirical testing of its portrayal in the public arena via mass media. This chapter has outlined research that pursued associated questions and, in so doing, has illustrated how portrayals of anthropogenic climate science have not been merely innocent reporting of scientific 'facts' and 'truths' (Boykoff and Boykoff, 2004; McChesney, 2008). Rather, this pattern of media representational practices has emerged from systematic and institutionalized journalistic routines, in particular through the norm of 'balanced reporting'.

As the previous chapters outlined, these routines do not operate in isolation, but take place in the context of interwoven political, economic, environmental, social and cultural influences. This empirical evidence has suggested that there have been some short-term improvements in media representations of anthropogenic climate change. However, over the long term, many institutional challenges persist for enhanced media reporting on the environment. The dynamic cultural politics are politicized and contested arenas where 'agents of definition' battle for recognition and discursive traction; and it is here where the implications for climate governance and action remain open considerations.

Three limitations to this empirical approach should be pointed out. First, William Freudenburg and Violetta Muselli have argued that

these findings have been a rather conservative assessment of journalistic practices over the last decade. In their study of media coverage
of anthropogenic climate change in four US newspapers from 1998
to 2002 and in 2008, they found that consensus assessments – and
media representations of them – were more conservative than new
and emergent research on anthropogenic climate change was actually documenting. They concluded that, 'the physical reality is significantly *more* ominous than has been widely recognized to date' (2010,
490). Therefore, taking the IPCC as an anchor for empirically testing
possibly divergent media coverage could be argued to have been a
comparatively conservative launching-off point.

Second, this research has placed an emphasis on interpretations
derived from coherent and systematic readings of media portrayals
of climate change. In so doing, the potential influence of a prominently placed article – generating a 'front-page thought' – or an attention-grabbing image accompanying an article or segment – and its
correspondence with text or transcript – has not been factored in or
weighted in the dataset. Moreover, the sometimes haphazard nature
of media consumption – from skimming articles to just hearing/
watching portions of a segment – has not been accounted for through
this approach. In other words, these studies struggle to account for
'selective listening' or 'selective reading' that we actually engage in
during our daily lives. These remain viable challenges that deserve
ongoing research attention as they are relevant inputs for ongoing
considerations of public awareness and potential engagement in various climate issues.

Connected to this point, a third limitation to this approach is that
quantitative interpretations of these patterns and trends can overlook
the phenomenon where doubts can be raised more readily than they
can be allayed. As Robert Costanza has said, 'All it takes is a little
muddying of the water so there's not a clear answer … it takes a lot less
money and effort to muddy the water than it does to clear the water'
(Peterka, 2010). Furthermore, William Freudenburg and colleagues
have described this as the power of 'Scientific Certainty Argumentation
Methods' or 'SCAMs' (2008). These factors were evidenced in a 2010
Wall Street Journal article entitled 'Heated exchange over climate'
(Glader, 2010). While the news hook was a recent journal article that
featured a century-long local weather record, the headline drew attention to the counter-claims of a 'self-described climate-change critic',

Anthony Watts. The Columbia University Lamont–Doherty Earth Observatory authors found that this weather station 'offered a powerful commentary on climate change'; however, the counter-claims about the placement of weather equipment were privileged by this demonstration of 'false equivalency', as *Climate Central* journalist Andrew Freedman put it (2010). In combination, views and perspectives on climate change are just as often gained from one particularly striking media representation of the issue as they are from cumulative media effects over time.

Nonetheless, these findings have illuminated how the undiscerning deployment of the journalistic norm of 'balance' has served to impede public and policy-maker understanding of anthropogenic climate change over time. Through this significant misapplication, evidence-based knowledge generated by those deemed 'experts' and 'authorities' through peer-review process has been put on a par with opinions and arguments offered by a voluble minority of claims-makers. Naomi Oreskes and Erik Conway have commented, 'The he said/she said framework of modern journalism ignores this reality. We think that if someone disagrees, we should give that someone due consideration. We think it is only fair. What we don't understand is that in many cases, that person has already received due consideration in the halls of science' through peer review (2010, 269).

Moreover, Ross Gelbspan has asserted, 'The professional canon of journalistic fairness requires reporters who write about a controversy to present competing points of view. When the issue is of a political or social nature, fairness – presenting the most compelling arguments of both sides with equal weight – is a fundamental check on biased reporting. But this canon causes problems when it is applied to issues of science. It seems to demand that journalists present competing points of views on a scientific question as though they had equal scientific weight, when actually they do not' (1998, 57–58). This work has therefore pointed to a clear need to more discerningly apply this and other journalistic norms and values – replacing 'false balance' with 'balance-as-accuracy' – when representing the various dimensions of climate science and governance.

The findings here have shown that the journalistic norm of 'balance' has served to amplify outlier views on anthropogenic climate change, and concurrently engendered an appearance of increased uncertainty regarding anthropogenic climate science. This, in turn, has entered into an already highly contested arena where it has permeated climate policy discourse and decision-making (McCright and Dunlap, 2010). When mass-media coverage distorts rather than clarifies scientific understanding of anthropogenic climate change, it can greatly impact how policy actors perceive, approach and prioritize actions and remedies (Trumbo, 1996). This can manifest subtly as well as explicitly.

For an example of subtleties, in 2006 Richard Harris of US *National Public Radio* covered the US House Energy and Commerce Subcommittee on Oversight and Investigations hearing entitled, 'Questions Surrounding the "Hockey Stick" Temperature Studies: Implications for Climate Change Assessments'. At the hearing, some members of Congress called into question more general climate science credibility regarding anthropogenic climate change. Representative Michael Burgess said, 'It is false to presume that a consensus exists today or that human activity has been proven to cause global warming…and that is the crux of this hearing.' Chairman Joe Barton added, 'My problem is that everybody seems to think that [anthropogenic climate change] is automatically a given and we shouldn't even debate the possibility of it or we probably shouldn't debate the causes of it and I think that's wrong.' In the report, Harris pointed out how these comments were viewed as outlier amongst the relevant expert policy and science communities. Nonetheless, these comments from Burgess and Barton found their way to the final cut in the segment on this influential US radio outlet (Harris, 2006).

Republican Senator James Inhofe provided an example of explicit influence in the policy arena when he interpreted these trends anecdotally from his perspective. In an interview with the *Tulsa World* – from Inhofe's home state of Oklahoma – the article also states, 'He blames the media for handing over an unfair amount of air time and coverage to the side that pushes the claim that links man to climate change' (Myers, 2006). In this case, journalist Jim Myers dutifully aired this claim from the prominent climate contrarian and therefore amplified Inhofe's anecdotal assertion.

These findings certainly do *not* suggest that journalists should censor views on various aspects of climate science and governance. Instead, the evidence outlined in this chapter seeks to improve efforts for greater media accuracy by more carefully and fairly representing *all* credible perspectives, findings, views and sides, in context. In other words, this calls for moving from a bipolar logic to a multi-polar one, where multiple considerations outlined in these chapters are taken into account when making journalistic decisions regarding 'who speaks for climate'. Stephen Schneider has commented that journalists 'don't have to avoid the contrarians. I have never said to leave the contrarians out, but they have to make sure that there is a perspective on their relative credibility' (quoted in Boykoff, 2007b, 482).

These findings have indicated that in certain places as well as a segment of the larger landscape of mass-media representations, there have been improvements. However, many challenges still remain. As a case in point, local television coverage of climate change on NBC station WJAR Providence/New Bedford (14 November 2009) provides a useful illustration of ongoing challenges in media representations of climate change. Host R. J. Heim hosted the show by framing the session in this way:

Today, on *Ten News Conference Special Assignment*, global warming – fact or fiction. If it is happening, what's the cause and what effect will it have on coastal areas like here in Southern New England... if you listen to the proponents, the atmosphere is warming, the glaciers are melting and sea levels are rising because of pollutants like carbon dioxide [that] man [sic] is putting into the air, and if we don't act now they say that changes to civilization will be catastrophic... if you listen to the opponents, they say man's not the cause of global warming, it's the sun. And all the hype and hysteria is to keep scientists awash in their $50 billion of research grants they receive from governments and corporations over the past two decades. What's really going on? ... We have both sides covered. (WJAR, 2009)

In this case, the nuance of evidence in the climate science to expert-based views on the efficacy of various policy measures and the urgency of action was inaccurately reduced to a mere two sides: proponents and opponents. In the debate that followed, a geologist and sociologist were cast as 'proponents' and the local weathercaster was put forward as the 'opponent'.

This work has served as a template for considerations of other climate science and policy issues. For instance, researchers Judy Curry, Peter Webster and Greg Holland wrote a piece for the *Bulletin of the American Meteorological Society* where they discussed how this 'bias-as-balance' issue has spilled over into media representations of climate change and hurricanes. They commented, 'Acrimony generated by the media debate has contributed to disruption of legitimate debates sponsored by professional societies...' and concluded that this can play a role in 'inflaming a scientific debate and the values gap between scientists and journalists' (2006, 1033).

It would be a mistake, however, to interpret these findings too broadly without further empirical research to test anecdotal claims. As was discussed in Chapter 3, all aspects of climate change should not be treated equally: there are facets of climate change where scientific agreement is strong (such as anthropogenic climate change), whereas for others, contentious disagreement garners worthwhile debate and discussion (such as whether the Copenhagen Accord is a worthwhile policy measure).

Yet, this analysis contributes to further discussions of an ongoing challenge at the science–practice interface, in that it further refines our understanding of media representations of anthropogenic climate change. In so doing, it has been important to remember, however, that science on anthropogenic climate change remains a historicized process and consensus does not represent the end of the tale, but rather a period in the ongoing story. Stephen Schneider argued, 'What needs to be done is go beyond platitudes about values embedded in science and to show explicitly, via many detailed and representative empirical examples, precisely how those social factors affected the outcome, and how it might have been otherwise if the process were differently constructed' (2001, 343).

7 | *Carbonundrums*
Media consumption in the public sphere

'[Media] is like a feral beast, just tearing people and reputations to bits' ~ statement by outgoing UK Prime Minister Tony Blair to the Reuters Institute, 12 June 2007 (Baldwin, 2007)

Mass-media representations of climate change move into the public sphere to fight for citizen attention alongside many pressing twenty-first century challenges. Through the framing of issues, predicaments and possibilities, a variety of 'actors' have undertaken variously embattled efforts to define the 'climate question'. The quip from former UK Prime Minister Tony Blair indicates how this is a battle-field, where actors can be adversarial in working to fulfil their roles in this public arena.

In particular, media workers – journalists, publishers, editors – shape these narratives through the application of journalistic norms and values, within a larger landscape of political, economic, environmental and cultures pressures (Gamson *et al.*, 1992). As such, selections from the steady stream of everyday events are captured as 'climate stories', thereby shaping public perception. Influences such as asymmetrical power and access to these discursive negotiations feed back through these social relationships and further shape emergent climate 'news', knowledge and discourse. In these ways, encoded messages – television/radio broadcasts, printed newspapers/magazines and internet communications – do not simply inform the public about the 'right' decision, but actually provide inputs into a dynamic and contested web of meaning-making and maintenance.

Anabela Carvalho and Jacquelin Burgess have developed 'circuits of communication' in order to illustrate three 'moments' or 'circuits' through which communications pass over time (2005). Media communications first originate and, second, disseminate into the public sphere before, third, entering the private sphere of individual engagement. Stories and reports are assembled, compete for attention, are taken up to varying degrees in our personal lives, and feed back again through ongoing interactions over time. These feedbacks shape news framing in subsequent moments, and inform ongoing environmental science, policy and practice interactions (Bord *et al.*, 2000).

This chapter turns centrally to the numerous complexities shaping the arena of interpretation, uptake or resistance to media representations of climate issues. I first explore key factors internal to media consumers and public citizens themselves, before appraising how public polling has captured the 'public mood' as well as how mass media have represented such polls. Then, I work through two conceptual models for understanding these communication processes: the Issue–Attention Cycle and the Public Arenas Model. Finally, building from previous discussions (see Chapter 4 in particular), I explore key questions involving external influences that seek to shape public understanding and engagement on climate change via mass media. To make this concrete, I focus on a heterogeneous group of NNSAs that have often been referred to alternatively as 'sceptics', 'contrarians' or 'denialists', whose political-economic and ideological approaches provide organizing and motivating forces behind their actions in the public sphere. These intertwined issues comprise the critical conditions for discursive and material battles for citizen perceptions. Anthony Leiserowitz – an expert in public understanding and climate change – has commented that these are factors that then 'fundamentally compel or constrain political, economic and social action to address particular risks' (2006, 45).

Complexities of human understanding and engagement

Amidst many present-day concerns – from global economic well-being to healthy local school lunches – the public traction of climate issues depends upon numerous contextual factors and a public 'caring capacity'. Aspects of these conditions have been variously referred to over time: for example, Sheldon Ungar has emphasized competing public issues, describing this as the 'attention economy' (2000), while Elke Weber has focused on limits to engagement because of a 'finite pool of worry' (2006). As Chapter 4 mentioned, in addition to scientific 'ways of knowing' about climate change, experiential, visceral and emotional factors play parts in public understanding and engagement with climate information. From one's deeply held environmental ethics, political persuasion or self-identified socio-economic class to more ephemeral issues of one's mood, stress levels, sleep deficits and penchants for conflict avoidance, numerous factors influence citizen views of climate science and governance.

While this volume largely focuses on the production of media representations in the public sphere, questions involving the multifarious ways in which individual understanding and engagement emerge through media representations remain vitally important (Kellstedt *et al.*, 2008). The previous chapters have focused on media representational practices themselves: the power of producing texts or segments, forms, icons and images that shape climate discourses in the public sphere. In so doing, they have worked through a number of hazards as well as footholds along the rocky terrain involving communication and climate-related attitudes and behaviours. This chapter briefly takes up considerations of how various aspects of the climate change issue can become salient.

Over time, many organizations have drawn on the power of claims in their efforts to influence public understanding and engagement in civil society. For example, the FrameWorks Institute has examined public discussions of climate change and the influence that language has had on public engagement in the US. Among their recommendations, FrameWorks Institute argued that climate communications need to focus more centrally on values-related themes – stewardship, responsibility and ingenuity – in order to achieve greater public engagement (2001).

As was discussed in previous chapters, the claims-makers can be as influential to the public citizenry as the claims themselves. For example, consider this statement:

Talk about climate change is not an ideological luxury but a reality. All of the industrialized countries, especially the big ones, bear responsibility for the global warming crisis. (Healy, 2010)

If this comment were emitted from the mouth of *Fox News* commentator Glenn Beck, it would certainly garner the interest of a different segment of civil society than if it were voiced by UN Secretary-General Ban Ki-moon. Moreover, these claims were in fact espoused by audiotape via *Al Jazeera* by Osama bin Laden. How comments get reconciled with the commentator in the minds of a public citizenry is certainly a complex and dynamic set of questions. These issues weave into psychological tenets of cultural cognition, where people's perceptions are found to be shaped largely by their values and by their role models (Kahan *et al.*, 2010). Dan Kahan has succinctly put it, 'People endorse whichever position reinforces their connection to others with whom they share important commitments' (2010, 1).

In addition, Matt Nisbet and John Kotcher have explored how opinion leaders have influenced public understanding and engagement in vastly different ways (2009). Along with journalistic norms and other contextual factors shaping media representations of climate change, reliance on the stances of these opinion leaders can help members of the public citizenry to stay safe from the anxieties and burdens of serious thought about personal choices regarding climate mitigation, adaptation and energy decarbonization. Moreover, this can lessen the burden of one's 'caring capacity' to then address what may be perceived as more immediate concerns, such as issues of job security, local school quality, crime and the economy. As Peter Taylor has described it, 'most people do not have problems of a global nature' (1997, 151). Furthermore, political cycles mean that policy actors are often more concerned by the next election, rather than the next generation. These expanded psychological considerations can help to explain apparent disconnects between convergent scientific agreement that humans contribute to climate change and divided opinions in the US public and policy communities (Pew Research Center, 2009a).

Intertwined here are important influences of ideological perspectives and preferences (see Chapter 4 for more). These can weave through fundamental perspectives on democracy, freedom, liberty and the role of government in society as well as humans in nature. In 2010, Matthew Feinberg and Rob Willer examined a dimension of this called a 'just world view' as it relates to representations about climate change. They found that people who resist doom-and-gloom portrayals of climate impacts may do so because they contradict their deep-seated beliefs in a cornucopian and just future. Moreover, they recommend 'framing global warming messages so they do not contradict individuals' deeply held beliefs' (Feinberg and Willer, 2011, 10). Considered in ways such as these, climate-change 'awareness' and 'knowledge', broadly construed, can prompt a range of responses in the public sphere (Burgess *et al.*, 1998). Media portrayals may drive one person towards behavioural change, while it can leave another person feeling overwhelmed or repulsed.

Public receptiveness to climate challenges invoked by opinion leader and former US Vice-President Al Gore provides clear examples of these many and complex interacting factors. For instance, some film-goers gain great inspiration from the messages in Al Gore's climate-change feature film *An Inconvenient Truth*, yet others found it to be the source of great political ire. This could partly be due to political ideology, as Gore had initially and primarily become known through his work as a left-of-centre Democratic political leader.

This was evident in a film review in the *Albuquerque Tribune*, which quoted Republican Oklahoma Senator James Inhofe, who compared the film to Adolf Hitler's *Mein Kampf*. In the article titled 'Republicans not warming up to Gore's polemic', Inhofe said, 'If you say the same lie over and over again, and particularly if you have the media's support, people will believe it' (Brosnan, 2006). As another example, media reporting on the Gore-led *Live Earth* July 2007 concerts may have inspired and motivated some people to strive for more low-carbon lifestyles, while they might have irked others and prompted them to surrender their carbon sacrifices when they learned of the high-carbon-intensity lifestyles of some of the performers.

One's personal ideological stance has also been found to influence their perception of the stance of journalists and news sources portraying the various dimensions of climate science and governance. In 2010, Kyun Soo Kim surveyed students in the US and found that individuals perceived a media bias from outlets whose coverage seemed to run counter to their own understanding of climate change. In particular, he found that 'the perception of bias was much higher among those who argue that global warming is [only] a natural pattern' (2010, 10). Consistent with this finding, Matt Nisbet and Chris Mooney have commented, 'Many scientists retain the well-intentioned belief that, if laypeople better understood technical complexities from news cover-age, their viewpoints would be more like scientists' and controversy would subside. In reality, citizens do not use the news media as sci-entists assume … faced with a daily torrent of news, citizens use their value predispositions (such as political or religious beliefs) as percep-tual screens, selecting news outlets and Web sites whose outlooks match their own' (2007, 56).

Furthermore, a 2006 study by Jon Krosnick and colleagues found that beliefs about climate change were actually a function of three main factors: possible relevant personal experiences (e.g. exposure to weather disasters), perceived consequences of climate change (e.g. relative vulnerability) and messages from informants (e.g. scientists via the mass media). Through this empirical research, the authors put forward a mechanism linking knowledge and action: 'knowledge may have increased certainty, which in turn increased assessments of national seriousness, which in turn increased policy support... knowledge about an issue *per se* will not necessarily increase support for a relevant policy. It will do so only if existence beliefs, attitudes, and beliefs about human responsibility are in place to permit the necessary reasoning steps to unfold' (2006, 36–37). In this way, media representations are one driver of awareness and engagement. Media coverage of an issue like 'Climategate' may grab one's attention, but the ways in which related themes are taken up in their lived cultures and social relations depend greatly on their philosophical, ideological, political and social perspectives and positions (Hulme, 2009a; Carvalho and Burgess, 2005).

Culture and physical geography also play into these psychologies. In the UK, the notion of 'global warming' has been a welcome thought to some, as relief from dank, rainy winters. In the *Express*, Zoe Nauman wrote, 'On balance, the weather's going to be wonderful' (2001, 17). As another example, Clare McKeon commented in the *Sunday Mirror*:

The consequences of global warming are supposed to be dire for everyone on the planet.

Mediterranean regions will become like central Africa, and will be too hot to visit. Water temperatures will rise and the Gulf Stream will alter its course. Well, October has been the warmest one on record, and it's been wonderful. Long balmy days with wonderful mild weather and sunshine. I planted tomatoes late this year and all the know-alls told me 'They'll never ripen.'

Guess what, they did, and this week and last I have had an abundance of sweet organic tomatoes.

Global warming can't be all that bad (2001, 27).

In contrast, in the Alaskan Inuit context, Sheila Watt-Cloutier addressed regional warming from a justice perspective by referring to it as 'the right to be cold' (Boswell 2007). Depending upon one's mental models and conceptions of 'an ideal climate' – from a drought-free Australian outback to a drier and warmer Zurich – priorities and perceptions are influenced by ongoing media representational practices.

On an individual level, conflicts between knowledge and behaviour – brought out by media representations of climate change – may also stir up anxiety between what we know we *ought* to do and what we actually do. This has been regularly called the 'attitude–behaviour' and 'value–action' gap (e.g. Ungar, 1994; Hobson, 2006; Ockwell *et al.*, 2009). This also interacts with Festinger's notion of cognitive dissonance (1957) in that tension arises when there are inconsistencies between beliefs and behaviours. Instead of modifying discourses or actions to mesh with beliefs, beliefs are in fact often adjusted to cohere with behaviours or articulations. Indeed, research by A. Ross Otto and Brad Love found that more information – by way of media representational practices or other communications – does not necessarily improve daily decision-making, particularly for long-term issues like climate change (2010). Birgitta Höijer has illustrated an aspect of this when she commented, 'we may regard climate change as something to collectively fear, but there is hope if we behave in a climate friendly fashion. If we do not, we should feel guilt' (2009, 11). These tendencies are consistent with many of the ambiguities and ambivalences, conflicts and contradictions that complicate the everyday cultural politics of climate change.

Furthermore, emotional and visceral dimensions of interpretation are important, in addition to what might be considered as rational appraisals of the climate-change information (Moser, 2007). Being 'emotional' has taken on negative connotations over time. For example, the *New York Times* journalist Andrew Revkin has commented that he works to distinguish 'between the potent "heat" generated by emotional content and the "light" of science and statistics' (2007, 156). Yet emotional and visceral interpretations inevitably function in tandem with rational considerations. These also combine with experiential problem-solving and learning devices, such as representativeness or a familiarity heuristic to aggregate notions of 'understanding' and 'concern' (Kahneman *et al.*, 1982).

Cass Sunstein's argument has been that, 'the availability heuristic ensures that some risks stand out as particularly salient, whatever their actual magnitude…If the United States is to take a stronger stand against climate change, it is likely to be a result of available incidents that seem to show that climate change produces serious and tangible harm' (2006, 195). Kari Marie Norgaard has also examined influences of self-protection, fear and risk to one's perceived security as reasons behind why people may resist information about anthropogenic climate change. As Norgaard has put it, 'Emotions of fear and helplessness can be managed through the use of selective attention' (2007). Through a case study in rural Norway, she has documented how individuals held climate information 'at a distance [as] an active strategy preformed by individuals as part of emotion management ... [a] process of collective avoiding as the social organizations of denial' (Norgaard, 2006, 372).

While these issues have been studied for many years within traditional disciplines (e.g. Kahneman and Tversky, 1973), it was not until 2009 that the American Psychological Association took up the interdisciplinary task of examining and articulating these connections in a report 'Psychology and global climate change'. Their stated entry point into the topic was that climate change is an issue 'not easily detected by personal experience, yet it invites personal observation and evaluation' (Swim *et al.*, 2009, 1).

Similarly, in 2009, the Institute for Public Policy Research published a report called 'Consumer Power: How the public thinks lower-carbon behaviour could be made mainstream' (Platt and Retallack, 2009). It was *not* a report on 'how lower-carbon behaviour could be made mainstream', but rather it was a study on perceptions of feasibility and desirability of lower-carbon choices. Regarding considerations of taking climate action to diminish climate impacts, journalist John Vidal of the *Guardian* pursued these issues when he posed the perennial question, 'We know what to do: why don't we do it?' (2009). In short, successful analyses of media representational practices and wider climate communication strategies must also take these many pathways to attitudes, intentions and behaviour (Ockwell *et al.*, 2009).

Polling and public sentiment

The previous section demonstrates how the 'public citizenry' is actually a much more complex and heterogeneous set of varied interests, perspectives, beliefs and concerns. Nonetheless, over time there have been many efforts to understand the 'public mood'. Despite its limits, the most readily accessible way to put one's proverbial finger on the pulse of public sentiment has been through polling data. However, explanatory power derived from polling data can be tricky.

Questions regarding public acceptability of various policy tools such as Cap-and-Trade or carbon taxation can provide helpful insights into questions of feasibility and latent public pressure. For example, the *Six Americas* studies conducted by Ed Maibach, Connie Roser-Renouf and Anthony Leiserowitz have sought to provide greater texture regarding US public views on numerous climate policy measures and personal actions. This work has provided useful insights into issues such as how religion, ideology and gender permeate support for climate action, as well as related issues such as energy-efficiency improvement measures (2009). Moreover, Chapter 2 mentioned how issues of public trust in climate science were usefully gauged through survey work by Anthony Leiserowitz and colleagues (Leiserowitz *et al.*, 2010).

Yet, pitfalls arise when science-based evidentiary questions are put on the same platform. In other words, it is fundamentally problematic when pollsters reduce expert-based science questions to the same domain as *vox populi* opinions or beliefs. For example, a February 2010 *BBC/Populus* poll posed the question, 'From what you know and have heard, do you think that the Earth's climate is changing and global warming is taking place?' Answers to such a question can be motivated by a range of influencing factors, from whether a respondent may wish it was not taking place to whether someone on the street or in mass media told them that it was not happening. Such a way of approaching the issue then privileges opinion at the expense of valuing relevant expert research and authority. In addition, such questions are further fuelled by issues of acquiescence, the wording of the questions and confusion between stated understanding and actual understanding of issues involved (Nisbet and Myers, 2007). Unless there is a global plebiscite or referendum on whether the climate is changing, such questions are at best distracting and at worst destructive to work that seeks to enhance public understanding and consistent, measured considerations of the range of climate policy alternatives.

In the context of newsroom cuts and shrinking funds for investigative journalism, the most recent poll might more readily make for an appealing news hook into making sense of public views and sentiments in the complex issues associated with climate change. Drawing again on the *BBC/Populus* polling example, three-quarters of respondents answered this question 'yes'. Even though this figure had dropped from 83 per cent just three months before, it remained an overwhelming majority. Nonetheless, media stories ran with headlines like 'Climate scepticism on the rise' (BBC, 2010) rather than 'Most people still feel climate change is happening', and thus powerfully shaped continued public discourse. Moreover, these chosen media framings demonstrated a penchant for mobilizing journalistic norms of drama and novelty for an attention-grabbing story (see Chapter 5 for more).

In this way, mass media do damage by reducing issues of risk and expert-based scientific understanding to that of mere opinion. To the point, polling agencies exhibit recklessness through such approaches, particularly when understaffed news agencies pick up their findings at face value in order to file a story on an ever-tightening deadline. While getting their latest polls picked up in the press may translate to commercial success, this carries the risk of giving potentially mistaken impressions of a fickle public view, devoid of important contextual factors (Marshall and Leber, 2010).

For example, a 2010 front-page article – above the fold – in the *New York Times* declared 'Climate Fears Turn to Doubts among Britons'. While polls conducted by the *BBC* and *Der Spiegel* provided useful news hooks for potentially discussing public views on climate risk management, the article instead proceeded to focus on opinions about the climate science. Journalist Elizabeth Rosenthal began the article, 'Last month hundreds of environmental activists crammed into an auditorium here to ponder an anguished question: If the scientific consensus on climate change has not changed, why have so many people turned away from the idea that human activity is warming the planet?' (2010, A1).

Furthermore, amid this perception of a fickle civil society regarding climate science and governance, there is the tendency for policy actors, scientists and other opinion leaders to over-compensate as a consequence. In the case of this 2010 perception of waning UK public 'belief' in climate change, Jon Krosnick warned, 'scientists are over-reacting' (Vergano, 2010). Journalist Dan Vergano also sagaciously argued that 'the public has its mind on more immediate problems in the midst of a global economic downturn' rather than the particulars of the 'Climategate' controversy or questions about Intergovernmental Panel on Climate Change (IPCC) claims of Himalayan glacier melt rate and climate impacts on Amazonian rainforests (2010). In fact, in spite of this enduring perception of a capricious public citizenry, through an aggregation of multiple decades of polling research, Roger Pielke Jr actually demonstrated that there has been consistent public support for climate policy action in the US and UK (2010).

Matt Nisbet and Teresa Myers summed up these polling and media reporting tendencies well, when they wrote, 'survey results often become an ideological Rorschach Test, with one side in the policy debate citing polls as reflective of a public demanding action on global warming, while the other side claiming that polls reveal... [a] citizenry unwilling to bear the economic costs of cutting greenhouse gas emissions' (2007, 445). To add further challenges to deriving useful information from polling questions on climate change, Jon Krosnick has pointed out that the *way* questions are asked has a critical bearing on results. He demonstrated this in an analysis of a range of polls from groups such as the Pew Research Center, *CNN*, *ABC News/ the Washington Post* and *Ipsos/McClatchy* (2010, A21). Krosnick posited that poll results can also be influenced by a person's mood when they are responding to the questions, their levels of attention to what the question is asking, and even to the weather outside when the respondent is completing the poll. He warned, 'Do not be a victim of the wording of the latest polls... Just because it happens doesn't mean it deserves coverage' (Wihbey, 2009).

On this point, numerous issues of climate risk – assessed through climate science measures – do not make for good questions upon which to poll a (representative) segment of the public citizenry. For the citizen-consumer to comment on this, polling groups call on the limited ability of a person to make judgments about quality of risk assessments through experiential knowledge and observations of our surrounding environment. Instead, pollsters would do well to focus on issues of risk management, where potential public support or resistance is important to decision-making processes.

Polls can indeed provide limited utility in terms of gauging possible public support for various policy actions on climate change. For example, it can be useful to document where 'global warming' ranks in public concern relative to other contemporary environmental issues, as well as where environmental issues rank relative to wider social issues (Jones, 2010). For a few years, AC Nielsen/Oxford University conducted online polling of over 26,000 people spanning fifty-two countries bi-annually, documenting changing public concern for climate change. The surveys have asked 'What is your biggest concern in the next six months?' as well as 'What is your second biggest concern in the next six months?' The scope of the polling was unparalleled and has therefore provided unique insights into an aggregated 'public mood' on climate change (AC Nielsen, 2008). However, key limitations may have affected and pervaded responses, thereby diminishing the explanatory power of the polling results. Limitations include varying levels of respondent acquiescence, differentiated interpretations of the term 'global warming' as the term was translated into multiple languages across cultures, and different socio-economic and educational levels of internet users in each country that make these response sets unrepresentative of larger public understanding in various countries. As another example, Ana Villar and Jon Krosnick have found that large majorities of people in Maine, Massachusetts and Florida have consistently supported government action to reduce GHG emissions (2010).

Overall, as John Wihbey has put it, 'Public opinion polls and surveys are attention getters, headline grabbers. Reporters and editors love them. Sometimes they should learn to hate them … or at least to approach each one with a healthy dose of skepticism' (2009).

Models to make sense of public understanding and engagement

Many factors such as those described above have contributed to perceptions and priorities regarding climate science and governance (Kingdon, 1995). Many attempts to theorize the role of mass media in shaping public awareness and engagement have relied mainly on two key theoretical models: the 'Issue–Attention Cycle' (1972) and the 'Public Arenas Model' (1988). Through distinct approaches, these conceptual models have helped to identify and distinguish patterns, appraise and assess influences, and gain insights from a swirl of contextual factors as well as embedded perspectives and viewpoints. For instance, in mapping the environmental policy-making process, Jane Roberts relied on Anthony Downs's 'Issue–Attention Cycle' to 'provide an explanation of the waxing and waning of issues within the policy environment' (2004).

In describing the Issue–Attention Cycle as it has related to issues in ecology, Downs argued that attention to environmental issues moves through five sequential stages. First is the 'pre-problem stage', when an ecological problem exists but has not yet captured public attention. Downs explained this as a stage where expert communities are aware of the risks, but they have not yet been disseminated more widely. The second phase was described by Downs as that of 'alarmed discovery and euphoric enthusiasm', where dramatic events make the public both aware of the problem and alarmed about it. He called the third stage the 'gradual-realization-of-the-cost stage' where key actors acknowledge sacrifices and costs incurred in dealing with the problem.

Fourth, there is the 'gradual-decline-of-intense-public-interest stage' where, according to Downs, actors become discouraged at the prospect of appropriately dealing with the issue, and crises are normalized through suppression, and in some cases boredom. Finally, Downs delineated a catch-all 'post-problem stage', where formerly 'hot' issues 'move into a prolonged limbo – a twilight realm of lesser attention or spasmodic reoccurrences of interest'. In this stage, Downs argued that when the issue is 'once elevated to national prominence [it] may sporadically recapture public interest'. Downs reasoned that this model has helped to better understand the nature of the problem as well as the 'way major communication media interact with the public' (1972).

This framework has helped to more carefully consider the intrinsic qualities of the issues themselves that influence ebbs and flows of media coverage over time. However, the Downs model has failed to adequately account for numerous contextual influences that shape how 'alarm' and 'costs' are determined and contested. Moreover, it has not accounted for the non-linear factors that shape dynamic interactions in climate politics via the mass media (Williams, 2000). As Chapter 4 discussed, it is important to consider how political-economic drivers as well as cultural pressures influence media representations themselves.

Riley Dunlap has argued that environmental issues have not conformed to Downs's Issue–Attention Cycle, since the problems have worsened, new problems have arisen and, most importantly, professionalized social movement organizations have been built to keep them alive (1992). Critics have also made the point that cycles may have both sped up in recent years, as well as become less apparent (e.g. Jordan and O'Riordan, 2000). Moreover, cross-cultural research has found evidence that while the Downs model appears to hold in some contexts, it does not hold in others. For instance, an examination of French and US contexts found divergent patterns of influences relative to the issues themselves as well as surrounding contextual factors (Brossard *et al.*, 2004).

In effect, the Downs model has provided helpful yet only partial, and overly linear, explanations and interpretations of the complexities of the multiple internal as well as external factors shaping representations of climate science and governance. Therefore, the entrenched use of this Downs model has enabled only limited understanding of *how* these media representations are constructed, and how these shape (and are shaped by) the ongoing cultural politics of climate change.

Despite these limitations, many scholars have continued to utilize this framework in seeking to understand the ebbs and flows of various discourses in the cultural politics of climate change. For instance, in his book *Climate for Change*, Peter Newell leaned heavily on this model as an 'all-embracing explanation for the nature of media coverage of global warming', despite acknowledgement that the model failed to 'accurately depict the complexity and challenging nature of the climate change problem' (Newell, 2000, 86). Perhaps the ongoing use of this Downs model might be partially attributed to its elegance and explanatory simplicity.

So, a second model – the 1988 'Public Arenas Model' by Stephen Hilgartner and Charles Bosk – has helped by attending to these additional considerations. This model has also accounted for 'the "arenas" where social problem definitions evolve, examining the effect of those arenas on both the evolution of social problems and the actors who make claims about them' (1988, 58). In this approach, mass media have been characterized as one of the key institutional arenas where these problems compete for attention and are negotiated, and where 'social problems are framed and grow' (1988, 58). This approach has therefore more capably examined both internal and external factors – as well as dynamic and non-linear influences – that have shaped mass-media representations of issues, events and information themselves, as well as the relevant and ongoing contextual inputs.

Furthermore, this conceptual model has helped to move analyses beyond static representations, where there has been a careful accounting for dynamic and competitive processes to define and frame 'climate stories'. In addition, this has accounted for considerations that not all audiences interpret things equally. At a minimum, the 'public' is a dynamic and heterogeneous community (Corfee-Morlot, 2007). This approach is therefore consistent with Tim Forsyth's assertion that, 'assessments of frames should not just be limited to those that are labelled as important at present, but also seek to consider alternative framings that may not currently be considered important in political debates' (2003, 78). Ultimately, the model has sought to organize and make sense of the 'institutional, political, and cultural factors that influence the probability of survival of competing problem formulations' within the mass media as well as climate politics, policy and practices (Hilgartner and Bosk, 1988).

Influential claims-makers in the public arena: a look at contrarian 'actors'

Questions regarding 'who speaks for the climate' involve considerations of how various perspectives – from climate scientists to business interests and ENGO activists – influence public discussions on climate change (see Chapter 1). 'Actors' in this theatre are ultimately all members of a collective public citizenry. However, differential access to media outlets is a product of differences in power. As Chapter 1 mentioned, this conception of power is a relational one that shapes interactions in the public arena. Michel Foucault has written, 'it is not the activity of the subject of knowledge that produces a corpus of knowledge, useful or resistant to power, but power-knowledge, the processes and struggles that transverse it and of which it is made up, that determines the forms of possible domains of knowledge' (1975, 27–28).

Further, power saturates social, political, economic and institutional conditions undergirding mass-media content production (Wynne, 2008). In this high-stakes, high-profile and highly contested milieu of climate science and governance, NNSAs have sought to access and utilize mass-media sources in order to shape perceptions on various climate issues contingent on their perspectives and interests (Nisbet and Mooney, 2007). In particular, 'contrarians', 'sceptics' or 'denialists' have gained discursive traction through the amplification of their claims in mass media over time (see Chapter 3 for more).

These voices can be traced back to asymmetrical power derived from control over the means of production since the eighteenth century Industrial Revolution. However, their views on the subject of climate change emerged prominently in media accounts in the late 1980s, primarily through an organizing force called the 'Global Climate Coalition' (Leggett, 2001). With roots in interests that sought to stop anti-tobacco legislation, this group was a consortium of primarily US-based coal and oil interests, and was set up to represent the anti-climate policy interests of the fossil-fuel burning industry (Oreskes and Conway, 2010; Michaels, 2008). Since that time, there have been reports exposing numerous tactics deployed by carbon-based industry interests to pursue media coverage in order to raise the visibility of their various brands of climate contrarianism (see Chapter 3 for more). For instance, in February 2007, the *Guardian* revealed that the US-based American Enterprise Institute – a group that receives funding from ExxonMobil Corporation – offered $10,000 'for articles that emphasized the shortcomings of [the Fourth Assessment] report from the UN IPCC' (Sample, 2007, 1).

While many have pointed out that 'scepticism' forms an integral and necessary element of scientific inquiry (e.g. Schneider, 2009), its use when describing outlier views on climate change is less positive. According to Peter Jacques, Riley Dunlap and Mark Freeman, the term 'sceptic' has been most commonly invoked to describe someone who denies the seriousness of an environmental problem, dismisses scientific evidence showing the problem, questions the importance and wisdom of regulatory policies to address them, and considers environmental protection and progress to be competing goals (2008). While these authors discuss 'environmental scepticism' more broadly, these attributes can be ascribed to those who have also focused more specifically on climate-change issues.

Aaron McCright has defined climate contrarians as those who vocally challenge what they see as a false consensus of mainstream climate science through critical attacks on climate science and eminent climate scientists, often with substantial financial support from fossil fuels industry organizations and conservative think tanks (2007). In 2010, University of Melbourne researcher Saffron O'Neill and I further developed a definition of 'climate contrarianism' by disaggregating claims-making to include ideological motives behind critiques of climate science, and exclude individuals who are thus far unconvinced by the science, or individuals who are unconvinced by proposed solutions, as these latter two elements can be more usefully captured through different terminology (2010b).

William Anderegg and colleagues have described climate sceptics and contrarians together as those who are unconvinced by the science (2010). Meanwhile, Kari Marie Norgaard has focused on the aspect of 'denial', and has developed three dimensions as they relate to environmental issues: literal (sheer refusal to accept evidence), interpretative (denial based on interpretation of evidence) and implicatory (denial based on the change/response that acceptance would necessitate) (2006). Taken together, these efforts have sought to provide greater texture to the motivations behind, and implications from, expressions of scepticism, contrarianism and denial regarding climate change. For example, Stephen Schneider observed how there is a great deal of difference between scepticism derived from ideology and scepticism derived from scientific evidence (Schneider, 2009).

It may be tempting to assemble a taxonomy of contrarianism, scepticism or denialism, and by extension trace the amount of media coverage of certain claims-makers in mass media. However, this approach risks underconsidering context and by excessively focusing on individual personalities at the expense of political, economic, social and cultural forces (see Chapter 5 for more). For example, Patrick Michaels, a professor at the University of Virginia, edits the Western Fuels Association-funded *World Climate Report* and is on advisory boards for the conservative groups such as the Greening Earth Society. In 2005 he wrote a book entitled *Meltdown: The Predictable Distortion of Global Warming by Scientists, Politicians and the Media*, published by Cato Institute Books. Michaels has received funding for his research from groups such as the Edison Electric Institute, The Intermountain Rural Electric Association and the Western Fuels Association (Beder, 2002; Gelbspan, 1998).

However, amid abundant evidence of ties between carbon-based industry and contrarian claims-making and climate-policy prioritization, it is a mistake to draw blanket conclusions based solely on their connections. The important issue is not necessarily the funding sources, but whether these ties influenced the content of the claims made by funding recipients. Naomi Oreskes has noted, 'the issue is that the research is supported by a sponsor who wants a *particular* result ... and the researchers know in advance what that outcome is, producing an explicit conflict of interest, which undermines the integrity of the research performed' (2004b).

For example, Professor William Freudenburg once accepted funding from ExxonMobil Corporation to research questions regarding damages relating to the Valdez oil spill. While admittedly burdened by the possibility of undue influence on his research methods and findings, Freudenburg recounted how his preliminary work was not primed for a particularly desired outcome. That said, when his tentative conclusions called for greater corporate transparency in order to achieve improved corporate behaviour, Exxon did not continue to fund the research (Liptak, 2008).

Moreover, this approach cuts both ways. Blanket assertions of climate 'scepticism', 'denialism' or 'contrarianism' across a range of distinct science and governance issues risk rejecting potentially legitimate and useful critiques out of hand by way of dismissing the individual rather than the arguments put forward. Thus, treatment of individuals through 'demonizing monikers' does little to illuminate the contours of their arguments; it actually has the opposite obfuscating effect in the public sphere. In other words, placing universalizing labels on claims-makers overlooks the varied and context-dependent arguments put forward. Media portrayals that pay attention to these subtleties do well to enhance public understanding and engagement with climate science and governance. Nonetheless, the fact that the anthropogenic climate dissenter and best-selling author of *State of Fear* – despite that it was a work of fiction – Michael Crichton was reported to have been consulted by President George W. Bush on climate policy (Janofsky, 2006) while the President ignored the advice of the NAS and EPA can be attributed in part to a convenient confluence of interests and objectives.

Through a study of newspaper coverage in twelve countries, James Painter found that views of climate sceptics were quoted regularly in Western outlets, but were absent from non-Western press accounts (2010). This group of dissenters has been particularly prominent in the US as many have been based in US universities and think tanks. Research by Aaron McCright and Riley Dunlap has focused on this opposition movement in the US, and has examined how certain individuals worked – at times through media attention – to develop competing discourses that disempowered top climate science during the Newt Gingrich-led 'Republican revolution' of 1994 to effectively gain a foothold in national and international discourse on the causes of climate change (2000; 2003; 2010). Such efforts have also continued to receive support from the US Chamber of Commerce, who have hired lobbyists and have spent millions of dollars on advertising of contrarian views about climate science and policy. The US Chamber of Commerce has received contributions from numerous carbon-based industry groups over the past decades to help fight climate legislation and question scientific understanding of the issues (Broder, 2009b).

Many similar contrarian initiatives in the US have been tied to carbon-based industry-funding sources. For example, there has been the 'CO$_2$ is Green' promotion. This turn of phrase was the centrepiece of an advertising campaign launched in the summer of 2010. Running in the *Washington Post*, the advert was a piece of an ongoing larger campaign by a group bearing the same name. In their words:

Our mission is to support scientifically and economically sound public policy on environmental issues. Currently, we are especially concerned with federal proposals that would interfere with nature's dependence on carbon dioxide (CO$_2$) ... CO$_2$ is Green is working to ensure that all federal laws or regulations are founded upon science and not politics or scientific myths. (co2isgreen.org, 2010)

The group has sought to contest the notion that carbon dioxide (CO$_2$) is a pollutant, and thus protest against legislation that aims to mitigate CO$_2$ emissions.

These particular claims have been enabled through financial backing by coal interests, and have been emitted by CO$_2$ is Green point source, H. Leighton Steward (Mulkern, 2010). *Forbes* magazine has listed Steward as having received many millions of US dollars in recent years through his work as Director of EOG Resources, a company committed to 'the exploration, development, production, and marketing of natural gas and crude oil primarily in the United States, Canada, the Republic of Trinidad, Tobago, the United Kingdom etc. [sic]' (Forbes, 2010). *Forbes* also has noted that, over the past two decades, Steward has worked in management roles associated with oil and gas exploration and production. This carbon-based industry career was punctuated by his role as Chair of the US Oil and Gas Association and the Natural Gas Supply Association. Beyond this legacy, it has been reported that Steward has remained an honorary Director of the American Petroleum Institute (Mulkern, 2010).

While far from universal, the Orwellian logic espoused by CO$_2$ is Green has been more representative than anomalous. The contemporary US context has been one where 'astroturf' groups have railed against the 'climate establishment' and where highly sophisticated and rapidly adaptive campaigns have sought to protect vested interests. The 2010 CO_2 is Green initiative has also shown similarities to other initiatives that have sought to influence public and policy-actor perceptions regarding connections between carbon-based industry activities and anthropogenic climate change. For example, a US-based conservative think tank called the Competitive Enterprise Institute launched a project in the spring of 2006 that targeted thirteen key cities in US states where climate legislation was being deliberated. The campaign argued that CO_2 is not a pollutant, and the slogan of that campaign was 'We Call It Life' (CEI, 2006).

While it may be tempting to dismiss such NNSA efforts as isolated, fringe, anomalous or geographically peculiar, they actually represent one of many contested spaces in the larger battlefield of decision-making regarding global political-economy and energy production as well as public understanding of climate change. Moreover, these spaces of contestation are growing. As evidence of this, in recent years the US has seen a 'climate-change lobby explosion' in Washington, DC. The Center for Public Integrity documented that there had been a 300 per cent increase in climate-change lobbyists (up to 2,340 in 2009) from 2005 to 2009, amounting to approximately $90 million in expenditure (Lavelle, 2009).

Conclusions

Steven Brechin has called climate change 'the ultimate collective action problem' (Smith, 2009). For everyday people, doing something about anthropogenic climate change is not a great priority. To many, climate change is perceived as a diffuse issue or distant and long-term threat (Leiserowitz, 2005). While we all are implicated to varying degrees as contributors of GHG emissions – through household activities, engagement in industrial activities through our consumption, transport – those who perceive themselves as experiencing concentrated impacts from climate change are much fewer in number. So, despite concern about climate change expressed by civil society across many country contexts, more immediate issues – such as job security, health and the economy – often take on greater importance in many people's everyday lives (Lorenzoni and Pidgeon, 2006).

Moreover, Sheldon Ungar pointed out a related consideration here when he cautioned, 'the public could very well be concerned but relatively ill informed' (2000, 309).

This chapter briefly discussed some of the important ways in which public perceptions and media representations interact, through complex and non-linear inputs and processes. For example, research by Yuki Sampei and Midori Aoyagi-Usui considered these interactions through their analyses of media coverage in *Yomiuri Shimbun*, *Asahi Shimbun* and *Mainichi Shimbun* in the Japanese context. In that study, they found that 'an increase in media coverage of global warming had an immediate influence on public awareness of global warming issues, but this effect did not last for more than a month' (2009, 210).

In the face of such evidence, many often turn to wider challenges of climate (il)literacy in civil society as an explanation for the lack of substantive engagement with climate-change causes and consequences. Clearly, without fundamental scientific literacy to help provide a foundation from which to face these issues, more journalism will not help (Miller *et al.*, 1997). However, climate literacy is not the necessary pathway to climate action. David Ropiek has cautioned, 'Don't put too much hope in the wisdom of a more informed public' (2010).

Furthermore, Anthony Leiserowitz offered important reminders when he commented, 'People are different and have different psychological, cultural, and political reasons for acting. Information is necessary, but insufficient' (quoted in Ropiek, 2010). Nonetheless, what is the role of mass media in promoting greater climate literacy? Are educational endeavours a component of one's journalistic responsibility? Or do such undertakings reach beyond the remit of mass-media workers, particularly in challenging economic times for journalism? Do advocacy journalists or new and social media-content producers have a new role to play? These can be contentious and highly debated considerations amidst the contemporary cultural politics of climate change. Yet they remain critical to ongoing considerations of 'who speaks for climate' and how.

Journalists and editors have consistently stated that their role is one of information dissemination rather than education. However, in practice, the distinction between these roles blurs. Media representational practices inevitably contribute to how people understand the world around them. Turning to climate science education in schools and university, it has generally been slow to permeate curricula amid the growing instrumental approaches to educational practices. Furthermore, relying on the leaders of tomorrow through education to tackle what many consider a pressing contemporary issue may be deemed a form of intergenerational irresponsibility. Journalist Bud Ward has commented, 'The late (great) science writer Victor Cohn...was fond of saying that journalists educate, but they are not educators. I agree: The verb applies, but the noun does not. It's more than just a difference of semantics.'

Meanwhile, political, economic pressures have contributed to tremendous pressures on and within the news industry, where these issues have become more, not less, challenging to cover (see Chapter 4 for more). And, media representations continue to have multifarious implications on relations between science, governance and public understanding/engagement. It is clear that climate issues themselves shape media reporting; however, it is also true that journalism shapes ongoing conceptions of climate change. These conceptions, in turn, shape associated politics, policy decisions and activities.

Yet, Administrator for the US National Oceanic and Atmospheric Administration Jane Lubchenco has commented, 'It's clear that there's been an insufficient job of communicating climate information to the public. I think much more needs to be done to communicate to policy-makers and citizens everywhere how important this issue is, what's at stake, and what the opportunities are for addressing climate change' (Lamb, 2010a).

At the end of the day, initiatives need to help the public *better understand how climate science and policy work*, in order to then more capably and critically evaluate their proposals, processes and products. Moving forward, it is our collectively diffuse yet shared responsibility to grapple with these challenges, and confront how to more effectively communicate the contours of climate change. As part of this, it is indispensably important to continue to critically interrogate how the variegated role of mass-media influences public understanding of climate science and policy implementation. Such are pervasive yet often invisible dimensions of today's 'Anthropocene Geopolitics' (Dalby, 2007).

8 | A light in the attic?
Ongoing media representations of climate change

There's a light on in the attic.
Though the house is dark and shuttered,
I can see a flickerin' flutter,
And I know what it's about.
There's a light on in the attic.
I can see it from outside,
And I know you're on the inside...looking out.
Shel Silverstein (1981)

As we collectively hurtle through the new millennium, the complex and multi-faceted issue of climate change cuts to the heart of humans' relationship with the environment. The cultural politics of climate change are situated – power-laden, media-led and recursive – in an ongoing battlefield of knowledge and interpretation (Boykoff *et al.*, 2009a). Mass media link these varied spaces together, as powerful and important interpreters of climate science and policy, translating what can often be alienating, jargon-laden information for the broadly construed public citizenry. Media workers and institutions powerfully shape and negotiate meaning, influencing how citizens make sense of and value the world. James Dearing and Everett Rogers have commented that many social problems never become issues because they 'require exposure – coverage in the mass media – before they can be considered "public issues"' (1996, 2; Matsaganis and Payne, 2005, 381).

Mike Hulme has observed, 'social, political and cultural dynamics at work around the idea of climate change are more volatile than the slowly changing and causally entangled climate dynamics of the Earth's biogeophysical systems' (2010). Amid these dynamics resides a set of questions regarding who – through media traction – become authorized to make sense of, translate and speak on behalf of climate change. This book has pursued these intertwined considerations, along with *why* and *how* these interactions have transpired over time, from place to place.

Overall, this book has endeavoured to help make sense of how media representations frame truth claims, how larger political contexts influence such framing processes, and how particularly amplified voices in these spaces shape ongoing interpretations of various climate challenges. Anthony Leiserowitz has written that these arenas of claims-making and framing are 'exercises in power...Those with the power to define the terms of the debate strongly determine the outcomes' (2005, 1433). In other words, discursive constellations – emergent through texts – work to challenge or sustain unequal power relations (Fairclough and Wodak, 1997). In this book I have appraised the Lorax-like role of media as a key interpreter and actor at the interface of humans and the climate.

More media coverage of climate change – even supremely fair and accurate portrayals – is not a panacea. In fact, increased media attention to the issue often unearths more questions to be answered, and *greater* scientific understanding actually can contribute to a *greater* supply of knowledge from which to develop and argue varying interpretations of that science (Sarewitz, 2004). Moreover, studies have shown that without some scientific knowledge to provide a foundation of understanding to follow ongoing issues, more journalism will not necessarily help (Miller *et al.*, 1997). *Columbia Journalism Review* journalist Cristine Russell has commented that issues associated with climate change become *more* challenging and complex to cover as understanding of its many dimensions develops (2008). At best, media reporting helps address, analyse and discuss the issues, *but not answer them.* While this can vary depending on which aspect of climate change one is focused on – from anthropogenic signals and noise to what should be done about it – the interacting factors can simultaneously illuminate and obfuscate connections between media coverage and public engagement.

Assessments of these media representational practices to date provide mixed feelings of both hope and despair. While Figure 1.1 at the beginning of the volume has shown a general increase in the amount of media coverage of climate change around the world, research explored here has shown that much work still remains to be done. While the 'light' may be on in this space, separations and communication difficulties remain. That said, improved reporting with greater specificity and contextualization through the combined efforts of journalists, editors, policy actors and scientists would help to more effectively engage the public, and would widen the spectrum of possibility for more informed decision-making.

New and social media

As an illustration of the dynamic nature of these interactions, new and social media are changing science, policy and citizen communications in unprecedented ways. In the last decade, there has been a significant expansion from consumption of traditional mass media – broadcast television, newspapers, radio – into consumption of new and social media, such as various uses of the internet, and through mobile phone communications. As mass media have been called the Fourth Estate, the significance of this development might deservedly earn the moniker 'Fifth Estate'.

This development of the Fifth Estate has signalled substantive changes in how people access and interact with information, who has access and who are content producers. At present, new/social media offers a platform for people to more democratically shape the public agenda. These communications are a shift from broadcast 'one-to-many' communications to interactive 'many-to-many' webs of communications (van Dijk, 2006; O'Neill and Boykoff, 2010a).

In January 2009, the Pew Research Center's Project for Excellence in Journalism (PEJ) began monitoring the content of the weekly 'news hole' in the US, distinguishing between traditional coverage (television, newspapers, radio) and new/social media (internet weblogs, Twitter). Through weekly content analysis, PEJ has shown how topics involving global warming have earned a much greater share of the news hole in new media: the topic has been one of the top five blog stories ten times since January 2009, but did not figure nearly as prominently during that time in traditional media (PEJ, 2010). For example, the Met Office Hadley Centre report in October 2009 mentioned earlier garnered overwhelming treatment on the blogs, while healthcare and the economy drove the bulk of coverage in traditional press. This may be due in part to the flexibility and potentially infinite nature of the news hole in new media, but may also mark the trends of diminishing traditional newsroom capabilities.

But with these shifts come numerous questions: does increased visibility of climate change in new/social media translate to improved communication or just more noise (as Neil Gavin calls it, the 'ranto-sphere' (2009, 5))? Do these spaces provide opportunities for new forms of deliberative community regarding questions of climate miti-gation and adaptation? Or has the content of this increased coverage shifted to polemics and arguments over measured analysis?

In this democratized space of content production, do new/social media provide more space for contrarian views to circulate? And through its interactivity, does increased consumption of news through new/social media further fragment a public discourse on climate miti-gation and adaptation, through information silos where members of the public can stick to sources that help support their already held views? Many questions such as these remain open at present.

Alex S. Jones has commented, 'Good journalism on the Web is a wondrous thing. Using all the tools that that web offers – words, sound, video, links, limitless data, search, graphics, interactivity – has produced an intoxicating ferment of creative journalistic thinking. If journalism is essentially storytelling, the potential is now comparable to a child being presented with a superdeluxe box of crayons that make the old, limited array of colors look paltry. Good "new" jour-nalism can take news to a level that none of the older forms of media can match' (2009, 179). Moreover, *Nature Climate Change Reports* editor Olive Heffernan has also commented, 'Web 2.0 is charting a new course for science communication, with much of the discourse on climate change now happening on blogs. Blogs may not yet have the breadth of readership of other media, but are none-the-less highly influential, as they are a source of information for journalists, as well as interested laypeople' (quoted in Boykoff, 2009b, 2). But Cass Sunstein has warned, 'A central task, in democratic societies, is for the print and broadcast media, and those who run and participate in Web sites, to combat self-segregation along political and other lines' (2009, 158).

Journalist Matt Ridley has argued that blogging on climate change represents a positive development for public understanding. In February 2010, he wrote that when the 'Climategate' scandal unfolded, 'It was amateur bloggers who scented the exaggerations, distortions and corruptions in the climate establishment; whereas newspaper reporters, even after the scandal broke, played poodle to their sources' (2010). In addition, George Brumfiel has noted that blogs have become a more prominent source for stories, and a greater influence on public discourse. He found that the percentage of journalists that have found stories on a scientist's blog has gone up to 63% from 18% in 2004 (Brumfiel, 2009, 276).

However, Sharon Dunwoody has cautioned that various modes of media production should not be considered equally. She said, 'because of their extensive reach and concomitant efficiencies of scale, mediated information channels such as television and newspapers have been the traditional channels of choice for information campaigns. But research on how individuals actually use mass-media information suggests that these channels may be better for some persuasive purposes than for others' (quoted in Boykoff, 2009b, 2). Furthermore, Cass Sunstein again offered a less rosy picture. He has warned of the likelihood of the 'echo chamber' effect where this interactivity actually walls off users from one another by merely consuming news that mesh with their world view and ideology (2007).

With these various hopes and concerns in mind for communications on climate change, the power of new and social media has already been harnessed in a variety of ways. For example, in India *Internews Europe* has engaged both rural farmers and urban slum dwellers through mobile phone technologies as a media communications platform for both literate and illiterate users through both text and images (West, 2008). The cost to purchase a SIM card and/or mobile handset has dropped significantly in India, and mobile phone ownership estimates range from 250 million to 400 million, while 'it is believed that 10,000 mobile phones are sold every hour' (West, 2008, 68). As an outgrowth of this trend, up-to-the-minute commercial weather forecasting and crop-pricing services have become increasingly available through mobile phone communications for Indian farmers.

The commodification and privatization of information associated with climate and agriculture (Pollard *et al.*, 2006) has been endorsed by institutions such as Indian Meteorological Department and the United Nations International Fund for Agricultural Development (IFAD), amid shrinking public services. IFAD Technical Advisor Jamie Anderson has enthused about these developments, claiming, 'commercialisation is inevitable and is not necessarily hurting the farmers' (Ghosh, 2009, 14). However, there are other spatial and temporal dimensions to these developments (and their implications) that must be taken up through ongoing research. Among them, can these new media tools work to inform a broader Indian citizenry? How might particular trends privilege certain ways of knowing, while marginalizing others? And how might various dominant discursive frames shape the perceived need in the heterogeneous Indian public for collective action in the face of anthropogenic climate change?

Speaking to a journalist from the *Hindustan Times*, India farmer Ramesh Shantaram Pawde remarked, 'I can't afford to suffer due to such frantic climate changes. I can't predict yields any more as my forefathers could. I have to depend on the SMS (short message service) communications', received from private weather forecasting firms (Ghosh, 2009, 14). Does the fact that he now looks to his mobile phone rather than to his environmental surroundings, and that the weakening of state support is 'normalized' in this way, provide signs of further entrenchment of divisions on climate action, or do they signify ways over the divide? The challenges and opportunities that this neo-millennial 'farmer Pawde' faces provide a compelling set of ongoing questions for media representations and communications of climate change.

As a quite different example, the US-based group Americans for Prosperity (AFP) have sought and gained an amplified media presence through producing their own media content online and by garnering media attention for the events they have sponsored in the public arena (Mayer, 2010). Through internet organizing – mass emails, web announcements, Tweets, Facebook communications, YouTube clips, blog posts – AFP has assembled a number of influential anti-climate legislation campaigns (Lean, 2009). Among them was the 2008 'Hot Air' tour. In 2009, *AFP* also began a web-based campaign called 'No Climate Tax' where constituents could send emails to their elected officials to encourage them to send a 'No Climate Tax Pledge'. In addition, *AFP* hosts ongoing web-based campaigns called 'Stop the Power Grab' to contest US EPA actions to regulate CO_2 emissions without the explicit support of US Congress.

AFP organizers have repeatedly touted the organization to be a 'grassroots group' (Fifield, 2009). However, examinations of these mobilizations have revealed that they have been more 'astroturf' than 'grassroots'. In other words, the social has been artificial, where AFP activities have been found to have grown through carbon-based industry funding, rather than authentic, community-based organization (Mayer, 2010; Mulkern, 2010). The group is registered as a non-profit, conservative think tank based in Washington, DC and receives ongoing funding from conservative foundations such as the Koch Family Foundation (Media Transparency, 2009). The Koch Family Foundation and its connected organizations have provided funding for the creation of a number of other conservative organizations, including the Cato Institute and Freedomworks. This Family Foundation has generated funds from the success of Koch Industries, which is the largest privately owned US-based energy company. At present, Koch Industries generates energy from fossil fuels and has a large stake in oil refining processes (Fifeld, 2009; Mayer, 2010). Nonetheless, AFP actions in new and social media provide an illustration of the amplification of perspectives and viewpoints in the public arena.

As new and social media representations and uses of climate change demonstrate, the boundaries between who constitute 'authorized' speakers (and who do not) in mass media as well as who are legitimate 'claims-makers' are consistently being interrogated, and challenged (Gieryn, 1999). For example, in the US there are current challenges to such democratic equality or 'net neutrality'. This 'net neutrality' push is one among many movements in recent years for broader reforms of journalistic freedom (e.g. McChesney, 1999) within the constructs of corporate media pressures. US legislation has been sponsored by *AT&T*, *Verizon*, *Comcast* and *TimeWarner* and proposes to create a tiered system of access speeds based on what a consumer pays and whether they use their content and services, or those of a competitor. The loss of 'net neutrality' could have a significantly detrimental impact on the ability of new/social media users to access a variety of sources and perspectives on climate science and governance. Through power, various actors in the cultural politics of climate change have harnessed the power of both traditional and new media to amplify their claims on issues from climate science to governance.

Meeting people where they are?

These trends in new and social media take place in the context of a wider and fundamental set of questions involving whether media representations of climate change are most effective when they meet people where they are, or when they are pushed to new considerations and behaviours. In a study of sustainable living practices in Australia, Kersty Hobson concluded, 'positive change is not about obtaining or instilling a new set of ethics or addressing public ignorance with information campaigns. Rather, it comes from fully investing in one's current position. That is, we can "start from where we are", to open up and explore the parts of us that want to live differently – the already ethical parts of us that are open to and already do think sustainably' (Hobson, 2008, 11).

For example, Pablo Suarez and colleagues at Red Cross/Red Crescent Climate Centre have worked to improve participatory approaches to knowledge sharing on climate adaptation among those most vulnerable to emergent climate-related impacts. Initiatives have engaged with community actors by way of collaborative and iterative communication practices. Climate adaptation strategies have been developed in this way in order to most effectively meet participants on their own terms as well as through what they deem meaningful to their lives and livelihoods. The researchers have found that through experimental learning through games as well as grassroots video production, risk management and decision-making on climate adaptation have been improved at the community level (Suarez *et al.*, 2011).

Yet, such undertakings are not without formidable – and sometimes fundamental – challenges. For instance, at the November 2008 launch of his 'culture strategy', Conservative London Mayor Boris Johnson embodied the promises and perils of such boundary work. In his remarks, Johnson argued that, 'arts chiefs must stop dumbing down culture for young people'. According to reporter Ian Drury, 'the Mayor of London pledged to stop targeting [young people] with hip-hop music and movies, and instead encourage them to enjoy opera and ballet' (2008). Importantly, this raised questions regarding whether such channels of communication might reach people where they *are* or where others think they *should be*. Yet, more fundamentally, Johnson's comments highlighted how political actors were prepared to wield and negotiate the contours of (popular) culture as a key means to various cultural and political, economic ends, in this case to try to foster greater cultural awareness in the lead-up to the London 2012 Olympics.

Another illustration of this push-pull came in October 2010. At that time, the group '10:10 UK' released a four-minute film called 'No Pressure'. This group was part of a Bill McKibben-led collective of initiatives in over forty countries around the world, where the premise was to 'encourage' people to cut their GHG emissions by 10 per cent in 2010. The film featured music from Radiohead, cameos by David Ginola, Gillian Anderson, Wilson Palacios and other members of Tottenham Hotspur Football Club. The vignette began with a school teacher explaining the campaign to a class of primary school children. She described potential carbon reduction activities as 'getting your dad to insulate the loft, or taking your next holiday by train instead of flying, or buying energy-saving lightbulbs'. She then followed by saying, 'No pressure at all, but it would be great to get a sense of who might do this...' After two children in the film identified themselves as non-participants, the teacher then revealed and pressed a red button. This then shockingly blew the two kids up in a blood-spattered mess in the room. Similar scenes then unfolded in an office gathering, on a football pitch, and in a recording studio.

The film generated many questions of appropriateness and morality, yet it undoubtedly garnered a great deal of attention in the public arena. Swift condemnation and disappointment was quickly emitted, from Glenn Beck at *Fox News* to Bill McKibben at the blog 'Climate Progress'. In addition, an apology followed from Eugenie Harvey, Director of 10:10 UK. In it she (perhaps cheekily) wrote, 'Last week, 10:10 made available a short film. Following the initial reaction to the film we removed it from our website and issued an apology... We will learn from this mistake... Meanwhile, our thanks go out to all those who support 10:10 and who work to combat the threat of climate change.' Sony Corporation Europe also disassociated themselves from the 10:10 campaign in the aftermath of negative video reactions. However, the genie was out of the bottle by this time and cynics argued that the public attention was already garnered.

These trends in media representations, images, messages and media channels may be harbingers of the ongoing cultural politics of climate change. Over the last decade, media coverage has grown more sophisticated, taking on textured considerations of governance and economics in addition to ongoing discussions about the basic science behind whether the climate is changing and to what extent humans play a role in climate change. For instance, the *New York Times* and *International Herald Tribune* journalist James Kanter has commented, 'Editors are becoming increasingly interested in follow-the-money stories. Editors want to know where money is generated in the new "green" economy and how it is spent... The burgeoning trade in carbon permits is a fruitful area for inquiry. In Europe, coal-fired

power utilities lobbied heavily for large quantities of free carbon permits...journalists are seeking to shed light on whether the policies
and technologies actually will work in the time frames identified by
scientists as necessary to take action that can curb climate change'
(quoted in Boykoff, 2009b, 7).

However, that does not mean that coverage of climate change has
moved beyond questions of the fundamental science. For example,
a 2010 *Discovery News* article online revisited the basic question,
'Is global warming real?' (Lamb, 2010b). While multi-scale political, economic, cultural, social and environmental forces – both inside
and outside media issues themselves – may cause the media 'light' of
insight to flicker and flutter, it continues to illuminate possibilities for
our collective future.

However, most research to date on media coverage of climate change
has focused on countries in the Group of Eight and other countries
of the Global North. This attention is consistent with the bulk of
media attention having been paid to climate change in these same
countries (see Figure 1.1). However, a lack of understanding of media
representations in countries of the Global South has been a problematic and ongoing challenge. Peter Newell has pointed out that those
in the Global South are often at the front line of climate impacts, and
those people often have the least voice in ongoing policy discussions
(2008). Ugandan journalist Patrick Luganda has said, 'Those most
at risk from the impacts of climate change typically have had access
to the least information about it through mass media. This short-
coming is detrimental to efforts to build resilient communities with
improved capacity to adapt to changes in the climate, address climate
impacts, and mitigate greenhouse gas emissions' (quoted in Boykoff,
2009b, 4). In terms of media visibility of climate-related challenges,
it harkens to the Robert Chambers classic intervention into 'whose
reality counts' (1997).

The lack of coverage of climate change, and research into coverage
of climate change, can be attributed in large part to capacity issues.
Philippines journalist Imelda Abano, from *Inter Press Service* and
Business Mirror, commented, 'While the threat of global warming
has only become more urgent and media interest in Asian countries increased, resources, skills and knowledge related to climate
change are limited. As a result, comprehensive discussions of climate
change and its effects on local environments rarely make it into the

mainstream news.' Furthermore, *Bankok Post* journalist Piyaporn Wongruang has commented how historical communist influences in developing countries such as Thailand 'have limited the ability of working journalists to cover emerging debates in climate change' (quoted in Boykoff, 2009b, 2).

However, there has been some emergent work that has looked at media and climate issues. Among them, the PANOS Institute surveyed forty-seven print, radio and television journalists from Honduras, Jamaica, Sri Lanka and Zambia (Harbinson *et al.*, 2006). The study documented low levels of coverage in each country context, and attributed it to three main issues that journalists and editors in these countries faced: first, low levels of knowledge of the issue – they linked this to a lack of access to 'timely, clear and understandable information on climate change'; second, financial resources – connections were made to constraints on first-hand reporting, as well as allocation of time to certain 'green' news beats; and third, incongruent habits and priorities – the report cited the penchant to cover stories of crime and violence 'primarily because these issues "sell" and so are preferred by editors and advertisers' (2006, 5).

Research is emerging from developing countries themselves. For example, through support from *Internews Network*, researcher Pham Huy Dung examined trends in media coverage of climate change in Vietnam from 2006 to 2008 (2008). Through content analysis and interviews with working journalists, Dung found that the number of stories on climate change is increasing as journalists and editors better understand the issues involved. However, in Vietnam, interviewees reported ongoing capacity challenges, from accessing relevant experts as story sources to having access to relevant peer-reviewed literature for background research. Mike Shanahan from the International Institute for Environment and Development has catalogued the scant studies and projects which examine media coverage of climate change in the Global South (2009).

Pioneering organizations and networks are seeking to overcome these challenges. Organizations such as the Climate Change Media Partnership, *Internews*, PANOS Institute and the *Earth Journalism Network* have come together to work to build capacity for media coverage of climate change in developing countries. Moreover, these groups are supporting workshops and other gatherings that build networks of support for journalists, editors and other content producers who are covering climate change for consumer-citizens in the Global South. For example, these organizations have partnered with the Network of Climate Journalists in the Greater Horn of Africa and begun holding workshops on climate communication for journalists and editors, climate scientists and various civil society organizations, in an effort to foster stronger networks of understanding through regions.

In addition, for countries of the Global South, and for populations that have not had great access to traditional news sources, techno-logical leap-frogging through new and social media (described above) represent opportunities to 'level the playing field' and become more frequent news consumers as well as content producers. For instance, in India, cell phone technologies are now used by over 400 million citizens, and 'experiments are sprouting with the goal of forging a new bond between citizen and state, through real-time, 24-hour cel-lular participation' (Giridharadas, 2009, A3). While these initiatives may offer 'lights' of hope, much more work needs to be done.

Meanwhile, many critical questions persist, such as:

→ What can we expect will be the future of mass media as a bridge between formal climate science and policy to our cafés, pubs, liv-ing rooms and kitchen tables amid the many challenges in the twenty-first century?

→ How will news and entertainment media differentially influence how climate issues are taken up or resisted in our everyday lives?

→ What are future roles that various claims-makers have in the crea-tion, maintenance or silencing of discourses on climate issues?

→ How will ongoing structures, laws and institutions continue to influence climate considerations?

→ What empirical work must be done to provide more textured understandings of media and climate?

→ How will these science–policy–media–public interactions play out differentially across different local, regional and national contexts?

→ How will varied cultural, social, political, economic and envir-onmental issues shape media representational practices from location to location?

→ What does the future hold for media representational practices shaping climate science and governance priorities?

→ How will such priorities shape ongoing media processes and practices?

→ How will these issues shape varied awareness and engagement across gender, age and socio-economic segments of the public citizenry?

These laundry lists of questions are only some of the many open considerations and sleeper issues that will be important as we collectively move forward.

Over the last decades, more expansive considerations of the role of science in society have been dramatic (Wynne, 2008). Meanwhile, the days of John Chancellor, Harry Reasoner and Walter Cronkite ('and that's the way it is') have given way to high-stakes, high-profile and highly contested claims on the complexities of climate change. However, as I mentioned in the Preface, there is promising research grappling with these burgeoning arenas of media portrayals of climate science and governance. For instance, James Painter at the Reuters Institute for the Study of Journalism at the University of Oxford examined trends in discourse and visibility of various claims-makers when he studied approximately 400 articles produced in newspapers in twelve countries at the time of the UN COP15 meeting in Copenhagen (2010).

This sort of approach has built upon previous and concurrent research in other contexts and conditions. For example, work by Astrid Dirikx and Dave Gelders explored coverage of UN Conference of Parties meetings in the Dutch and French newspapers – *De Volkskrant*, *NRC Handelsblad*, *Le Monde* and *Le Figaro*. Consistently, across the sources, they found more prevalent discussions of responsibility for and consequences of climate action, yet there was scant evidence of discourses regarding the impacts of climate action on the climate across the UN COP meetings from 2001 to 2007 (2010). Similarly, Lars Kjerulf Petersen examined Danish television coverage of the UN Rio Summit in 1992 and Rio+10 in 2002, and found similar results that he attributed to the ongoing entrenchment of 'economistic discourse' (2007, 227). These three examples illustrate research efforts to document where there has been discursive traction as well as Derridean silences via mass media, as well as what may be implications from such trends. Carl Grundy-Warr and James Sidaway have reminded us that examinations of 'the political geographies of … silence and erasure demand our critical and careful scrutiny' (2006, 481).

Conclusions

When Joe Smith assembled the valuable edited book *The Daily Globe: Environmental change, the public and the media* just over a decade ago, the science–media–policy/practice landscape looked very different. At that time, Smith asserted that climate issues were 'routinely underreported', and connected this to a lack of prioritization in addressing environmental degradation. However, now that climate change is often widely reported through mass-media outlets, many questions remain as to how media representations will contribute to multi-scale action, from individual to international mitigation and adaptation practices.

As was discussed in the previous chapters, the road from information acquisition via mass media to various forms of engagement and action is far from straightforward, and is filled with turns, potholes and intersections. This is a complex arena: mass-media portrayals simply do not translate truths or truth claims, nor do they fill knowledge gaps for citizens and policy actors to make 'the right choices'.

Moreover, media representations clearly do not dictate particular behavioural responses. For example, research has shown that fear-inducing and catastrophic tones in climate-change stories can inspire feelings of paralysis through powerlessness and disbelief rather than motivation and engagement. Jon Krosnick and colleagues have found that, 'knowledge about an issue *per se* will not necessarily increase support for a relevant policy. It will do so only if existence beliefs, attitudes, and beliefs about human responsibility are in place to permit the necessary reasoning steps to unfold' (2006, 37). Furthermore, through analyses of fifteen years of climate-change perception polling and research, Irene Lorenzoni and Nick Pidgeon have found that the extent to which people perceive that they can make a difference significantly determines levels of ongoing (dis)engagement, amid the complexities of perceptions about climate change. They concluded, 'Successful action is only likely to take place if individuals feel they can and should make a difference...' (2006, 88).

Yet, media portrayals continue to influence – in non-linear and dynamic ways – individual to community- and international-level perceptions of climate science and governance (Wilby, 2008). As this volume has shown, mass media have constituted key interventions in shaping the variegated, politicized terrain within which people perceive, understand and engage with climate science and policy (Bord *et al.*, 2000; Krosnick *et al.*, 2006; Leiserowitz, 2006). Moreover, mass media comprise a community where climate science, policy and politics can readily be addressed, analyzed and discussed. The way that these issues are covered in media can have far-reaching consequences in terms of ongoing climate scientific inquiry as well as policymaker and public perceptions, understanding and potential engagement. In this contemporary environment, numerous NNSAs also compete to influence decision-making and policy prioritization at many scales of governance (Liverman, 2004). These factors all contribute to the perceived range of possibilities for action.

Sonja Boehmer-Christiansen has asserted, 'The environmental policy problem facing societies is twofold: (1) how to ensure that useful knowledge informs policy without being misused and distorted; and (2) how to respond to this knowledge in the context of existing patterns of interests, perceptions and commitments' (1994, 140). Over time, these sorts of intersecting challenges have played out in a variety of ways. For example, in 2004 author Michael Crichton published the novel *State of Fear*. This was a tale about an antagonistic and extremist environmental group peddling what he characterized as the 'myth' of anthropogenic climate change. Behind the veil of science fiction, Crichton provided highly selective referencing of climate science. This then provided a vehicle through which oppositional views – irrespective of their validity – were smuggled or paraded into the policy and public sphere.

State of Fear gained a great deal of discursive traction with policymakers in the US during the time of the George W. Bush administration. For instance, then-Chair of the US Senate Environment and Public Works Committee, James Inhofe (Republican, Oklahoma), called for it to be required reading for committee members (Janofsky, 2005). Moreover, in 2006 President George W. Bush (and Karl Rove) invited Crichton to the White House to discuss climate policy (Janofsky, 2006). Furthermore, in the same year, Crichton was awarded the American Association of Petroleum Geologists Journalism Award for his novel. Despite convergent agreement in expert communities that humans contribute to climate change (see Chapter 6), systemic mobilizations of power through the success of this book fuelled an atmosphere of confusion.

This *State of Fear* example also raises perennial questions about the interactions – and potential trade-offs – between scientific accuracy and effectiveness through media communications in civil society. As the issue of climate change moved onto the public agenda in the late 1980s, Stephen Schneider commented to *Discover Magazine* about this challenge. He said:

On the one hand, as scientists we are ethically bound to the scientific method, in effect promising to tell the truth, the whole truth and nothing but – which means that we must include all doubts, the caveats, the ifs, ands and buts. On the other hand, we are not just scientists but human beings as well. And like most people we'd like to see the world a better place, which in this context translates into our working to reduce the risk of potentially disastrous climate change. To do that we need to get some broad-based support, to capture the public's imagination. That, of course, means getting loads of media coverage. So we have to offer up scary scenarios, make simplified, dramatic statements, and make little mention of any doubts we might have. This 'double ethical bind' we frequently find ourselves in cannot be solved by any formula. Each of us has to decide what the right balance is between being effective and being honest. *I hope that means being both.* (quoted in Schell, 1989, 47, emphasis added)

While Schneider's statement has been misappropriated and taken out of context on numerous occasions since that utterance, the challenges that he picked up on remain relevant in the high-stakes contemporary environment of communicating climate change. Schneider had rightly argued many times that the 'double ethical bind' can and should be overcome in order to do justice to the scientific work that undergirds it. However, with numerous examples at the interface of climate science, policy, media and the public, these issues can often become trade-offs – either inadvertently or through deliberate actions (see Chapter 3 for more).

As another example, we can consider the 2006 promotional poster that was often used to advertise the film *An Inconvenient Truth* featuring former US Vice-President Al Gore. The poster prominently showed a hurricane emerging from a smokestack. While the film's promoters likely did not mean for this to be interpreted literally, the imagery did suggest a causal connection between industrial GHG emissions and hurricane activity. Thought of the other way around, the poster implied that by shutting the power plant down, so goes the hurricane (Pielke Jr, 2010). Roger Pielke, Jr pointed out, 'One of the chief problems with this imagery is that the primary driver of increasing disaster losses around the world is not climate change, human caused or otherwise' (2010, 167). Such attention-getting imagery may have boosted ticket sales. However, this effectiveness came at the expense of accuracy, as Chapter 3 briefly discussed the ongoing debate regarding connections between hurricanes and climate change. Moreover, Saffron O'Neill and Sophie Nicholson-Cole found that while images of industrial smokestacks may have raised awareness and concern about climate change, they have been one of the images that make people feel most disempowered about doing something to combat it (2009).

While these two examples may have focused on individuals, the critiques put forward in this book have not been meant as attacks on individual journalists, editors, publishers, scientists, policy actors or other non-nation-state actors. This perspective aligns with Michel Foucault's view that 'individuals are the vehicles of power, not its points of application'.

Examples abound: individual journalists can heroically swim upstream to provide fair and accurate reporting, but they paddle against a strong current of political economics (e.g. shrinking newsrooms); individual policy actors can push for greater accountability regarding lobbying interactions on US Capitol Hill, yet the absence of codified restrictions in US politics contributes to tremendous ongoing carbon-based-industry influence on decision-making; uncle Mike may want high-speed, low-cost, low-pollution transport, but he votes against his own interests in supporting political parties that oppose such measures in their ideological chants for smaller government and lower taxes.

There are numerous unresolved tensions here. While these critical analyses focus on how political, economic and cultural factors from many sources and at many levels contribute to this historically-infused tapestry of interactions, these are woven together by everyday choices. In other words, institutional and long-term improvements ultimately derive from individual and daily changes in attitude, intention and behaviour.

Furthermore, responsibilities for enhanced media representations of climate change certainly do not rest solely with media actors and media institutions themselves. Rather, necessary, sustained and long-term improvements involve recasting relationships between and within the realms of science, policy, media and civil society. The focus has been on examining the institutional features of the news media in its coverage of this issue as it provides an important bridge between the formal spaces of climate science–policy interactions and our everyday lives.

Dramatic improvements can be gained, however, through more consistent interactions between science, policy, media and consumer-citizen communities. For instance, climate scientists can more effectively help journalists, publishers and editors understand nuances in climate science. Reciprocally, media workers can help scientists to better appreciate pressures that media communities face with story deadlines, language, translation, negotiations in the newsroom and so on.

Furthermore, enhanced understanding will spill over to greater public understanding of both process and product. Scientific papers, policy measures and media representations are not viewed as reified markers of culture, but rather windows into the processes that contribute dynamically to the formation and maintenance of cultural identity as well as the cumulative characteristics of society (Maleuvre, 2004). The *New York Times* journalist Andrew Revkin has commented, 'The more scientists and journalists talk, the more likely it is that the public – through the media – will appreciate what science can (and cannot) offer as society grapples with difficult questions about how to invest scarce resources. An intensified dialogue of this sort is becoming ever more important as science and technology increasingly underpin daily life and the progress of modern civilization' (2007, 158).

Revkin's comment also provides insights into the need for more dialogical models of communication, and expanded engagement between the climate-controlled and formal spaces of science and policy and the elements of civil society (e.g. Forsyth, 2003; Nisbet *et al.*, 2010). Policy actors and scientists must recognize that dialogical and iterative interactions with media and public are increasingly a fabric of their professional obligations and responsibilities rather than an annoyance that can be avoided while the science or the policy 'speaks for itself'.

A case in point here arose in July 2010 when it was revealed that IPCC Chair Rajendra Pachauri had circulated an email to the Intergovernmental Panel on Climate Change (IPCC) Fifth Assessment Report authors stating, 'My sincere advice would be that you keep a distance from the media…' (Brainard, 2010), and included a document assembled by the group 'Resource Media' providing 'tips for responding to the media' (Curtis, 2010). These tips demonstrated an archaic view of science in society and also inflamed rather than assuaged concerns regarding IPCC openness, transparency, effective communications and dialogue (Revkin, 2010b).

Cross-community wariness can, of course, cut both ways. Despite calls for better communication from scientists, the *New York Times* journalist Andrew Revkin has posited, 'There are exceptions, but over the years I have learned to be skeptical of scientists who are adept at speaking in sound bites' (2007, 152). Meanwhile, one's own scientific colleagues may harbour resentment towards the articulate and outspoken expert. Journalist Robert Wyss has observed, 'Many scientists have not liked show-offs' (2008, 73).

For scientists, or anyone working on a specific set of research questions, fair and accurate communication can feel like a massive challenge. As was discussed in Chapter 3, it can be very difficult to compress the complexities of time and space into succinct yet accurate sound bites as well as crisply worded commentary. These portrayals are typically valued by policy actors, mass media and public citizens who are in a hurry to keep going with the rest of their lives. This process of compressing complexity into climate stories can seem akin to trying to adequately summarize the contours of one's specialization in the space of a picture postcard. Yet, one's ability to do so does not guarantee communication success. In addition to the many cultural, political, economic, social and environmental issues of context described earlier, eloquent speakers can still be met with suspicion by journalists and the public. Some members of the public may gravitate to the self-effacing claims-maker over the well-groomed and telegenic spokesperson.

Nonetheless, heroic scientists-as-communicators such as Stephen Schneider have continued to speak to policy actors, NNSAs and the public about various aspects of climate science and policy. Schneider also developed a website that discussed challenges involved in media portrayals of climate change, which he dubbed 'Mediarology'. Furthermore, The Aldo Leopold Leadership Program and the American Academy for the Advancement of Science have provided institutional support to encourage interactions between science and society. Chris Mooney and Sheril Kirshenbaum have called for greater institutional support for these 'culture-crossing' activities (2009), and

Thomas Bowman and colleagues have called for institutional support to provide new initiatives aimed at improved and sustained communications about climate change (2009).

The 'fossils' of climate science and policy decision-making among us speak of communications with the public as a 'dumbing down' of complex science and governance information for public consumption. However, these institutions and organizations have clearly overcome these pockets of resistance, and have instead noted these endeavours as critical efforts to 'smarten up' climate communications.

There remain many approaches to these interactions. Some of them provide short-term gains, but may come at the cost of long-term benefits between climate science, policy, media and the public. As an example, University of Leeds researcher Simon L. Lewis was drawn into the heavily politicized arena of climate science policy in January 2010, when he was asked to respond to IPCC claims regarding the effects of changing precipitation patterns on Amazonian forests. To his chagrin, the responses he offered to the *Sunday Times* regarding the IPCC claims were 'heavily edited and misleadingly taken out of context' (2010, 7). However, Lewis was frustrated by how his efforts to correct the record fell far short of the influence that his misrepresented views had in traditional and new media ('reproduced over 20,000 times on the Internet'). Perceiving this as a challenge to his expert credibility, Lewis contacted the *Guardian*, as well as influential US blogger Joe Romm, and published articles about his complaints through those sources. Lewis was more satisfied by this pro-active approach, commenting that, 'For a scientist to take such an active media role was unorthodox, but it felt good. And it worked' (2010, 7). And additional sources such as the *New York Times*, and the *Sunday Times* itself, gave coverage to Lewis's claims.

In Lewis's recounting through the *Nature* commentary, 'How to beat the media in the climate street fight', this battle may have been won. However, in the longer relationship between science, media and the public, casting these interactions through such language may actually have had a detrimental effect on future connectivity to media communities. By arguing that 'researchers must take a more aggressive approach to counter shoddy journalism and set the scientific record straight', Lewis may have fanned the flames of ongoing adversarial experiences, rather than quelling the heat in favour of the more open and dialogical interactions that are needed to expand capabilities both through policy action and in everyday decision-making.

Ultimately, this book has sought to explore how media representations – from articulations to silences – (re)shape and (re)configure discourses which, in turn, can expand or constrict alternatives for decision-making (Swyngeduow, 2007). Mass media are influential and heterogeneous conduits to both informal and formal discourses and imaginaries within the spaces of cultural politics and geopolitics (Dalby, 1996; Castree, 2006). Media contribute to, and often embody, articulations of political identity and culture in society (Dittmer, 2005), and significantly influence ongoing public understanding of climate science and policy (Wilson, 1995). Ways of knowing – both challenged and supported through media depictions – shape ongoing discourses and imaginaries, circulating in various cultural and political contexts. Furthermore, varying media representational practices contribute – amid a complex web of factors – to divergent perceptions, priorities and behaviours.

On this battlefield of knowledge, understandings and interpretations, and amidst the many social referents in our daily lives – our families, workplaces, communities etc. – media representations of climate-change actors, action, predicaments and progress remain key influences that shape discourses and considerations for possible climate action. This book has helped us ponder how climate science and policy inform the everyday spaces of civil society, as well as how these everyday spaces feed back on formal science and policy processes and priorities.

The mantra of 'more science' or reducing uncertainty will not resolve these communication challenges between science, policy and civil society. Mike Hulme has commented that 'scientific inquiry is no substitute for political argument' (2009b). Sheila Jasanoff has warned, 'it will not be enough for climate scientists to be still more scrupulous and transparent toward their peers. Adding more new forms of expertise may increase the credibility of the field, but it will not fully address the third component of accountability, which involves relations between science and its publics' (2010, 696).

The focus on media and climate change – arguably the most heavily politicized scientific issue at the turn of the new millennium – provides a number of opportunities. Among them, examinations of these amplified interactions can inform and anticipate other current science issues, such as ongoing concerns for toxins or genetically modified organisms in the environment, nanotechnology risks and increased threats to water quantity and quality. By unpacking and analyzing interactions that focus on climate change, representative challenges ranging from extrinsic issues (e.g. political economics) to intrinsic issues (e.g. uncertainty) can inform perceptions and decision-making in these associated environmental challenges.

These considerations of 'who speaks for climate' via mass media may be as important as formal climate governance architectures themselves to the long-term success or failure of efforts to take carbon out of the atmosphere or keep it out. We ignore or dismiss the influence of media representations – cultural politics more broadly – in shaping climate science and governance at our peril. The many 'actors' in this theatre of cultural politics – from climate scientists to business industry interest and ENGO (pro)activists to artists, union workers, farmers, teachers, television and movie stars – are ultimately all members of a public citizenry. In short, a more informed public and more wisely supported links between science, policy and media are in our collective self-interest.

References

Abramson, Rudy 1992. 'Ice cores may hold clues to weather 200,000 years ago', *Los Angeles Times* December 2: A1.

AC Nielsen 2008. *Global omnibus survey.* Oxford, UK.

ActionMedia 2005. *Naming global warming.* ActionMedia, Minneapolis, MN.

Adam, David 2010. 'Climategate review clears scientists of dishonesty over data', *Guardian*, July 7, Retrieved August 15, 2010, www.guardian. co.uk/environment/2010/jul/07/climategate-review-clears-scientists-dishonesty.

Adger, W. Neil, Benjaminsen, Tor A., Brown, Katrina and Svarstad, Hanne 2001. 'Advancing a political ecology of global environmental discourses', *Development and Change* 32(4): 681–715.

Allan, Stuart, Adam, Barbara, and Carter, Cynthia (eds.) 2000. *Environmental risks and the media.* New York, NY: Routledge.

Allen, Myles 2008. 'Minority report', *Nature* 1, April: 209.

Allen, Myles R., Stott, Peter A., Mitchell, John F.B., Schnur, Reiner and Delworth, Thomas L. 2000. 'Quantifying the uncertainty in forecasts of anthropogenic climate change', *Nature* 407: 617.

Anderegg, William R.L., Prall, James W., Harold, Jacob and Schneider, Stephen H. 2010. 'Expert credibility in climate change', *Proceedings of the National Academy of Sciences* 107: 12107–12109.

Anderson, Alison 1997. *Media, culture and the environment.* New Brunswick, NJ: Rutgers University Press.

Andreadis, Eleni and Smith, Joseph 2007. 'Beyond the ozone layer', *British Journalism Review* 18(1): 50–56.

Andrews, Wyatt 1990. 'Environment, global warming, Bush', *CBS Evening News*, February 5.

Antilla, Liisa 2005. 'Climate of scepticism: US newspaper coverage of the science of climate change', *Global Environmental Change* 15: 338–352.

2010. 'Self-censorship and science: a geographical review of media coverage of climate tipping points', *Public Understanding of Science* 19(2): 240–256.

Applebome, Peter 2010. 'Ignoring the planet won't fix it', *New York Times* October 28: A22.

Argrawala, Shardul 1998. 'Structural and process history of the Inter-governmental Panel on Climate Change', *Climatic Change* **39**: 621–642.

Atkinson, Rick 1995. 'Reaching a consensus is the hot topic at global climate conference', *Washington Post* March **28**: A10.

Audit Bureau of Circulations 2010. Standard certificates of circulation: US newspapers.

Bagdikian, Ben H. 2004. *The new media monopoly*. Boston, MA: Beacon Press.

Bailey, Ian 2007. 'Neoliberalism, climate governance and the scalar politics of EU emissions trading', *Area* **39**(4): 431–442.

Baldwin, Katherine 2007. 'Blair attacks "feral" media he once tamed', *Reuters*, June 12.

Ball, Jeffrey 2005. 'California sets emissions goals that are stiffer than US plan', *Wall Street Journal*, A4.

   2009. 'The earth cools, and fight over warming heats up', *Wall Street Journal* October 30: A21.

BBC 2010. 'Climate scepticism on the rise', *BBC News*, February 7, http://news.bbc.co.uk/2/hi/8500443.stm.

Beck, Ulrich 1992. *Risk society: towards a new modernity*. London, UK: Sage.

Beder, Sharon 2002. *Global spin: the corporate assault on environmentalism*. White River Junction, VT: Chelsea Green Publishing Company.

Bennet, James 1997. 'Warm globe, hot politics', *New York Times* December 11: A1.

Bennett, W. Lance 2002. *News: the politics of illusion*. New York, NY: Longman.

Bernstein, Richard 2005. 'The view from abroad', *New York Times* September 4: D5.

Billett, Simon 2010. 'Dividing climate change: global warming in the Indian mass media', *Climatic Change* **99**(1/2): 525–537.

Blackman, Oonagh 2006. 'Climate is threat to economy', *Mirror* October 28: 12.

Blaikie, Piers 1985. *The political ecology of soil erosion in developing countries*. London, UK: Longman Scientific and Technical.

Blaikie, Piers and Brookfield, Harold 1987. *Land degradation and society*. London, UK: Methuen.

Boehmer-Christiansen, Sonja 1994. 'Global climate protection policy: the limits of scientific advice part 1', *Global Environmental Change* **4**: 140–159.

Bolin, Bert 2007. *A history of the science and politics of climate change: the role of the Intergovernmental Panel on Climate Change*. Cambridge, UK: Cambridge University Press.

Booker, C. 2009. 'Climate change: this is the worst scientific scandal of our generation', *Telegraph*, November 28, Retrieved August 12, 2010, www.telegraph.co.uk/comment/columnists/christopherbooker/6679082/Climate-change-this-is-the-worst-scientific-scandal-of-our-generation.html.

Bord, Richard J., O'Connor, Robert E. and Fischer, Ann 2000. 'In what sense does the public need to understand global climate change?', *Public Understanding of Science* 9: 205–218.

Borenstein, Seth 2009. 'Impact: statisticians reject global cooling', *Associated Press*, October 26.

Boswell, Randy 2007. 'Inuit activist awaits Nobel call: Watt-Cloutier may just snag peace prize along with Gore', *Winnipeg Free Press* October 7: 1.

Bowen, Jerry 2004a. 'Global warming: movie debate', *CBS Evening News*, May 20.

2004b. 'What does it mean to you? (global warming)', *CBS Evening News*, October 27.

Bowman, Thomas E., Maibach, Edward, Mann, Michael E., Moser, Susanne C. and Somerville, Richard C.J. 2009. 'Creating a common climate language', *Science* 324, April 3: 36–37.

Boykoff, Maxwell 2007a. 'Flogging a dead norm? Newspaper coverage of anthropogenic climate change in the United States and United Kingdom from 2003–2006', *Area* 39(4): 470–481.

2007b. 'From convergence to contention: United States mass media representations of anthropogenic climate change science', *Transactions of the Institute of British Geographers* 32(4): 477–489.

2008a. 'The cultural politics of climate change discourse in UK tabloids', *Political Geography* 27(5): 549–569.

2008b. 'Lost in translation? United States television news coverage of anthropogenic climate change, 1995–2004', *Climatic Change* 86(1): 1–11.

2008c. 'The real climate swindle', *Nature Reports Climate Change* 2(2): 31–32.

2008d. 'Fight semantic drift!? Mass media coverage of anthropogenic climate change', In Michael K. Goodman, Maxwell T. Boykoff, and Kyle T. Evered (eds.), *Contentious geographies: environmental knowledge, meaning, scale*. Hampshire, UK and Burlington, VT: Ashgate Publishing Ltd.

2009a. '"We speak for the trees": media reporting on the environment', *Annual Review of Environment and Resources* **34**: 431–458.

2009b. 'A discernible human influence on the COP15? Considering the role of media in shaping ongoing climate science', Copenhagen Climate Congress Theme 6, Session 53.

Boykoff, Maxwell and Boykoff, Jules 2004. 'Bias as balance: global warming and the U.S. prestige press', *Global Environmental Change* **14**(2): 125–136.

2007. 'Climate change and journalistic norms: a case-study of U.S. mass-media coverage', *Geoforum* **38**(6): 1190–1204.

Boykoff, Maxwell and Goodman, Michael K. 2009. 'Conspicuous redemption? Reflections on the promises and perils of the "celebritization" of climate change', *Geoforum* **40**: 395–406.

Boykoff, Maxwell and Mansfield, Maria 2008. '"Ye olde hot aire": reporting on human contributions to climate change in the UK tabloid press', *Environmental Research Letters* **3**(2): 1–8.

Boykoff, Maxwell and Rajan, S. Ravi 2007. 'Signals and noise: mass-media coverage of climate change in the USA and the UK', *European Molecular Biology Organization Reports* **8**(3): 1–5.

Boykoff, Maxwell, Goodman, Michael K. and Curtis, Ian 2009. 'Cultural politics of climate change: interactions in everyday spaces', In Maxwell Boykoff (ed.), *The politics of climate change: a survey*. London, UK: Routledge/Europa, 136–154.

Boykoff, Maxwell, Bumpus, Adam, Liverman, Diana and Randalls, Samuel 2009b. 'Theorising the carbon economy: introduction to the special issue', *Environment and Planning A* **41**(10): 2357–2379.

Bozell, Brent 1992. 'Environment: global warming', *NBC Nightly News*, March 9.

Brainard, Curtis 2008. 'Global cooling, confused coverage', *Columbia Journalism Review – The Observatory*, November 26.

2010. 'Mediaphobia at the IPCC', *Observatory – Columbia Journalism Review*, 12 July, retrieved 1 October, 2010, www.cjr.org/the_observatory/mediaphobia_at_the_ipcc.php.

Bray, Dennis and von Storch, Hans 1999. 'Climate science: an empirical example of post-normal science', *Bulletin of the American Meteorological Society* **80**(3): 439–455.

Bridge, Gavin 2010. 'Resource geographies I: making carbon economies, old and new', *Progress in Human Geography* doi: 10.1177/0309132510385524: 1–15.

Briggs, Asa and Burke, Peter 2005. *A social history of the media: from Gutenberg to the internet*. Cambridge, UK: Polity Press.

Broder, John M. 2009a. 'Seeking to save the planet, with a thesaurus', *New York Times* May 2: A11.

2009b. 'Storm over the chamber', *New York Times* November 19: F1.

2010a. 'Climate fight is heating up in deep freeze', *New York Times* February 11: A1/A18.

2010b. 'Skepticism on climate change is article of faith for tea party', *New York Times* October 21: A1.

Brokaw, Tom 1990. 'Atmosphere, global warming', *NBC Nightly News*, March 29.

Brosnan, James W. 2006. 'Report: first half of '06 was warmest for US', *Albuquerque Tribune/Scripps Howard News Service*, July 15.

Brossard, Dominique, Shanahan, James and McComas, Katherine 2004. 'Are issue-cycles culturally constructed? A comparison of French and American coverage of global climate change', *Mass Communication & Society* 7(3): 359–377.

Brown, Campbell 2009. 'Global warming: trick or truth', *CNN*, December 7.

Brownstein, Ronald 2010. 'GOP's new Senate class could be conservative vanguard', *National Journal*, September 25.

Brulle, Robert J. 2010. 'From environmental campaigns to advancing a public dialogue: environmental communication for civic engagement', *Environmental Communication – A Journal of Nature and Culture* 4(1): 82–98.

Brumfiel, Geoff 2009. 'Supplanting the old media?', *Nature* 458(March 19): 274–277.

Bryant, Raymond L. 2009. 'Born to be wild? Non-governmental organisations, politics and the environment', *Geography Compass* 3(4):1540–1558.

Bumpus, Adam and Liverman, Diana 2008. 'Accumulation by decarbonisation and the governance of carbon offsets', *Economic Geography*, 84(2): 127–55.

Burgess, Jacquelin 1990. 'The production and consumption of environmental meanings in the mass media: a research agenda for the 1990s', *Transactions of the Institute for British Geography* 15: 139–161.

2005. 'Follow the argument where it leads: some personal reflections on "policy-relevant" research', *Transactions of the Institute of British Geographers* 30(3): 273.

Burgess, Jacquelin, Harrison, Carolyn and Filius, Petra 1998. 'Environmental communication and the cultural politics of environmental citizenship', *Environment and Planning A* 30: 1445–1460.

Burkeman, Oliver 2003. 'Memo exposes Bush's new green strategy', *Guardian* March 4, 1.

Bustillo, Miguel 2005. 'Gov. vows attack on global warming', *Los Angeles Times* (June 2): B1.

Carroll, John S. 2006. 'What will become of newspapers?', Working paper: Shorenstein Center for the Press, Politics, Public Policy. Cambridge, MA: Harvard University.

Carvalho, Anabela 2005. 'Representing the politics of the greenhouse effect', *Critical Discourse Studies* 2(1): 1–29.

2007. 'Ideological cultures and media discourses on scientific knowledge: re-reading news on climate change', *Public Understanding of Science* 16: 223–243.

2008. 'Media(ted) discourse and society', *Journalism Studies* 9(2): 161–177.

Carvalho, Anabela and Burgess, Jacquelin 2005. 'Cultural circuits of climate change in UK broadsheet newspapers, 1985–2003', *Risk Analysis* 25(6): 1457–1469.

Cass, Loren 2007. 'Measuring the domestic salience of international environmental norms: climate change norms in American, German and British climate policy debates', In Mary E. Pettenger, *The social construction of climate change*. London, UK: Ashgate Ltd., 24–50.

Castree, Noel 2004. 'Differential geographies: place, indigenous rights and "local" resources', *Political Geography* 23(2): 133–167.

2006. 'From neoliberalism to neoliberalisation: consolations, confusions, and necessary illusions', *Environment and Planning A* 38: 1–6.

CEI 2006. 'We call it life', Competitive Enterprise Institute, retrieved 8 January, 2007, www.cei.org.

Chambers, Robert 1997. *Whose reality counts?: putting the first last.* London, UK: Intermediate Technology Publications.

Chapman, Jane L. 2005. *A comparative media history: an introduction, 1789 – present.* London, UK: Polity Press.

Clarkson, Jeremy 2000. 'Tony's gas tax makes me fume', *Sun* February 25: 25.

2004. 'Ewe-reek-a!', *Sun* September 23: 25.

CNN 2006. Headline news: live today, June 26.

Co2isgreen.org 2010. 'More CO_2 results in a greener earth: about us', Retrieved 1 October, http://co2isgreen.org/default.aspx/MenuItemID/138/MenuGroup/Home.htm.

Collins, H.M. and Evans, Robert 2002. 'The third wave of science studies: studies of expertise and experience', *Social Studies of Science* 32: 235–296.

Columbia Journalism Review 2004. 'Brits vs. Yanks: who does journalism right?', *Columbia Journalism Review* May/June: 44–49.

Compton, Ann 1990. 'Environment, global warming and Bush', *ABC World News Tonight*, February 5.

Connell, Ian 1998. 'Mistaken identities: tabloid and broadsheet news discourse', *Javnost-The Public* 5(3): 11–31.

Corbett, Julia B. and Durfee, Jessica L. 2004. 'Testing public (un)certainty of science: media representations of global warming', *Science Communication* 26(2): 129.

Corfee-Morlot, Jan, Maslin, Mark and Burgess, Jacquelin 2007. 'Global warming in the public sphere', *Philosophical Transactions of the Royal Society A* 365(1860): 2741–2776.

Cosgrove, Denis 1983. 'Towards a radical cultural geography: problems of theory', *Antipode* 15: 1–11.

1994. 'Contested global visions: one world, whole Earth and the Apollo space photographs', *Annals of the Association of American Geographers* 84: 270–294.

Cottle, Simon 2000. 'TV news, lay voices and the visualisation of environmental risks', In Stuart Allan, Barbara Adam and Cynthia Carter (eds.), *Environmental risks and the media*. London, UK: Routledge, 29–44.

Cowen, Robert C. 1957. 'Are men changing the Earth's weather?', *Christian Science Monitor* December 4: 13.

Cox, J. Robert 2006. *Environmental communication in the public sphere.* Thousand Oaks, CA: Sage Publications.

Cronin, Tim and Santoso, Levania 2010. 'REDD+ politics in the media: a case study from Indonesia', Center for International Forestry Research working paper 49, www.cifor.cgiar.org/publications/pdf_files/WPapers/WP-49Santoso.pdf.

Crowley, Thomas 2000. 'Causes of climatic change over the past 1000 years', *Science* 289(July 14): 270–277.

Crutzen, Paul J. 2002. 'The anthropocene', *Journal de Physique IV France* 10: 1–5.

Cunningham, Brent 2003. 'Re-thinking objectivity', *Columbia Journalism Review* 42: 24–32.

Curran, James 2002. *Media and power.* London: Routledge.

Curry, Judith, Webster, Peter and Holland, Gregory 2006. 'Mixing politics and science in testing the hypothesis that greenhouse warming is causing a global increase in hurricane intensity', *Bulletin of the American Meteorological Society* August: 1025–1037.

Curtis, K. 2010. *Background & tips for responding to the media.* Media Backgrounder for Working Group 2, Resource Media, April.

Cushman, John H. 1998. 'Industrial group plans to battle climate treaty', *New York Times*, April 26: A1.

Dahlgren, Peter and Sparks, Colin (eds.) 1992. *Journalism and popular culture*. London, UK: Sage.

Daily Mail Reporter 2010. 'Donald Trump: climate campaigner Al Gore should be stripped of Nobel Peace Prize after record snow storms', *Daily Mail Online*, 15 February, Retrieved 5 October 2010, www.dailymail. co.uk/news/article-1251283/Donald-Trump-Climate-campaigner-Al-Gore-stripped-Nobel-Peace-Prize-record-snow-storms.html.

Dalby, Simon 1996. 'Reading Rio, writing the world: The New York Times and the "Earth Summit"', *Political Geography* 15(6/7): 593–613.

2007. 'Anthropocene geopolitics: globalisation, empire, environment and critique', *Geography Compass* 1: 1–16.

de Certeau, Michel 1984. *The practice of everyday life*. Translated by S. Rendall, Berkeley, CA: University of California Press.

Dearing, James W. and Rogers, Everett 1996. *Communication concepts 6: agenda-setting*. Newbury Park, CA: Sage Publications.

Debord, Guy 1983. *Society of the spectacle*. New York: Zone Books.

Delasky, Kathleen 1990. 'Environment, Earth day', *ABC World News Tonight*, April 15.

Delingpole, James 2009. 'Climategate: the final nail in the coffin of "anthropogenic global warming"?,' *Telegraph*, November 20, Retrieved 28 September 2010, http://blogs.telegraph.co.uk/news/jamesdelingpole/100017393/climategate-the-final-nail-in-the-coffin-of-anthropogenic-global-warming/.

Demeritt, David 2001. 'The construction of global warming and the politics of science', *Annals of the Association of American Geographers* 912: 307–337.

2006. 'Science studies, climate change and the prospects for constructivist critique', *Economy and Society* 35(3): 453–479.

Derrida, Jacques 1978. 'Structure, sign, and play in the discourse of the human sciences', In Jacques Derrida, *Writing and difference*. Chicago, IL: University of Chicago Press, 278–293.

Deuze, Mark 2005. 'Popular journalism and professional ideology: tabloid reporters and editors speak out', *Media, Culture and Society* 27(6): 861–882.

Dipensa, Jaclyn and Brulle, Robert 2003. 'Media's social construction of environmental issues: focus on global warming – a comparative study', *The International Journal of Sociology and Social Policy* 23(10): 74–105.

Dirikx, Astrid and Gelders, Dave 2010. 'To frame is to explain: a deductive frame-analysis of Dutch and French climate change coverage during the annual UN Conferences of the Parties', *Public Understanding of Science* 1: 1–11.

Disney, H. 2002. 'Leader as scientists predict that damage to the atmosphere may be repaired in 50 years', *Express* September 19: 13.

Dittmer, Jason 2005. 'Captain America's empire: reflections on identity, popular culture, and post-9/11 geopolitics', *Annals of the Association of American Geographers* 95(3): 626–643.

Djupsund, Göran and Carlson, Tom 1998. 'Trivial stories and fancy pictures? Tabloidization tendencies in Finnish and Swedish regional and national newspapers, 1982–1997', *Nordicom* 19(1): 101–115.

Dobbs, Lou 2009. 'Climate change battle', *CNN Lou Dobbs Tonight*, January 31.

Dolan, Maura and Lawrence, Mark 1988. 'Greenhouse effect: stratosphere becoming a hot topic', *Los Angeles Times* September 1: A1.

Downs, Anthony 1972. 'Up and down with ecology – the issue-attention cycle', *Public Interest* 28: 38–50.

Doyle, Gillian 2002. *Media ownership: the economics and politics of convergence and concentration in the UK and European media*. London, UK: Sage Publications.

Doyle, Julie 2007. 'Picturing the clima(c)tic: Greenpeace and the representational politics of climate change communication', *Science as Culture* 16(2): 129–150.

  2008. 'Seeing the climate? The problematic status of visual evidence in climate change campaigning', In Sidney I. Dobrin and Sean Morey (eds.), *Ecosee: image, rhetoric, nature*. New York: State University of New York Press, 279–298.

Drury, Ian 2008. 'Boris orders arts chiefs to stop "dumbing down" culture for young people', *Mail on Sunday Online*, 24 November, Retrieved 15 December 2008, www.mailonsunday.co.uk/news/article-1088956/Boris-orders-arts-chiefs-stop-dumbing-culture-young-people.html.

Dung, Pham Huy 2008. 'Climate change coverage by the Vietnamese media: three-year trend 2006–2008', Institute of Health, Environment and Development working paper, Hanoi, Vietnam.

Dunlap, Riley E. 1992. 'Trends in public opinion toward environmental issues: 1965–1992', In Riley E. Dunlap and Angela G. Mertig (eds.), *American environmentalism. The U.S. Environmental Movement 1970–1990*. Philadelphia, PA: Taylor and Francis, 89–115.

  2008. 'Climate-change views: Republican-Democrat gaps extend', *Gallup*, May 29.

Dunwoody, Sharon and Griffin, Robert J. 1993. 'Journalistic strategies for reporting long-term environmental issues: a case study of three

Superfund sites', In Anders Hansen (ed.), *The mass media and environmental issues*. Leicester, UK: Leicester University Press, 22–50.

Dunwoody, Sharon and Peters, Hans Peter 1992. 'Mass media coverage of technological and environmental risks', *Public Understanding of Science* 1(2): 199–230.

Edwards, Arthur 1999. 'Scientific expertise and policy-making: the intermediary role of the public sphere', *Science and Public Policy* 26(3): 163–170(8).

Eilperin, Juliet 2005. 'Severe hurricanes increasing, study finds', *Washington Post* (September 16): A13.

Einsiedel, Edna and Coughlan, Eileen 1993. 'The Canadian press and the environment: reconstructing a social reality', In Anders Hansen (ed.), *The mass media and environmental issues*. Leicester, UK : Leicester University Press, 134–149.

Entman, Robert M. 1989. *Democracy without citizens: media and the decay of American politics*. Oxford, UK: Oxford University Press.

   1993. 'Framing: toward clarification of a fractured paradigm', *Journal of Communication* 43(4): 51–58.

Ereaut, Gill and Segnit, Nat 2006. 'Warm words: how are we telling the climate story and can we tell it better', *Institute for Public Policy Research*, August.

Fairclough, Norman 1995. *Media discourse*. London, UK: Edward Arnold.

Fairclough, Norman and Wodak, Ruth 1997. 'Critical discourse analysis', In Teun A. van Dijk (ed.), *Discourse as social interaction: Volume 1*. London, UK: Sage, 258–284.

Feinberg, Matthew and Willer, Robb 2011. 'Apocalypse soon? Dire messages reduce belief in global warming by contradicting just world beliefs', *Psychological Science*, forthcoming.

Festinger, Leon 1957. *A theory of cognitive dissonance*. Stanford, CA: Stanford University Press.

Fialka, John J. 2002. 'U.S. backs Indian to head climate panel after Exxon Mobil opposes American', *Wall Street Journal* April 4: C18.

Fifeld, Anna 2009. 'US rightwing activists curb efforts to cut CO2 emissions', *Financial Times*, November 3.

Finnegan, Michael 2006. 'Election 2006: California races, California elections, a landslide for Feinstein and governor', *Los Angeles Times* (November 8): A1.

Fleischer, Ari 2001. 'Press briefing', The James S. Brady Briefing Room, March 28.

Fleming, James Roger 1998. *Historical perspectives on climate change*. Oxford, UK: Oxford University Press.

Forbes 2010. 'EOG resources', retrieved, 28 September 2010, http://finapps.forbes.com/finapps/jsp/finance/compinfo/CIAtAGlance.jsp?tkr=EOG.

Forsyth, Timothy 2003. *Critical political ecology: the politics of environmental science.* London, UK: Routledge.

Foucault, Michel 1975. *Discipline and punish.* Translated by A. Sheridan, New York, NY: Pantheon.

1980. *Power/knowledge.* New York, NY: Pantheon.

1984. 'Space, knowledge and power', In Paul Rabinow (ed.), *The Foucault reader.* New York, NY: Pantheon Books, 239–256.

Frame Works Institute 2001. *Talking Global Warming (Summary of Research Findings).* Washington, DC: Frame Works Institute.

Freedman, Andrew 2010. 'Falling off the climate reporting 'balance' beam', *Climate Central,* May 6.

Freudenburg, William R. 2000. 'Social construction and social constrictions: toward analyzing the social construction of "the naturalized" and well as "the natural"', In G. Spaargaren, Arthur Mol and Frederick Buttel (eds.), *Environment and global modernity.* London, UK: Sage, 103–119.

Freudenburg, William R. and Muselli, Violetta 2010. 'Global warming estimates, media expectations, and the symmetry of scientific challenge'. *Global Environmental Change* 20: 483–491.

Freudenburg, William R., Gramling, Robert and Davidson, Debra J. 2008. 'Scientific certainty argumentation methods (SCAMs): science and the politics of doubt', *Sociological Inquiry* 78: 2–38.

Friedman, Thomas 2010. 'Global weirding is here', *New York Times* February 17: A23.

Funtowicz, Silvio O. and Ravetz, Jerome R. 1993. 'Science for the post-normal age', *Futures* 25: 739–755.

Galtung, Johan and Ruge, Mari Holmboe 1965. 'The structure of foreign news: the presentation of the Congo, Cuba and Cyprus crises in four foreign newspapers', *Journal of International Peace Research* 1: 64–90.

Gamson, William A. and Modigliani, Andre 1989. 'Media discourse and public opinion on nuclear power: a constructionist approach', *American Journal of Sociology* 95(1): 1–37.

Gamson, William A., Croteau, David, Hoynes, William and Sasson, Theodore 1992. 'Media images and the social construction of reality', *Annual Review of Sociology* 18: 373–93.

Gans, Herbert J. 1979. *Deciding what's news.* New York, NY: Pantheon.

Gavin, Neil 2009. 'The web and climate change politics: lessons from Britain?', In Tammy Boyce and Justin Lewis (eds.), *Climate change and the media.* London, UK: Peter Lang Publishing, 129–144.

Gelbspan, Ross 1998. *The heat is on: the climate crisis, the cover-up, the prescription*. Boston, MA: Perseus Press.

Ghosh, Aditya 2009. 'The sunshine industry', *Hindustan Times* 5 April: 14.

Gieryn, Thomas F. 1999. *Cultural boundaries of science: credibility on the line*. Chicago, IL: University of Chicago Press.

Gillis, Justin 2010. 'In weather chaos, a case for global warming', *New York Times* August 15: A1.

Giridharadas, Anand 2009. 'A pocket-size leveller in an outsize land', *New York Times* May 17: A3.

Gitlin, Todd 1980. *The whole world is watching*. Berkeley, CA: University of California Press.

Glacken, Clarence 1967. *Traces on a Rhodian shore: nature and culture in western thought from ancient times to the end of the eighteenth century*. Berkeley, CA: University of California Press.

Glader, Paul 2010. 'Heated exchange over climate', *Wall Street Journal*, May 6.

Goffman, Erving 1974. *Frame analysis: an essay on the organization of experience*. Cambridge, MA: Harvard University Press.

Goldacre, Ben 2008. 'Don't let the facts spoil a good story', *Guardian*, September 13: 21.

Gottlieb, Robert 2002. *Environmentalism unbound: exploring new pathways for change*. Cambridge, MA: MIT Press.

Graber, Doris 2000. *Media power in politics*. Washington, DC: CQ Press

Gregory, David 2003. 'Environment: EPA report', *NBC Evening News*, June 19.

Gross, Alan G. 1994. 'The roles of rhetoric in the public understanding', *Public Understanding of Science* 3: 3–23.

Grove, Richard H. 2003. *Green imperialism*. Cambridge, UK: Cambridge University Press.

Grundy-Warr, Carl and Sidaway, James D. 2006. 'Political geographies of silence and erasure', *Political Geography* 25(5): 479–481.

Gupta, J. (2001). *Our simmering planet: what to do about global warming?* New York, NY, Zed Books.

Hager, Robert 2002. 'In depth – Bush, global warming policy change', *NBC Nightly News*, June 3.

Hajer, Maarten 1993. 'Discourse coalitions and the institutionalization of practice: the case of acid rain in Britain', in Frank Fisher and John Forester (eds), *The argumentative turn in policy analysis and policy-making*. Durham, NC: Duke University Press.

    1995. *The politics of environmental discourse: ecological modernization and the policy process*. Oxford, UK: Clarendon Press.

Hall, Stuart 1988. *The hard road to renewal: Thatcherism and the crisis of the left*. London, UK: Verso.

1997. *Representation: cultural representation and signifying practices*. Thousand Oaks, CA: Sage.

Halpert, Julie 2009. 'Nonprofit journalism model: a future of environmental reporting?', *Yale Forum on Climate Change and the Media*, September 15.

Hansen, Anders 1991. 'The media and the social construction of the environment', *Media, Culture and Society* 13: 443–458.

Hansen, Anders and Machin, David 2008. 'Visually branding the environment: climate change as a marketing opportunity', *Discourse Studies* 10: 777–794.

Harbinson, Rod 2006. 'Whatever the weather: media attitudes to reporting climate change', *Panos Institute Report*, London, February.

Harris, Richard 2006. 'Global warming a hot topic in congressional hearing', *National Public Radio*, 20 July, www.npr.org/templates/story/story.php?storyId=5569901.

Hart, David M. and Victor, David G. 1993. 'Scientific elites and the making of US policy for climate change research', *Social Studies of Science* 23: 643–680.

Harvey, David 1990. 'Between space and time: reflections on the geographical imagination', *Annals of the Association of American Geographers* 80: 418–434.

Harvey, Fiona 2010. 'Research says climate change undeniable', *Financial Times* July 28: 1.

Healy, Jack 2010. 'Bin Laden adds climate change to list of grievances against U.S.', *International Herald Tribune* January 30: A6.

Hebert, H. Josef 2005. 'White House climate-report editor now works for Exxon', *Associated Press*, June 14.

Herman, Edward S. and Chomsky, Noam 1988. *Manufacturing consent: the political economy of the mass media*. Toronto, CA: Pantheon Books.

Herrick, Thaddeus 2001. 'Weighing the evidence of global warming: a scientist's work on ocean becomes fodder for skeptics – much to his dismay', *Wall Street Journal* March 22: B1.

Hilgartner, Stephen and Bosk, Charles L. 1988. 'The rise and fall of social problems: a public arenas model', *The American Journal of Sociology* 94(1): 53–78.

Hitchens, Peter 2006. 'The green fanatics...and a nice little earner', *Mail on Sunday* November 5: 25.

Hobson, Kersty 2006. 'Bins, bulbs and shower timers: on the 'techno-ethics' of sustainable living', *Ethics, Environment, and Place* 3: 317–336.

2008. 'Reasons to be cheerful: thinking sustainably in a (climate) changing world', *Geography Compass* **2**: 1–16.

Hoggan, James and Littlemore, Richard 2009. *Climate cover-up: the crusade to deny global warming*. Vancouver CA: Greystone Books.

Höijer, Birgitta 2009. 'Emotional anchoring and objectification in the media reporting on climate change', *Public Understanding of Science* **1**: 1–15.

Homans, Charles 2010. 'Hot air: why TV weathermen are climate skeptics', *Columbia Journalism Review* January/February: 24–28.

Houghton, John T., Filho, L.G. Meiro, Callander, B.A., Harris, N., Kattenburg, Arie, and Maskell, Kathy (eds.) 1995. *Climate change 1995: the science of climate change*. Geneva: Intergovernmental Panel on Climate Change.

Houghton, John T., Ding, Yihui, Griggs, David, Noguer, Maria, van der Linden, Paul and Xiaosu, Dai 2001. *Climate change 2001: the scientific basis*. Geneva: Intergovernmental Panel on Climate Change.

Huck, Peter 2006. 'Burning issues', *Guardian* December 13: 10.

Hudson, Paul 2009. 'What happened to global warming?', *BBC News*, 13 October, Retrieved 7 October 2010, http://news.bbc.co.uk/2/hi/8299079.stm.

Hulme, Mike 2006. 'Chaotic world of climate truth', *BBC News*, November 4.

2007. 'Newspaper scare headlines can be counter-productive', *Nature* **445**(February 22): 818.

2009a. *Why we disagree about climate change: understanding controversy, inaction and opportunity*. Cambridge, UK: Cambridge University Press.

2009b. 'Laboratories' outer limits', *Guardian*, December 4.

2010. 'The year climate science was redefined', *Guardian*, November 17.

Inhofe, James M. 2003. 'The science of climate change Senate floor statement', *Chair: Committee on Environment and Public Works*, July 28.

Irwin, Alan and Wynne, Brian (eds.) 1996. *Misunderstanding science? the public reconstruction of science and technology*. Cambridge, UK: Cambridge University Press.

Iyengar, Shanto 1991. *Is anyone responsible?* Chicago, IL: University of Chicago Press.

Jacques, Peter J., Dunlap, Riley E. and Freeman, Mark 2008. 'The organization of denial', *Environmental Politics* **17**: 349–385.

Janofsky, Michael 2005. 'Michael Crichton, novelist, becomes Senate witness', *New York Times*, Sept 29.

2006. 'Bush's chat with novelist alarms environmentalists', *New York Times* (February 19): A1.

Jasanoff, Sheila 1996. 'Beyond epistemology: relativism and engagement in the politics of science', *Social Studies of Science* 26(2): 393–418.

Jasanoff, Sheila (ed.) 2004. *States of knowledge: the co-production of science and social order.* London, UK: Routledge.

2005. *Designs on nature: science and democracy in Europe and the United States.* Princeton, NJ: Princeton University Press.

2010. 'Testing time for climate science', *Science* 328, May 7: 695–696.

Jasanoff, Sheila and Wynne, Brian 1998. 'Science and decisionmaking', In Steve Rayner and Elizabeth L. Malone (eds.), *Human choice and climate change.* Columbus, OH: Battelle Press, 1–87.

Johansen, Bruce E. 2002. *The global warming desk reference.* Westport, CT: Greenwood Press.

Joint Science Academies Statement 2005. Global response to climate change.

Jones, Alex S. 2009. *Losing the news: the future of the news that feeds democracy.* Oxford, UK: Oxford University Press.

Jones, Jeffrey M. 2010. 'In US, many environmental issues at 20-year-low concern', *Gallup*, 16 March, www.gallup.com/poll/126716/environmental-issues-year-low-concern.aspx.

Jordan, Andrew and O'Riordan, Timothy 2000. 'Environmental politics and policy processes', In Timothy O'Riordan, *Environmental science for environmental management.* Harlow: Prentice Hall.

Kaempffert, Waldemar 1956. 'Science in review: warmer climate on Earth may be due to more carbon dioxide in the air', *New York Times* October 28: 191.

Kahan, Dan M., Jenkins-Smith, Hank and Braman, Donald 2010. 'Cultural cognition of scientific consensus', *Journal of Risk Research* 9(2): 1–28.

Kahneman, Daniel and Tversky, Amos 1973. 'On the psychology of prediction', *Psychological Review* 80: 237–251.

Kahneman, Daniel, Slovic, Paul and Tversky, Amos (eds.) 1982. *Judgment under uncertainty: heuristics & biases.* Cambridge, UK: Cambridge University Press.

Karl, Thomas R. and Trenberth. Kevin E. 2003. 'Modern global climate change', *Science* 302(December 5): 1719–1723.

Kaufman, Leslie 2010. 'On global warming, science and weathercasters at odds over climate change', *New York Times* March 29: A16.

Kellstedt, Paul M., Zahran, Sammy and Vedlitz, Arnold 2008. 'Personal efficacy, the information environment, and attitudes toward global warming and climate change in the United States', *Risk Analysis* 28(1): 113–126.

Key, Ivor 2000. 'North Pole melts for the first time in 50M years', *Express* August 21: 25.

Kim, Kyun Soo 2010. 'Public understanding of the politics of global warming in the news media: the hostile media approach', *Public Understanding of Science* 1: 1–17.

Kingdon, John W. 1995. *Agendas, alternatives, and public policies.* New York, NY: Longman.

Krauss, Clifford and Mouawad, Jad 2007. 'Exxon chief defends oil industry', *International Herald Tribune*, February 14.

Kroll, Gary 2001. 'The "silent springs" of Rachel Carson: mass media and the origins of modern environmentalism', *Public Understanding of Science* 10: 403–420.

Krosnick, Jon A. 2010. 'The climate majority', *New York Times* June 9: A21.

Krosnick, Jon A., Holbrook, Allyson L. Lowe, Laura and Visser, Penny S. 2006. 'The origins and consequences of democratic citizens' policy agendas: a study of popular concern about global warming', *Climatic Change* 77(1): 7–43.

Krugman, Paul 2006. 'A false balance', *New York Times*, January 30.

Laclan, Ernest and Mouffe, Chantal 2001. *Hegemony and Socialist Strategy: Towards a Radical Democratic Politics.* Verso, London.

Lahsen, Myanna 2005. 'Technocracy, democracy, and US climate politics: the need for demarcations', *Science, Technology & Human Values* 30(1): 137–169.

    2008. 'Experiences of modernity in the greenhouse: a cultural analysis of a physicist "trio" supporting the backlash against global warming', *Global Environmental Change* 18: 204–219.

Lakoff, George 2010. 'Why it matters how we frame the environment', *Environmental Communication – A Journal of Nature and Culture* 4(1): 70–81.

Lamb, Gregory M. 2010a. 'As climate change debate wages on, scientists turn to Hollywood for help', *Christian Science Monitor*, March 15.

Lamb, Robert 2010b. 'Is global warming real?', *Discovery News*, June 8.

Latour, Bruno 2004. *Politics of nature.* Cambridge, MA: Harvard University Press.

Lavelle, Marianne 2009. 'The climate change lobby explosion', Center for Public Integrity, February 24.

Lean, Geoffrey 2005. 'Attack on London: Gleneagles may yet prove to be Blair's finest hour and leave a lasting legacy to the world', *Independent* (July 10): 18.

    2009. 'American economists recognise the climate change threat', *Telegraph*, November 6.

Leggett, Jeremy 2001. *The carbon war: global warming and the end of the oil era.* New York, NY: Routledge.

Leiserowitz, Anthony A. 2005. 'American risk perceptions: is climate change dangerous?', *Risk Analysis* 25: 1433–1442.

2006. 'Climate change risk perception and policy preferences: the role of affect, imagery, and values', *Climatic Change* 77(1): 45–72.

Leiserowitz, Anthony, Maibach, Edward W., Roser-Renouf, Connie, Smith, Nicholas and Dawson, Erica 2010. 'Climategate, public opinion, and the loss of trust', working paper, http://ssrn.com/abstract=1633932.

Lewis, Simon L. 2010. 'How to beat the media in the climate street fight', *Nature* 468(7): 7–8.

Lippmann, Walter 1922. *Public opinion.* New York, NY: The MacMillan Company.

Liptak, Adam 2008. 'From one footnote, a debate over the tangles of law, science and money', *New York Times*, November 25.

Littler, Jo 2009. *Radical consumption: shopping for change in contemporary culture.* London, UK: Open University Press.

Liu, Xinsheng, Vedlitz, Arnold and Alston, Letitia 2008. 'Regional news portrayals of global warming and climate change', *Environmental Science and Policy* 11: 379–393.

Liverman, Diana 2004. 'Who governs, at what scale and at what price? Geography, environmental governance and the commodification of nature', *Annals of the Association of American Geographers* 94(4): 734–738.

Liverman, Diana and Sherman, Douglas 1985. 'Natural hazards in novels and films: implications for hazard perception and behaviour', In Jacquelin Burgess and John R. Gold (eds.), *Geography, the media and popular culture.* London, UK: Croom Helm, 86–95.

Lorenzoni, Irene and Pidgeon, Nick F. 2006. 'Public views on climate change: European and US perspectives', *Climatic Change* 77(1/2): 73–95.

Lovely, Erika 2008. 'Scientists urge caution on global warming', *Politico*, November 25.

Lowe, Thomas D. and Lorenzoni, Irene 2007. 'Danger is all around: eliciting expert perceptions for managing climate change through a mental models approach', *Global Environmental Change* 17 (1): 131–146.

Luke, Timothy 1997. *Ecocritique: contesting the politics of nature, economy, and culture.* Minneapolis, MN: Minnesota University Press.

1999. 'Environmentality as green governmentality', In Éric Darier (ed.), *Discourses of the environment.* Oxford, UK: Blackwell.

2008. 'The politics of true convenience or inconvenient truth: struggles over how to sustain capitalism, democracy, and ecology in the 21st century', *Environment and Planning A* **40**(8): 1811–1824.

Luntz, Frank 2003. *The environment: a cleaner, safer, healthier America.* Washington, DC: The Luntz Research Companies – Straight Talk, 131–146.

Luscombe, Richard 2008. 'Surge in fatal shark attacks blamed on global warming', *Observer* April 5: 34.

Maibach, Ed, Roser-Renouf, Connie and Leiserowitz, Anthony 2009. 'Global warming's six Americas: an audience segmentation analysis' *Yale Project on Climate Change and George Mason University*

Mail on Sunday 2002. 'Greens own goal', *Mail on Sunday* August 11: 24.

Maleuvre, Didier 2004. 'Beyond culture', *Journal of Human Values* **10**(2): 131–141.

Manzo, Kate 2010. 'Imaging vulnerability: the iconography of climate change', *Area* **42**(1): 96–107.

Marshall, Christa and Leber, Jessica 2010. 'Climate science and public opinion "can be a bit messy"', *Energy and Environment*, February 24.

Marx, Karl 1891. *The Eighteenth Brumaire of Louis Bonaparte.* New York, NY: International Publishers.

Mastrandrea, Michael and Schneider, Stephen H. 2004. 'Probabilistic integrated assessment of dangerous climate change', *Science* **304**: 571–575.

Matsaganis, Matthew D. and Payne, J. Gregory 2005. 'Agenda-setting in a culture of fear', *American Behavioral Scientist* **49**(3), 379–392.

Mayer, Jane 2010. 'Covert operations: the billionaire brothers who are waging a war against Obama', *The New Yorker*, August 30.

Mazur, Allan and Lee, Jinling 1993. 'Sounding the global alarm: environmental issues in the US national news', *Social Studies of Science* **23**(4): 681–720.

McChesney, Robert W. 1999. *Rich media, poor democracy: communication politics in dubious times* Chicago; IL: University of Illinois Press.

2008. *The political economy of media: enduring issues, emerging dilemmas.* New York, NY: Monthly Review Press.

McCright, Aaron M. 2007. 'Dealing with climate contrarians', in Susanne C. Moser and Lisa Dilling (eds.), *Creating a climate for change: communicating climate change and facilitating social change.* Cambridge, UK: Cambridge University Press, 200–12.

McCright, Aaron M. and Dunlap, Riley E. 2000. 'Challenging global warming as a social problem: an analysis of the conservative movement's counter-claims', *Social Problems* **47**(4): 499–522.

2003. 'Defeating Kyoto: the conservative movement's impact on U.S. climate change policy', *Social Problems* 50(3): 348–373.

2010. 'Anti-reflexivity: the American conservative movement's success in undermining climate science and policy', *Theory Culture Society* 27(2/3): 100–133.

McFarling, Usha Lee 2001. 'Studies point to the human role in global warming', *Los Angeles Times* April 13: A1.

McKeon, Clare 2001. 'I like it warm', *Sunday Mirror* November 21: 27.

McManus, Phil A. 2000. 'Beyond Kyoto? media representation of an environmental issue', *Australian Geographical Studies* 38(3): 306–319.

McPhee, John 1998. *Annals of the former world*. London, UK: Farrar Straus Giroux.

McQuail, Denis 2005. *Mass communication theory*. Thousand Oaks, CA: Sage Publications.

Media Transparency 2009. Conservative transparency, Retrieved 26 November 2009, http://mediamattersaction.org/transparency/.

Michaels, David 2008. *Doubt is their product: how industry's assault on science threatens your health*. Oxford, UK: Oxford University Press.

Milbank, Dana and Richburg, Keith 2001. 'Bush, EU clash over climate policy: Europeans plan to pursue Kyoto curbs despite U.S. stance', *Washington Post* June 15: A1.

Miller, Jon, Pardo, Rafael and Niwa, Fujio 1997. *Public perceptions of science and technology: a comparative study of the European Union, the United States, Japan, and Canada*. Madrid, Spain: BV Foundation.

Monbiot, George 2009. 'Pretending the climate email leak isn't a crisis won't make it go away', *Guardian*, 25 November. Retrieved 18 August 2010, www.guardian.co.uk/environment/georgemonbiot/2009/nov/25/monbiot-climate-leak-crisis-response.

Mooney, Chris and Kirshenbaum, Sheril 2009. *Unscientific America: how scientific illiteracy threatens our future*. New York, NY: Basic Books.

Morello, Lauren 2009. 'Obama and his aides phase "greenhouse gases" out of their vocabulary', *Energy & Environment*, September 23.

Moser, Susanne 2007. 'More bad news: the risk of neglecting emotional responses to climate change information', In Susanne Moser and Lisa Dilling (eds.), *Creating a climate for change*. Cambridge, UK: Cambridge University Press, 64–80.

2009. 'Costly politics – unaffordable denial: the politics of public understanding and engagement in climate change', In Maxwell Boykoff (ed.), *The politics of climate change: a survey*. London, UK: Routledge/Europa, 155–182.

Moser, Susanne and Dilling, Lisa (eds.) 2007. *Creating a climate for change: communicating climate change and facilitating social change.* Cambridge, UK: Cambridge University Press.

Mulkern, Anne C. 2010. 'Oil group, climate bill supporters clash in summer campaigns', *Energy and Environment,* 17 August, Retrieved 5 September, www.eenews.net/Greenwire/print/2010/08/17/1.

Murdock, Graham 2002. 'Media, culture, and modern times: social science investigations', In Klaus Bruhn Jensen (ed.), *A handbook of media and communication research.* London, UK: Routledge, 40–61.

Myers, Jim 2006. 'Heat wave has senator sticking to beliefs', *Tulsa World,* July 22.

Nabiyeva, Komila 2010. 'The British media and climate change: representation of the Climategate scandal in the British national newspapers.' Unpublished MSc thesis, Berlin: Humboldt University.

Nature 2009. 'Filling the void', *Nature* 458, March 19: 260.

Nauman, Zoe 2001. 'On balance, the weather's going to be wonderful', *Express* July 27: 17.

Nelkin, Dorothy 1987. *Selling science: how the press covers science and technology.* New York, NY: W.H. Freeman.

Newell, Peter 2000. *Climate for change: non-state actors and the global politics of the greenhouse.* Cambridge, Cambridge University Press.

2008. 'Civil society, corporate accountability and the politics of climate change', *Global Environmental Politics* 8(3): 122–153.

News of the World 2002. 'Just 100 years to go folks!', *News of the World,* February 3.

Newspaper Marketing Agency 2010. 'Facts and figures', Retrieved September 26, 2007, www.nmauk.co.uk/nma/do/live/factsAndFigures.

Newton, Kenneth 1999. 'Mass media effects: mobilization or media malaise?', *British Journal of Political Science* 29: 577–599.

Nisbet, Matthew C. 2009. 'Communicating climate change: why frames matter for public engagement', *Environment magazine* March/April: 12–23.

Nisbet, Matthew C., Hixon, Mark A., Moore, Kathleen Dean and Nelson, Michael 2010. 'Four cultures: new synergies for engaging society on climate change', *Frontiers in Ecology and the Environment* 8(6): 329–331.

Nisbet, Matthew C. and Kotcher, John E. 2009. 'A two-step flow of influence? Opinion-leader campaigns on climate change', *Science Communication* 30(3): 328–354.

Nisbet, Matthew C. and Mooney, Chris 2007. 'Framing science', *Science* **316**: 56.

Nisbet, Matthew C. and Myers, Teresa 2007. 'The polls—trends: twenty years of public opinion about global warming', *Public Opinion Quarterly* **71**(3): 444–470.

Nordhaus, William D. 1994. 'Expert opinion on climatic change', *American Scientist* **82**(1): 45–51.

Norgaard, Kari Marie 2006. '"People want to protect themselves a little bit": emotions, denial, and social movement nonparticipation', *Sociological Inquiry* **76**(3): 372–396.

2007. 'Understanding the climate ostrich', *BBC News*, November 15.

O'Connor, Martin 1999. 'Dialogue and debate in a post-normal practice of science: a reflection', *Futures* **31**: 671–687.

Ockwell, David, Whitmarsh, Lorraine and O'Neill, Saffron 2009. 'Reorienting climate change communication for effective mitigation: forcing people to be green or fostering grass-roots engagement?', *Science Communication* **30**: 305–327.

Olausson, Ulrika 2009. 'Global warming – global responsibility? media frames of collective action and scientific uncertainty', *Public Understanding of Science* **18**(4): 421–436.

Olson, Randy 2009. *Don't be such a scientist: talking substance in an age of style*. Washington, DC: Island Press.

O'Neill, Saffron J. and Boykoff, Maxwell 2010a. 'The role of new media in engaging the public with climate change', In Lorraine Whitmarsh, Saffron J. O'Neill and Irene Lorenzoni (eds.), *Engaging the public with climate change: communication and behaviour change*. London, UK: Earthscan.

2010b. 'Climate denier, skeptic, or contrarian?', *Proceedings of the National Academy of Sciences* **107**(39): doi/10.1073/pnas.1010507107.

O'Neill, Saffron and Hulme, Mike 2009. 'An iconic approach for representing climate change', *Global Environmental Change* **19**(4): 402–410.

O'Neill, Saffron and Nicholson-Cole, Sophie 2009. '"Fear won't do it": promoting positive engagement with climate change through visual and iconic representations', *Science Communication* **30**: 355–379.

O'Reilly, Bill 2009. 'The Climate Feud', *The O'Reilly Factor, Fox News*, December 9.

Oreskes, Naomi 2004a. 'Beyond the ivory tower: the scientific consensus on climate change', *Science* **306**(5702): 1686.

2004b. 'Science and public policy: what's proof got to do with it?', *Environmental Science and Policy* **7**: 369–385.

Oreskes, Naomi and Conway, Erik M. 2010. *Merchants of doubt: how a handful of scientists obscured the truth on issues from tobacco smoke to global warming*. New York, NY: Bloomsbury Press.

Otto, A. Ross, and Love, Bradley C. 2010. 'You don't want to know what you're missing: when information about forgone rewards impedes dynamic decision making', *Judgment & Decision-Making* 5(1): 1–10.

Painter, James 2010. 'Summoned by science: reporting climate change at Copenhagen and beyond', Reuters Institute for the Study of Journalism, University of Oxford, November 15.

Palin, Sarah 2009. 'Sarah Palin on the politicization of the Copenhagen climate conference', *Washington Post*, 8 December. Retrieved 2 October 2010, www.washingtonpost.com/wp-dyn/content/article/2009/12/08/AR2009120803402.html.

Parkinson, Dan 2005. 'Jaws...off Hartlepool', *Daily Mail* September 5: 4.

Pearce, Fred 1989. *Turning up the heat: our perilous future in the global greenhouse*. London, UK: Bodley Head.

PEJ 2006. *The state of the news media 2006*. Project for Excellence in Journalism, Retrieved 11 January, 2007, www.stateofthenewsmedia.org.

2009. *State of the news media: an annual report on American journalism*. Project for Excellence in Journalism, www.stateofthemedia.org.

2010. 'Bloggers focus on two favorite subjects: health care and global warming', Project for Excellence in Journalism, 29 March–2 April, Retrieved 2 October 2010, www.journalism.org/index_report/bloggers_focus_two_favorite_subjects_health_care_and_global_warming.

Peterka, Amanda 2010. 'Scientists scramble to bridge the uncertainty gap', *Energy & Environment*, November 9.

Peters, Hans Peter, Brossard, Dominique, de Cheveigné, Suzanne, Dunwoody, Sharon, Kallfass, Monika, Miller, Steve and Tsuchida, Shoji 2008. 'Science communication: Interactions with the mass media', *Science* 321(5886): 204–205.

Petersen, Lars Kjerulf 2007. 'Changing public discourse on the environment: Danish media coverage of the Rio and Johannesburg UN summits', *Environmental Politics* 16(2): 206–230.

Peterson, Collin 1989. 'Experts, OMB spar on global warming: "greenhouse effect" may be accelerating, scientists tell hearing', *Washington Post* May 9: A1.

Pew Research Center 2009a. 'Fewer Americans see solid evidence of global warming', *Pew Center for People and the Press*, October 22.

2009b. *Pew Research Center's Project for Excellence in Journalism state of the news media: an annual report on American journalism*. Retrieved 18 January 2010, www.stateofthemedia.org/2009/index.htm.

Phillips, Nelson and Hardy, Cynthia 2002. *Discourse analysis: investigating processes of social construction*. Thousand Oaks, CA: Sage Publications.

Pidgeon, Nick and Gregory, Robin 2004. 'Judgment, decision-making and public policy', in Derek J. Koehler and Nigel Harvey (eds.), *Handbook of judgment and decision-making*, Oxford, UK: Blackwell, 604–623.

Pielke Jr, Roger A. 2005. 'Misdefining "climate change": consequences for science and action', *Environmental Science and Policy* 8: 548–561.

2007. *The honest broker: making sense of science in policy and politics*. Cambridge, UK: Cambridge University Press.

2010. *The climate fix: what scientists and politicians won't tell you about global warming*. New York, NY: Basic Books.

Pielke Jr, Roger A. and Sarewitz, Daniel 2002. 'Wanted: scientific leadership on climate', *Issues in Science and Technology* Winter: 27–30.

Platt, Reg and Retallack, Simon 2009. *Consumer power: how the public thinks lower-carbon behaviour could be made mainstream*. London, UK: Institute for Public Policy Research.

Pollack, Henry 2003. 'Can the media help science?', *Skeptic* 102: 73–80.

Pollard, Jane S., Oldfield, Jonathan, Randalls, Samuel and Thornes, John E. 2006. 'Firm finances, weather derivatives and geography', *Geoforum* 39(2): 616–624.

Pooley, Eric 2009. *How much would you pay to save the planet? The American press and the economics of climate change*. Discussion Paper Series #D-49. Joan Shorenstein Center for Press, Politics, Public Policy, Kennedy School, Harvard University.

Prudham, Scott 2007. 'The fictions of autonomous invention: accumulation by dispossession, commodification, and life patents in Canada', *Antipode* 39(3): 406–429.

Pulver, Simone 2007. 'Making sense of corporate environmentalism: an environmental contestation approach to analyzing the causes and consequences of the climate change policy split in the oil industry', *Organization and Environment* 20(1): 44–83.

Quart, Alissa 2010. 'The trouble with experts', *Columbia Journalism Review* July/August: 17–18.

Quinn, Kathleen 1992. 'Courting the great gray lady', *Lingua Franca* April/May: 27–29.

Rajan, S. Ravi 2006. *Modernizing nature*. Oxford, UK: Oxford University Press.

Rayner, Steve 2006. 'What drives environmental policy?', *Global Environmental Change* 16(1): 4–6.

Revkin, Andrew C. 2002. 'Can global warming be studied too much?', *New York Times* December 3: F1.

2005a. 'Bush aide edited climate reports', *New York Times*, A1.

2005b. 'Former Bush aide who edited reports is hired by Exxon', *New York Times* June 15: A21.

2007. 'Climate change as news: challenges in communicating environmental science', In Joseph F.C. DiMento (ed.), *Climate change: what it means for us, our children, and our grandchildren*. Cambridge, MA: MIT Press.

2010a. 'The distracting debate over climate certainty', *Dot Earth, New York Times*, 10 February, http://dotearth.blogs.nytimes.com/2010/02/10/the-distracting-debate-over-climate-certainty/.

2010b. 'Climate panel struggles with media plan', *Dot Earth, New York Times*, 10 July, retrieved 22 September 2010, http://dotearth.blogs.nytimes.com/2010/07/10/climate-panel-struggles-with-media-plan/.

Revkin, Andrew C. and Broder, John M. 2009. 'Facing skeptics, climate experts sure of peril', *New York Times* December 7: A1.

Rice, Doyle 2008. 'Climate now shifting on a continental scale – study: migration patterns adjust, plants bloom early', *USA Today* May 15: 11B.

Ridley, Matthew 2010. 'Global warming guerrillas', *Spectator UK*, 3 February Retrieved 4 October 2010, www.spectator.co.uk/essays/all/5749853/the-global-warming-guerrillas.thtml.

Robbins, Paul 2001. 'Fixed categories in portable landscape: the causes and consequences of land cover categorization', *Environment and Planning: A* 33(1): 161–179.

2004. *Political ecology: a critical introduction*. London, UK: Blackwell Publishers.

Roberts, Bob 2004. 'Blair: it's doomsday, PM warning on climate', *Mirror* September 15: 2.

Roberts, Jane 2004. *Environmental policy*. London, UK: Routledge.

Robinson, James 2008. 'Top gear on the road to global domination', *Observer*, July 9.

Rooney, Dick 2000. 'Thirty years of competition in the British tabloid press', In Colin Sparks and John Tulloch (eds.), *Tabloid tales: global debates over media standards*. Lanham, MD: Rowman and Littlefield: 91–110.

Ropiek, David 2010. 'Climate change literacy won't be enough', *Climate Central*, 20 October, www.climatecentral.org/breaking/blog/climate_change_literacy_wont_be_enough

Rosati, Clayton 2007. 'Media geographies; uncovering the spatial politics of images', *Geography Compass* 1(5): 995–1014.

Rosenthal, Elisabeth 2010. 'Climate fears turn to doubts among Britons', *New York Times* May 25: A1.

Roston, Eric 2008. *The carbon age*. New York, NY: Walker Publishing Company.

Royal Society of London 2010. 'Climate change: a summary of the science', Royal Society of London, September 30, http://royalsociety.org/climate-change-summary-of-science/.

Russell, Cristine 2008. 'Climate change: now what?', *Columbia Journalism Review*, July/August.

Rutherford, Stephanie 2007. 'Green governmentality: insights and opportunities in the study of nature's rule', *Progress in Human Geography* 31: 291–307.

Sampei, Yuki and Aoyagi-Usui, Midori 2009. 'Mass-media coverage, its influence on public awareness of climate-change issues, and implications for Japan's national campaign to reduce greenhouse gas emissions', *Global Environmental Change* 1: 203–212.

Sample, Ian 2007. 'Scientists offered cash to dispute climate study', *Guardian* February 2: A1.

Sarewitz, Daniel 2004. 'How science makes environmental controversies worse', *Environmental Science and Policy* 7: 385–403.

Sartor, Tricia and Page, Dana 2009. 'Global warming generates little heat in the media', *Pew Research Center's Project for Excellence in Journalism*, retrieved 18 January 2010, www.journlism.org/numbers_report/global_warming_generates_little_heat_media.

Schell, Jonathan 1989. 'Our fragile Earth', *Discover Magazine* October: 47.

Schlesinger, James 2003. 'Climate change: the science isn't settled', *Washington Post* July 7: A17

Schmidt, Gavin 2008. 'To blog or not to blog?', *Nature* 1(April): 208–209.

Schneider, Stephen H. 1993. 'Degrees of certainty', *National Geographic Research and Exploration* 9(2): 173–190.

2001. 'A constructive deconstruction of deconstructionists: a response to Demeritt', *Annals of the Association of American Geographers* 91(2): 338–344.

2009. *Science as a contact sport: inside the battle to save Earth's climate*. Washington, DC: National Geographic.

Schoenfeld, A. Clay, Meier, Robert F. and Griffin, Robert J. 1979. 'Constructing a social problem: the press and the environment', *Social Problems* 271: 38–61.

Seymour, Julia A. and Gainor, Dan 2008. *Global warming censored: how the major networks silence the debate on climate change*. Washington, DC: Business & Media Institute.

Shabecoff, Philip 1988. 'Global warming has begun, expert tells Senate', *New York Times* June 24: A1.

Shanahan, Mike 2009. 'Time to adapt? Media coverage of climate change in nonindustrialised countries', In Tammy Boyce and Justin Lewis (eds.), *Climate change and the media*. London, UK: Peter Lang Publishing, 145–157.

Shanahan, James and Good, Jennifer 2000. 'Heat and hot air: influence of local temperature on journalists' coverage of global warming', *Public Understanding of Science* 9: 285–295.

Shapiro, Harold T., Diab, Roseanne, de Brito Cruz, Carlos Henrique, Cropper, Maureen, Fang, Jingyun, Fresco, Louise O., Manabe, Syukuro, Mehta, Goverdhan, Molina, Mario, Williams, Peter, Winnacker, Ernst-Ludwig and Zakri, Abdul Hamid 2010. *Review of the IPCC: an evaluation of the procedures and processes of the Intergovernmental Panel on Climate Change*. Amsterdam: InterAcademy Council.

Silverstein, Shel 1981. *A light in the attic*. New York, NY: Harper Collins.

Simon, Richard 2006. 'Green laws no slam-dunk in new Congress', *Los Angeles Times* (December 18): A12.

Singer, Sally 2002. 'Warrior one', *Vogue*, October.

Slocum, Rachel 2004. 'Polar bears and energy-efficient lightbulbs: strategies to bring climate change home', *Environment and Planning D* 22: 413–438.

Smith, Joe (ed.) 2000. *The Daily Globe: Environmental change, the public and the media*. London, UK: Earthscan Publications Ltd.

Smith, Joe 2005. 'Dangerous news: media decision making about climate change risk', *Risk Analysis* 25: 1471.

Smith, Kerri 2009. 'The wisdom of crowds', *Nature Reports Climate Change*, 30 July, www.nature.com/climate/2009/0908/full/climate.2009.73.html.

Smith, Nicholas and Joffe, Helene 2009. 'Climate change in the British press: the role of the visual', *Journal of Risk Research* 12(5): 647–663.

Solomon, Susan, Qin, Dahe, Manning, Martin, Chen, Zhenlin, Marquis, Melinda, Averyt, Kristen, Tignor, Melinda and Miller, Jr, Henry LeRoy (eds.) 2007. *Climate change 2007: the physical science basis, summary for policymakers*. Intergovernmental Panel on Climate Change, Cambridge, UK: Cambridge University Press.

Somerville, Richard C.J. 2006. 'Medical metaphors for climate issues', *Climatic Change* 76:1–6.

Soraghan, Mike 2010. 'Companies play 'name that disaster' with an eye on posterity', *Energy and Environment*, 9 September, Retrieved 20 September, 2010, www.eenews.net/public/Greenwire/2010/09/09/1.

Spencer, Miranda 2010. 'Environmental journalism in the Greenhouse Era: looking for climate news beyond corporate media' *Fairness and Accuracy in Reporting Extra*, February.

Starr, Paul 2004. *The creation of the media: political origins of modern communications*. New York, NY: Basic Books.

Stocking, Holly and Leonard, Jennifer P. 1990. 'The greening of the media', *Columbia Journalism Review* December, 37–44.

Stone, Clarence N. 1980. 'Systemic power in community decision making: a restatement of stratification theory', *American Political Science Review* 74: 978–990.

Suarez, Pablo, Benn, Justin and Macklin, Colleen 2011. 'Putting vulnerable people at the center of communication for adaptation: the case for knowledge sharing through participatory games and video tools' *World Resources Report*, www.worldresourcesreport.org/printpdf/responses/putting-vulnerable-people-center-communication-adaptation-case-knowledge-sharing-through-p

Sunstein, Cass R. 2006. 'The availability heuristic, intuitive cost-benefit analysis, and climate change', *Climatic Change* 77: 195–210.

2007. *Republic.com 2.0*. Princeton, NJ: Princeton University Press.

2009. *Going to extremes: how like minds unite and divide*. Oxford, UK: Oxford University Press.

Swim, Janet, Clayton, Susan, Doherty, Thomas, Gifford, Robert, Howard, George, Reser, Joseph, Stern, Paul and Weber, Elke 2009. 'Psychology and global climate change: addressing a multi-faceted phenomenon and set of challenges', Report by American Psychological Association Task Force, www.apa.org/releases/climate-change.pdf.

Swyngedouw, Erik 2007. 'Impossible sustainability and the post-political condition', In Rob J. Kreuger and David Gibbs (eds.), *The sustainable development paradox: urban political economy in the United States and Europe*. New York, NY: Guildford Press, 13–40.

Taylor, Peter 1997. 'How do we know we have global environmental problems? Undifferentiated science-politics and its potential reconstruction', in Saul E. Halfon, Paul N. Edwards and Peter J. Taylor (eds.), *Changing life: genomes, ecologies, bodies, commodities*. Minneapolis, MN: University of Minnesota Press, 149–174.

Taylor, Peter and Buttel, Frederick 1992. 'How do we know we have global environmental problems? Science and the globalization of environmental discourse', *Geoforum* 23(3): 405–416.

Tett, Simon F.B., Stott, Peter A., Allen, Myles R., Ingram, William J. and Mitchell, John F.B. 1999. 'Causes of twentieth-century temperature change near the Earth's surface', *Nature* 399: 569.

Thacker, Paul D. 2006. 'Climate change and American exceptionalism', *Environmental Science and Technology online*, February 21.

The New York Times 1932. 'Next great deluge forecast by science', *New York Times*, **4**.

The Onion 2005. 'Actual expert too boring for TV', *The Onion* May 4: 1.

Trenberth, Kevin E. 2008. 'Observational needs for climate prediction and adaptation', *WMO Bulletin* 57(1): 17–21.

Trumbo, Craig 1996. 'Constructing climate change: claims and frames in US news coverage of an environmental issue', *Public Understanding of Science* 5: 269–283.

Ungar, Sheldon 1992. 'The rise and (relative) decline of global warming as a social problem', *Sociological Quarterly* 33: 483–501.

  1994. 'Apples and oranges: probing the attitude-behaviour relationship for the environment', *Canadian Review of Sociology and Anthropology* 31: 288–304.

  2000. 'Knowledge, ignorance and the popular culture: climate change versus the ozone hole', *Public Understanding of Science* 9: 297–312.

USA Today 2005. 'Yes, the globe is warming, even if Bush denies it', *USA Today* June 17: 10A.

Van Belle, Douglas A. 2000. 'New York Times and network TV news coverage of foreign disasters: the significance of the insignificant variables', *Journalism and Mass Communication Quarterly* 77(1): 50–70.

Van Dijk, Jan 2006. *The network society*. London, UK: Sage.

Van Dijk, Teun A. 1988. *News as discourse*. Hillsdale, NJ: Laurence Erlbaum.

VandeHei, Jim 2005. 'President holds firm as G-8 Summit opens: Bush pledges to help Africa, but gives no ground on environmental policy', *Washington Post* (July 7): A14.

van Zoonen, Liesbet 1998. *A tyranny of intimacy? women, femininity and television news*. London, UK: Sage.

Vergano, Dan 2005. 'The debate's over: globe is warming', *USA Today*, A1.

  2010. 'Some scientists misread poll data on global warming controversy', *USA Today*, March 9.

Vidal, John 2009. 'We know what to do: why don't we do it?', *Guardian* May 30: 32.

Villar, Ana and Krosnick, Jon 2010. 'American public opinion on global warming in American states: an in-depth study of Florida, Maine and Massachusetts', Woods Institute for the Environment, Palo Alto, CA.

Ward, Bud 2008. *Communicating on climate change: an essential resource for journalists, scientists and editors*. Providence, RI: Metcalf Institute for Marine and Environmental Reporting, University of Rhode Island Graduate School of Oceanography.

2009. 'Reporter Revkin's "worst misstep": aftermath of a climate reporting gaffe', *Yale Forum on Climate Change and the Media*, May 5.

Warrick, Joby 1997. 'The warming planet: what science knows', *Washington Post* November 12: A1.

Weart, Spencer R. 2003. *The discovery of global warming*. Cambridge, MA: Harvard University Press.

Weaver, Andrew 2008. *Keeping our cool*. Toronto, Ontario: Viking Canada.

Weber, Elke 2006. 'Evidence-based and description-based perceptions of long-term risk: why global warming does not scare us (yet)', *Climatic Change* 77: 103–120.

Weingart, Peter, Engels, Anita and Pansesgrau, Petra 2000. 'Risks of communication: discourses on climate change in science, politics, and the mass media', *Public Understanding of Science* 9: 261–83.

Weiskel, Timothy C. 2005. 'From sidekick to sideshow: celebrity, entertainment, and the politics of distraction', *American Behavioral Scientist* 49(3): 393–409.

Weisskopf, Michael 1988. 'Two Senate bills take aim at "greenhouse effect"', *The Washington Post* July 29: A17.

1990. 'Environmentalists try to cut Sununu down to size', *Washington Post* February 22: A21.

1992. 'Bush to attend Rio "Earth Summit" in June: decision follows U.S.-won concessions in draft language on limiting pollution', *Washington Post* 13 May: A3.

West, John 2008. *The promise of ubiquity: mobile as media platform in the Global South*. Paris, France: Internews Europe.

Westen, Drew and Lake, Celinda 2009. 'Speaking with Americans about energy and climate: from the think tank to the kitchen table', *Huffington Post*, 20 May, www.huffingtonpost.com/drew-westen/speaking-with-americans-a_b_205598.html.

Whatmore, Sarah 2002. *Hybrid geographies: natures, cultures, spaces*. London, UK: Sage.

Whitmarsh, Lorraine 2008. 'What's in a name? Commonalities and differences in public understanding of "climate change" and "global warming"', *Public Understanding of Science* 1: 1–20.

Wigley, Tom M.L. 1999. *The science of climate change: global and US perspectives*. Washington, DC: Pew Center on Global Climate Change.

Wihbey, John 2009. 'Polls and surveys grab media headlines: but beware polling pitfalls on climate change', *Yale Forum on Climate Change and the Media*, June 16.

Wilby, Peter 2008. 'In dangerous denial', *Guardian* June 30: 9.

Wilkins, Lee 1993. 'Between the facts and values: print media coverage of the greenhouse effect, 1987–1990', *Public Understanding of Science* 2(1): 71–84.

Wilkins, Lee and Patterson, Philip 1987. 'Risk analysis and the construction of news', *Journal of Communication* 37(3): 80–92.

1991. *Risky business: communicating issues of science, risk, and public policy*. Westport, CT: Greenwood Press.

Wilkinson, Katharine K. 2010. 'The Earth's salvation? How evangelical Christians are engaging with climate change', *Environment magazine* March/April: 47–57.

Williams, Jerry 2000. 'The phenomenology of global warming: the role of proposed solutions as competitive factors in the public arenas of discourse', *Human Ecology Review* 7(2): 63–72.

Williamson, Elizabeth and King Jr, Neil 2010. 'Snow adds to political drift', *Wall Street Journal*, February 11.

Wilson, Kris M. 1995. 'Mass media as sources of global warming knowledge', *Mass Communications Review* 22(1&2): 75–89.

2000. 'Communicating climate change through the media: predictions, politics, and perceptions of risks', in Stuart Allen, Barbara Adam, and Cynthia Carter (eds.), *Environmental risks and the media*. New York, NY: Routledge, 201–217.

2007. 'Television weathercasters as potentially prominent science communicators', *Public Understanding of Science* 17: 73–87.

WJAR 2009. 'Global warming: fact or fiction?', Providence/New Bedford, NBC Affiliate, November 14.

Woodside, Christine 2009. 'Scientist Rosenzweig weighs in on New York, media coverage, outlook ahead', *Yale Climate Media Forum*, January 20.

Wynne, Brian 1992. 'Uncertainty and environmental learning', *Global Environmental Change* June: 111–127.

1994. 'Scientific knowledge and the global environment', In Ted Benton and Michael Redclift (eds.), *Social theory and the global environment*. London, UK: Routledge, 169–189.

2008. 'Elephants in the rooms where publics encounter "science"?', *Public Understanding of Science* 17: 21–33.

Wyss, Robert L. 2008. *Covering the environment: how journalists work the green beat*. London, UK: Routledge.

Zehr, Stephen C. 2000. 'Public representations of scientific uncertainty about global climate change', *Public Understanding of Science* 9: 85–103.

Index